Music, History, and Ideas

Music, History, and Ideas

BY

HUGO LEICHTENTRITT

CAMBRIDGE, MASSACHUSETTS

HARVARD UNIVERSITY PRESS

1961

Twelfth Printing

Distributed in Great Britain by
Oxford University Press
London

414

PRINTED AT THE HARVARD UNIVERSITY PRINTING OFFICE

CAMBRIDGE, MASS., U. S. A.

To

My Distinguished Colleagues

IN THE DIVISION OF MUSIC OF HARVARD UNIVERSITY
IN GRATEFUL RECOGNITION OF THE ENCOURAGE-
MENT THEY HAVE GIVEN THIS BOOK

ACKNOWLEDGMENT

-》》-》》-》》-》》❖《《-《《-《《-《《

The present book had its origin in two series of twelve public lectures on music as a part of general culture, given at Harvard University in 1934–35. To serve as material for a book, the subject matter in those lectures was considerably enlarged, supplemented, and rounded off. I am indebted to Mrs. Elizabeth Johnson for valuable assistance in the revision of the text.

H. L.

HARVARD UNIVERSITY
CAMBRIDGE, MASSACHUSETTS
January 1938

CONTENTS

CONTENTS

INTRODUCTION

->>>->>>->>>->>>-❖-<<<-<<<-<<<-<<<

THE study of music is generally pursued from one particular point of view: a certain instrument is learned, or the art of singing is cultivated; the technique of composition is studied, or the history of music is surveyed more or less carefully. In the course of a general musical education one may even combine the study of several of the topics just mentioned. Yet specialized studies of this type cut music off from its natural connection with the spiritual and material world, and leave out of consideration the fact that it is only one part of general culture. The state of general culture in a particular epoch is, in turn, dependent on the state of social life, on the political history, the geographic conditions, and the language of a country. Music consequently has an essential relationship to all these subjects. Furthermore, it rests on an underlying scientific basis that involves physics and mathematics, and it has ties, more or less close, with literature and the other arts. Poetry, architecture, sculpture, painting, dancing, acting, and the industrial arts have affected music and have in their turn been affected by it. Philosophy, aesthetics, and meditation on the inner meaning of human life and art also draw music into their compass. But as it is generally studied nowadays music has too much the status of an anatomical preparation. We look at it very minutely — microscopically, in fact; we dissect it and analyze its appearance, but the true object of our study forever escapes us.

There cannot be any doubt that this peering at minutiae keeps the student from grasping the larger aspects of his subject and prevents him from acquiring an insight into certain essential properties of the art of music. Many of these essential properties can only be perceived when we put music back into its natural connection with the physical and spiritual world of which it is a mere fragment. When we see it as part of a larger whole, a new question confronts us. What does this fragment of music mean in the vast symphony of nature, in the immense compass of culture?

In the attempt to find a solution it may be helpful to remember a maxim of modern medicine: A disease of a certain organ indicates that the entire organism is out of order, and accordingly local treatment must be supplemented by a fitting general treatment that goes back to the real cause. Similarly in the study of music or any other art certain symptoms, although not those of disease, ought to be traced back to their ultimate cause, as far as possible beyond the immediate local reaction. In the following investigations it is proposed to supplement the customary curriculum of musical study by inviting the reader to look through the holes in the fence we have built around music in order to see what has been going on beyond its confines. In other words, we shall try to connect the facts of the history of music with the history of the human spirit, with general culture in its varied aspects, and with the history of political and social conditions, which are of preëminent importance for art and science.

This will help us to understand better not only what has happened in the art of music but also why it happened in a certain way, at a certain time, in a certain locality, and we may succeed in recognizing some of the laws of natural growth and evolution that govern all aspects of life, music among them. Of course, the outlook into so vast a panorama is not easy to acquire. One has to climb high to gain a comprehensive view, and the road upward is full of difficulties and obstacles. The professional student of the history of music ought to be cultivated and widely read, scholarly in many directions, in order to grasp the complicated and fascinating problems that present themselves as he progresses on his slow and roundabout way.

A hasty survey of the auxiliary sciences needed may indicate the nature and importance of the problems involved. Languages may be considered first. An acquaintance with Latin is needed, especially for the study of medieval music. Our knowledge of medieval music is derived almost exclusively from a number of theoretical treatises written in Latin by learned monks in various countries. Most that are known are to be found in several important collections, edited in 1784 by Martin Gerbert, the celebrated abbot of the Benedictine monastery of St. Blasien in the Black Forest, and in 1864–1876 by Coussemaker, the greatest French authority on medieval music. Hardly any of these treatises has been translated into other languages. They do not, in fact, lend themselves easily to translation, and one's understanding would hardly be increased by translations which, in view of the abstract subject matter, would be unidiomatic and forced in any modern language that does not possess the characteristic terseness and logical precision of Latin. A knowledge of Latin, however, is needed not only by the specialist in medieval music but by anyone who wants to study Catholic church music, for Latin is the universal language of the Catholic Church all the world over. Starting with Gregorian chant in the Middle Ages, the immense literature of motets and masses down to the present time makes use almost exclusively of Latin texts. The majority of these texts are taken from the Latin Bible, though a number of hymns make use of the wonderful Latin poetry written by medieval poets. No one who is not well versed in Latin can acquire a satisfactory acquaintance with Palestrina's works, which are the glory of Catholic church music.

Still more important for the student of musicology is a knowledge of German. It may be stated without exaggeration that three-quarters of the important standard works on all subjects connected with the history and theory of music are written in German. One may even go so far as to say that modern musicology is in the main a German science; certainly all through the nineteenth century the predominance of German musicology was undisputed. Only a few of the fundamental books have been translated into English, the bulk of this extensive literature being available only in German. Moreover, a great many of the world's finest compositions were written to German words. Some two hundred Bach cantatas and the German operas of Mozart, *Die Entführung aus dem Serail* and *Die Zauberflöte*, reveal their real meaning only to those thoroughly familiar with the language. German song in the nineteenth century, one of the most precious treasures of music, loses most of its immediate appeal if not sung in German and properly understood. Of Schubert's nearly seven hundred songs, of the thousand songs of Mendelssohn, Schumann, Robert Franz, Brahms, Hugo Wolf, and Richard Strauss — exquisite marvels of lyric art — only a few have been translated into English and French. And these few translations are so inadequate that they can never replace the original German poetry; in fact, they destroy many of the most delightful, expressive, and picturesque traits of great masters in the art of coördinating word and tone. As for opera, no one who is unable to understand and appreciate the German dramatic story can claim a close acquaintance with Weber, Wagner, and Strauss. Wagner, especially, makes so intimate a connection between the single word and the music that it is quite impossible to appreciate his art fully without a profound knowledge of the German language.

The part Italy has played in the history of musical art is so important and rich, especially in older times, that Italian, too, is inseparably tied to our study. In order to acquire a knowledge of the Italian madrigal, a vast subject, far from being exhausted, one needs some acquaintance with Italian poetry from Dante to the poets of the Renaissance — Petrarch, Tasso, Sannazaro, and others. The Italian language is no less important for the study of opera, which originated in Italy in the seventeenth century and for more than two hundred years was dominant in all European countries. Furthermore, an immense literature of Italian monodic vocal music, chamber cantatas, still remains to be explored, beginning with Caccini's manifesto of the new style, the celebrated *nuove musiche* of 1602, and extending into Mozart's time. Barely one-quarter of this literature has been studied in detail.[1] Later writers of opera — Mozart, Rossini, Verdi, and Puccini

---

[1] It was my privilege to open to students the charming paths of these *bel canto* gardens in the chapter concluding my revision and completion of the posthumous fragmentary fourth volume of Ambros' unsurpassed *Geschichte der Musik*.

— have a fair chance of showing their artistic powers to the best advantage only if sung in Italian to an appreciative audience thoroughly familiar with this language.

Similarly, the genuine masterpieces of French music can reveal all their charm and refinement of taste only to listeners who respond quickly to every word, every accent of the language. How this vivacious and eloquent language influenced music in various directions is manifest in the lively part songs of that witty *causeur*, Clément Jannequin, early in the sixteenth century. One hundred years later the grandiloquent language of classical French tragedy in the epoch of Louis XIV determines the musical style of the opera of Lully, and in the eighteenth century Rameau's operatic style has something both of baroque pathos and of the fragile charms, the limpid, over-refined grace of rococo diction. Gluck's heroic opera, Cherubini's post-revolutionary musical drama, the romantic grand opera of Meyerbeer, Halévy, and Gounod, the picturesque emotionalism of Bizet's *Carmen*, the delicately curved, faintly whispered *arioso* of Debussy's *Pelléas et Mélisande* — all these depend for their telling effect on the listener's familiarity with the French language.

Moreover, an important theoretical and historical literature is written in French, starting with Mersenne's fundamental *Harmonie universelle* in 1636 and continuing down to the bulky tomes of Lavignac's *Encyclopédie* in our own time. In this French literature are included such fundamental books as Rameau's *Traité de l'harmonie* (1722), in which the modern theory of chords and harmony is presented for the first time, Couperin's *L'Art de toucher le clavecin* (1717), Rousseau's *Dictionnaire de musique* (1767), *Lettre sur la musique moderne et française*, and, in the nineteenth century, the highly important historical works of François Fétis and C. E. H. Coussemaker.

Various sciences also claim attention in the professional education of the adequately taught musician. An elementary acquaintance, at least, with the physical laws of acoustics is indispensable for everyone working in the field of musical theory and for everyone who is interested in the history and construction of various musical instruments. The theory of music has to deal with the nature of the musical tone, the laws of the vibrations of strings, of sound waves, of the propagation of sound, of the formation of intervals and of scales. Practical music is also concerned with the various systems of tuning, with the acoustic qualities of buildings and halls, the laws of resonance, of harmonic and disharmonic overtones, and with such matters as the sounds of various sorts of organ pipes, as well as the tubes of the wind instruments. What causes various sound-colors or timbres, why a flute differs in sound from an oboe and clarinet, a violin from a viola, are important problems for the theory and practice of music. Further, the anatomy of the human ear and of the vocal apparatus has a certain importance. In this complex of physical knowledge which forms the basis of music, mathematics is included to a certain extent. The inner relationship of mathematics and music has often been remarked. For ordinary purposes it is certainly not necessary to master the intricacies of differential calculus and higher mathematics in order to be an able musicologist; an elementary arithmetical and mathematical knowledge is all that is actually needed unless one becomes a specialist in research on the border line of music and mathematics, where a number of interesting problems still await solution. But what the student of music needs is a certain mathematical bent of mind, an ability to think and observe in terms of ratios, proportions, quantities, linear extensions. This mathematical method is of use especially in analytical work. The principles of logical construction and progression and the problem of making music logically coherent, subjects of especial importance for the composer, also belong in this complex.

Political history, geography, and the history of general culture in fine arts and literature are likewise important auxiliary sciences for musicology. It is impossible, for instance, to understand the development of music in Germany since 1500 without knowing about the Reformation and the beginnings of the Protestant Church, without knowing about the antagonism between Catholic southern Germany and the Protestant north. In the seventeenth century the Thirty Years' War (1618–1648) was of the greatest importance for German music. It meant a fight for supremacy between the Catholic and Protestant powers, but it finally came to a close without a clear decision. Thenceforth, even more than before, music in Germany grew in two separate branches. Protestant music in middle and northern Germany gradually became what we now call genuine German music. The Catholic music of South Germany, Bavaria, and Austria preserved more of an international, cosmopolitan character; it always maintained close relations with Italian art and was actually dominated by Italian masters in the service of the imperial court in Vienna and the Munich court. We must know something of the cultural state of Germany between 1500 and 1600 in order to understand the artistic importance of cities like Nuremberg and Augsburg. The wealth and the extensive international commerce of these and other German cities during the sixteenth century stand in glaring contrast to the general poverty all over Germany in the next century, the ruin of arts and culture caused by the Thirty Years' War. Unless one knows this, one cannot properly understand the mission and importance of the modest, yet genuine art of the Protestant cantors in Saxony, the artistic ancestors of J. S. Bach. Great artists like Heinrich Schütz in Dresden and Buxtehude in Lübeck cannot be comprehended merely through their music. One must also know something about the districts and the cities in which they lived, the political and historical events which contributed to the shaping of their lives and artistic careers. One cannot appreciate Bach's historical position without knowing of the part which Saxony and Thuringia played in German music, or without understanding the cultural importance of cities like Dresden, Leipzig, Hamburg, and Lübeck. With the ascent of Frederick the Great to the Prussian throne the cities of Berlin and Potsdam acquire importance for the history of music. To be familiar with the peculiar predilection of the king for French and Italian art helps one to comprehend many musical events in Berlin. Similarly, in order to enter into the spirit of Haydn's and Mozart's art it is useful to be acquainted with the cultural conditions of Austria, where magnates and princes of immense wealth patronized music and maintained their private opera houses and orchestras, engaging famous artists as *Kapellmeister*. An acquaintance with the rococo spirit in vogue toward 1750, with its superrefinement, its artificial grace, its extremely cultivated taste, its love for the dainty and ornamental, helps us to catch the spirit of Mozart's minuets and other little pieces of so fragile, delicate, and amorous a character. Haydn's music, too, has the elegant stamp of the *mondaine* society of his time, for which a great many of his productions were written to order. But a stronger element in Haydn was a healthy, fresh, vigorous, rustic tone, his inheritance from the Austrian village where he was born. Haydn's music combines in an unusual way the vigor of Austrian popular dance and song with the refinement and social culture characteristic of Vienna.

A clear insight into Italian music cannot be gained without a knowledge of the history of the Renaissance and its forerunners, from Dante to Michelangelo. It is important to know what the Roman popes meant for art, what the state of social culture was, what the leading cities — Rome, Florence, Venice, and later Naples — accomplished in politics, culture, and the arts. Palestrina cannot be properly comprehended unless one is familiar with the Catholic Counter Reformation of the late sixteenth century, destined to counteract and diminish the dangerous growth of the new Protestant Church. Madrigal and opera in Italy are inseparable from Italian Renaissance poetry and from the aesthetic views that dominate this epoch. Italian *opera buffa* and the amusing Italian dramatic intermezzi, like Pergolesi's *La Serva Padrona*, can be properly appreciated only through an acquaintance with the popular *commedia dell'arte*, the half-improvised play of the Italian comedians, with its traditional comic characters — Pantalone, Brighella, Gratiano, and others. The witty Venetian comedies of Goldoni explain the intellectual and social atmosphere in which a masterpiece like Rossini's *Barber of Seville* could come into existence. And what Italy itself meant for the artists of all countries from about 1600 to 1900 must be appreciated if one is to reach an approximately correct estimate of the immense influence exercised by Italian culture all over the civilized world. During these three centuries musicians, sculptors, painters, and architects everywhere considered their artistic education incomplete unless they had spent several years in Italy. Bach, who never was in Italy, is an exception to this rule, all the more remarkable for being solitary. Great masters like Hans Leo

Hassler, the Dutchman Sweelinck, the German composers Heinrich Schütz, Handel, Hasse, Graun, Gluck, and scores of others owe a great deal to their years of study with the leading Italian masters. The pilgrimage of the world's greatest painters to Italy for centuries had its purpose and its consequences. Goethe's Italian journeys definitely shaped his art. A curious German novel, *Hildegard von Hohenthal*, written by Goethe's contemporary, Wilhelm Heinse, shows a most interesting aspect of the Italian operatic atmosphere of the late eighteenth century. The adventures of a young German musician traveling in Italy are described here with a welcome abundance of detail, crowned by an apotheosis of Neapolitan opera toward 1780, with an exceedingly instructive and psychologically remarkable analysis of the operas of Traetta, Maio, Jomelli, Piccini, Paesiello, Cimarosa, and other musicians of the period.

The historical development of French music, as well, is closely tied up with the events of French history and with changes in cultural conditions. France enters musical history about 1200 with the great Paris school, headed by two masters of universal reputation, Leoninus and Perotinus. In its aesthetic tendencies and in its entire organization this age of the *ars antiqua* is an outcome of the scholastic system which at that time reached its climax in philosophy, theology, fine arts, and literature, everything being made subservient to ecclesiastic supremacy. The second branch of older French music, the songs of the troubadours, trouvères, and minstrels, is the product of the chivalrous culture of Normandy, Burgundy, and the southern Provençal region at the time of the Crusades. Later, in the sixteenth century in the time of King Henri IV, the French Renaissance finds its peculiar expression in music in conjunction with the famous group of poets called *La Pléiade*, one of whom was Pierre de Ronsard. Henry Expert has given us a valuable survey of the charming chansons of this epoch by Certon, Claudin de Sermisy, Jean Courteois, and Jannequin. French music of the seventeenth century is even more closely connected with the political ascent of France in the age of Louis XIV. The royal court in Versailles and in Paris becomes the center of French culture in all the sciences and arts. French opera is identical with royal court opera. Lully, its first great master, is closely allied with his librettist Quinault and the great dramatists Molière, Corneille, and Racine. The rise of French church music and instrumental music is also inspired by the patronage of the royal court. The great clavecinist Couperin, for example, was court pianist. In the eighteenth century French music is characterized by three different styles, intelligible from their close connection with the leading ideas of this epoch. The fanciful, playful, rococo attitude in the harpsichord music of Couperin, Rameau, and Daquin represents the earliest stage. Toward 1760 this style begins to disappear. The new rational spirit of the French encyclopedists — Voltaire, Diderot, Marmontel — and Jean Jacques Rousseau's cry, "Back to nature and simplicity," become evident in the rather simple, straightforward, inartificial music that supersedes it, especially in the comic operettas of Rousseau, Philidor, Duni, and Monsigny. Gluck, too, must be classed here, although his creative power lifts him immensely above his more modest predecessors, and though his great last works form a transition to the third French style of this century, foreshadowing the spirit of the French Revolution with its grand sweep, its passionate cry for equality, fraternity, humanity. Big proportions, powerful climaxes, exciting crescendi, profound and passionate expression characterize Gluck's style, and Cherubini's music also shows these traits, an expression of the revolutionary spirit which later gained fuller expression in the work of Beethoven.

As to French music of the nineteenth century, one can easily show how its style and tendencies are connected with great political changes. The Emperor Napoleon, the Restoration about 1830, the Revolution of 1848, the Second Empire under Napoleon III, the fall of the French Empire after the Franco-Prussian War, the new Republic — all these changes are reflected also in music. A few names may suggest these changes, characteristic of the spirit of the age. Take Cherubini, Auber, Boieldieu, Meyerbeer, Berlioz, Halévy, Adam, Gounod, Liszt, Chopin, Offenbach, Bizet, Saint-Saëns, Massenet, César Franck, d'Indy, and Debussy, and one has all the tendencies and varying styles of French music in this century. The classicist Cherubini is followed by the romantic school, led by Berlioz, Meyerbeer, Liszt, Chopin. Offenbach is a kind of miniature Aristophanes, mocking at the frivolities of Parisian society in the sixties. A new rise comes with the Republic, with Bizet and Saint-Saëns. The sensuous and agreeable but sentimental Massenet and the severe César Franck show the contrasting tendencies of their age.

A glance at geography will show that this science also has some importance for music. What "east," "west," "south," and "north" mean in the various countries, where the important cities are situated, the names and situations of the great rivers and chains of mountains are significant matters. For Netherlandish art it is helpful to be acquainted with the differences between the Flemish and the Dutch provinces, between cities like Antwerp, Brussels, and Amsterdam, in location and culture. One gets a clearer notion of Italian music by knowing where the Italian districts are located, how far Venice is from Milan, Bologna, Florence, Rome, and Naples. It helps in understanding the musical history of Austria and southern Germany if one knows that of all the Italian centers of music Venice lies nearest to Germany and Austria, that it is reached by the oldest and most frequented road across the Alps, the Brenner Strasse, well known to all travelers from Munich through the Tyrol to Italy, and that at times the Venetian provinces were a part of the German empire. The constant connection between Venice and Vienna, Munich, Augsburg, and Nuremberg not only in commercial but also in artistic matters is thus explained; we understand why the German emperors residing in Vienna always called great Venetian conductors and composers of opera to Vienna, why Munich is full of Italian musicians, why so many young German artists went to Venice to study. The nature of German music becomes clearer if one realizes that the country falls into two geographical districts of especial importance. The first is the Catholic southern district, south of the river Main on both sides of the Danube, which comprises cities like Salzburg (Mozart's home), Augsburg, Munich, Nuremberg, and Mannheim, where the Danube landscape has already lost its characteristic traits, and where we come into touch with the Rhine, flowing to the north, with places like Basel, Mayence, Frankfort, Bonn,

Cologne, all of importance in the history of German music. All these Danube and Rhine districts have a close natural connection in culture, tradition, and the arts. Everywhere here we notice that the Italian influence is much stronger than in the Saxo-Thuringian region in central Germany, the other district of main importance for German music. This district is situated between the rivers Elbe and Weser, both flowing to the north. Here we approach the heart of German Protestant music. Cities like Dresden, Leipzig, Wittenberg (Luther's home) Halle (Handel's birthplace), Weimar, Eisenach (Bach's birthplace), Rudolstadt, Zwickau (Schumann's native town), Zittau, Gotha, Köthen (known in connection with Bach), Weissenfels, and many other smaller towns are full of musical recollections. One cannot, in fact, get a clear notion of the growth of German Protestant music from about 1525 to 1700 and its climax in Bach without having an idea of the geographical characteristics of this district. It is a great help to have actually visited in a leisurely way these lovely old quaint towns, to have seen this peaceful landscape with its magnificent pine forests, its little mountain rivulets, its charming valleys between chains of hills and mountains. How much better one understands the idyllic portions of Bach's music, many of the preludes of the *Well-Tempered Clavichord*, and the delightful dance music of the piano suites after one has become acquainted with the quiet spirit of this Thuringian landscape, the ancient culture of its thoroughly German towns! When thirty years ago work for the publication of the *Denkmäler Deutscher Tonkunst* (*Monuments of German Music*) was organized systematically, all the towns and villages of this district were searched for musical relics, and everywhere, even in remote villages far in the Thuringian forest and the Saxon Erzgebirge, old organs, fragments of old musical libraries, many musical manuscripts of surprising value, and books dating back to the seventeenth century were found in abundance, even though two hundred and fifty years had passed and much valuable material had perished. A third German region of considerable musical importance runs along the coast of the Baltic Sea and the North Sea in North Germany. Here the Baltic Sea with its many ports and its wealthy commercial cities forms the connecting link. From the Middle Ages this Baltic district had been the seat of a highly developed culture. Independent, free cities, each a little republic, had formed a powerful league, the Hansa, extending far beyond the present German frontiers to Denmark, Norway, Sweden, Finland, and to the former Baltic provinces of Russia, now called Lithuania and Esthonia. In Germany cities like Hamburg, Bremen, and Lübeck have retained to the present day their old designation of "Hansa" cities. Add to these famous cities places like Rostock, Danzig, Königsberg, Copenhagen, Helsingfors, the famous Swedish university towns Lund, Upsala, and Riga, Dorpat in the former Russian-Baltic district, and a whole extensive, coherent, and characteristic chapter of musical history is awakened in the recollection of one well versed in musical events down to the eighteenth century.

As to the relation of music to general culture, the fine arts, social conditions, and the structure of society in different ages, a few casual, unsystematic remarks must suffice here by way of introduction. Terms like antique, medieval, Romanesque, Gothic, Renaissance, baroque, rococo, empire, romantic, neo-romantic, conservative, futuristic, modernistic, impressionistic, expressionistic, nationalistic, radical, and so on, have special well-defined meanings in the history of culture, fine arts, and literature. Those meanings are also reflected in music, and a long list might be given of composers and works that illustrate these terms. The same spirit, for example, which produced Gothic architecture shaped intellectual life in general during the last centuries of the Middle Ages. There are Gothic science, philosophy, and literature in the scholastic period, and in music the Gothic spirit is revealed in the rise and development of the linear polyphonic style. Similar observations regarding the Romanesque attitude of mind and the characteristic reflections in music of the Renaissance, baroque, and rococo styles in architecture and painting will be presented in more detail in the later chapters of this book.

A few remarks on romanticism here may emphasize the especial musical importance of the romantic spirit. The romantic music of the early nineteenth century cannot be properly comprehended without a familiarity with the romantic movement in poetry, drama, and fiction of the years 1830–1860 in Germany and France. Schumann, Chopin, Berlioz, Meyerbeer, Liszt, Wagner have their literary companions in Jean Paul, Heine, Eichendorf, Mickiewicz, Victor Hugo, Alfred de Musset, George Sand, Byron, Shelley. The Louvre and the Musée du Luxembourg in Paris contain magnificent collections of the French romantic painters, led by Delacroix, the friend of Chopin, and it is not hard to see in their paintings something very similar in spirit to Chopin, Liszt, and Berlioz. The romantic spirit is a revolt against the cold imitation of classical antiquity of the preceding epoch. It aims at freedom from the rules of the schools, at individual development, at an extension of the compass of the single arts by crossing the frontier to other neighboring arts, at passionate expression of the emotional element; it craves rich, glowing colors, fantastic vistas into distant countries and ages, especially the medieval period, into exotic, Oriental regions. All this holds true in poetry, drama, and painting as well as music. In Schumann, for instance, there is a close alliance with poetry not only in his songs, the ideal musical translation of Heine and Eichendorf, but also in his piano music. The *Papillons*, the *Faschingschwank aus Wien*, the *Carnival*, the *Fantasy*, with its mottoes from Schlegel, the *Jugend Album*, and many other beautiful works are full of poetic allusions inspired by the romantic spirit.

It is appropriate here also to hint at the connection of philosophy with music and at the intimate connection of social conditions with art. Certain epochs are dominated by certain methods of thinking. Thus, for instance, Aristotle is the great authority for the Middle Ages, and the Aristotelian logic is as evident in the medieval Latin treatises on music as in the compositions of the great Parisian school, the *ars antiqua*, of about 1200. It is not necessary that a composer should ever have studied philosophy, should ever have meditated on the systems of Plato, Spinoza, Kant, or Schopenhauer, for he grows up in a certain intellectual atmosphere, saturated with the powerful ideas of great philosophers. Thus Kant's categorical imperative finds its musical parallel in Beethoven's music; Wagner translates Schopenhauer's pessimism in terms of musical art; and in Brahms's music one may see a similarity to Fichte's idealistic philosophy.

Finally, as to social conditions, it is quite evident that the arts, being a luxury of life, can only flourish where considerable wealth prevails, where there is a stable state of affairs, a refinement of culture, and an intellectual intensity. Russian Communism and the mental attitudes developed under Hitler leave their imprint in artistic matters. American prosperity has shaped the musical conditions in this country. And if we look backwards in history we perceive that the French Revolution of 1789, the English civil war of the seventeenth century, and the Thirty Years' War deeply affected all the arts, including music.

In short, wherever one looks one perceives how closely art is connected with the physical conditions of life, with the actual happenings of political history, and with the world of the spirit. To show this intimate relation in detail is the aim of the following chapters, which turn the general remarks of this introductory sketch into a more concentrated study of certain schools of music and epochs of musical art.

CHAPTER ONE

THE MUSIC OF THE GREEKS

WHAT is called the history of music starts with the music of the Christian Church in the later Middle Ages. Our knowledge of music in antiquity, in Egypt, Palestine, Persia, in Greece and Rome, is too fragmentary and disconnected to be called historical and is, moreover, almost totally lacking in actual musical documents. At least two thousand years have passed since the gradual decline of the art of music as practiced by the civilized European nations of the ancient world, the Greeks and Romans. And we should have to go back three thousand years in order to come into direct touch with the musical art of Egypt, of the Hebrew people of Biblical times, of Babylon, and of the great nations of the Far East, India, China, Japan. This long lapse of time explains to a certain extent why the monuments of ancient music have perished almost entirely. Much of it was never written down at all, because most of the ancient nations did not possess what we call a system of musical notation. Music was handed down merely by oral tradition from one generation to the next one. It was only very late, comparatively speaking, that a practically useful notation of music was invented, certainly thousands of years after the invention of the letters of the alphabet. But even after the development of such a notation the chances for a long survival of musical documents were slight enough. Music had for its preservation no material like the bronze and marble of sculpture, the stones and bricks of architecture, which under favorable circumstances may survive a couple of thousand years or longer. It was written down on parchment or paper, a material easily destroyed by fire, by the influences of weather, by careless treatment; a material easily lost, not of any apparent value to uneducated people. Yet the documents of ancient literature which were subject to the same risks survived to a considerable extent. We still possess the Bible, the many sacred books of the East, the poetry of Homer, the Greek dramas; we have the works of the great philosophers and historians of antiquity, of Plato and Aristotle, of Herodotus, Thucydides, Livy, Tacitus, Cicero, Virgil. Though perhaps three-quarters of Greek and Latin classical literature has disappeared beyond hope of recovery, one-quarter at least has been preserved, and this small part is regarded as one of the priceless treasures of human culture.

If literature has been preserved, at least in part, why should ancient music have disappeared so completely? It is not easy to answer this question. Still, a few reasons may be given in explanation. One must remember that even our oldest manuscripts of Greek and Roman literature do not go back to antiquity. They are late medieval copies of still older manuscripts, now lost, and it was only through long generations and whole chains of copies that classical literature was transmitted. Some ancient Greek manuscripts must have contained musical notation as well as words. A thousand years later, in the Middle Ages, the Latin and Greek texts could still be read and copied. But, since the Greek art of music had been dead for centuries, the musical notation was no longer understood. Thus the musical signs, which were utterly meaningless to the medieval scribes, were considered as superfluous, a disturbing ballast, and were finally left out of the copies entirely. All traces of the ancient manuscripts have vanished, and with them the music has perished. We may explain the loss of ancient music in still another manner. We are justified in assuming that music in antiquity had no standing comparable to that of literature. It was only an adornment, a servant to poetry, and had nothing like the importance it has acquired in modern times. There can be no doubt that, in comparison with architecture, sculpture, and poetry, it held only a secondary rank, which it shared with painting. It seems probable, therefore, that in later times less care was spent on preserving the music than on preserving the poetry. Yet even this secondary art of music — in Greece, especially — must have been a glorious achievement, judging by the numerous enthusiastic references to it scattered through Greek and Latin literature and uttered by the greatest poets, philosophers, and historians. A few fragments of genuine Greek music have been found occasionally in the last two hundred years, and thanks to the assiduous labor and ingenious research of able scholars they have been deciphered satisfactorily.

Yet how little idea this scanty harvest gives us of what Greek music really was! Imagine that in two thousand years from now all traces of our present music should have perished and that learned philologists of the year 4000 should hail with pride and enthusiasm the sensational discovery of a few scraps from the nineteenth and twentieth centuries: phrases from Gershwin's *Rhapsody in Blue*, a couple of motives from Wagner's *Meistersinger*, six measures from Schubert's "Unfinished" Symphony, snatches from an Italian folk song, a bit of American jazz, and slight fragments of Beethoven's "Eroica." A noted critic and historian of the year 4000 would then work up a lecture on the primitive state of music as it existed in 1900.

We find ourselves in a similar position with regard to ancient music. We try to judge that lost art from a few fragmentary scraps that chance to have come down to our age. All we possess of ancient Greek music at present is a series of disconnected little fragments, like a finger, half a nose, or an elbow joint of a statue broken into a thousand pieces which may some day be dug out of the earth somewhere in Greece. The entire treasure of Greek music known at present can be collected in a little booklet containing hardly more than four or five printed pages. The table of contents is quickly exhausted. We have (1) the beginning of Pindar's first Pythian Ode; (2) three short hymns of Mesomedes; (3) a few fragments of instrumental *études*; (4) the tombstone of Seikilos in Asia Minor, with a popular melody on the marble slab; (5) two fairly well preserved hymns to Apollo found in Delphi; (6) a fragment from Euripides' *Orestes*; (7) a papyrus from Egypt with a hymn to Apollo; (8) an early

Christian hymn, from the third century of our era, which is written in Greek notation.

But it is not on account of these few remnants that Greek music has gained so much importance for later ages. After all, these fragments, thrown together by chance, are not much more to us than an interesting curiosity. They are too few, too short, and too fragmentary to give us any adequate idea of the state of Greek music at its height. We have, however, left over from antiquity, quite a number of important Greek theoretical treatises on music; we have highly interesting accounts of musical matters in the writings of Greek philosophers like Plato and Aristotle, historians like Plutarch, Boethius, and Cassiodorus. So it happens that we are quite well instructed in the theory and aesthetics of Greek music, though the actual monuments have been almost entirely lost. One might consider this a poor consolation, a meager substitute, and in a certain sense it is. On the other hand, these theoretical, historical, and aesthetic writings by ancient authors acquire a very considerable importance because without them we could not understand the growth of medieval music. Furthermore, our own theory of music is based on the musical laws derived from ancient Greek music and transmitted to us by the Middle Ages. We possess at least a part of the treatises of Aristoxenus of Tarentum, the greatest exponent of the Greek theory of rhythm. Pausanias, who has been called a kind of Greek Baedeker on account of his description of the memorable sights in the various Greek provinces, wrote important chapters on music at the Pythian plays and on Greek folk song. Ptolemy, the great geographer and astronomer, left us a mathematical theory of Greek music. The Alexandrian encyclopedists Athenaeus and Julius Pollux made valuable extracts from lost older treatises on music and compiled a sort of musical dictionary. A treatise attributed to Plutarch even gives us a sketch of the historical development of Greek music — alas, without the musical illustrations, the actual works of art, which alone could make that historical survey really alive and fertile for research. From all these sources fundamental facts may be extracted which are necessary for understanding the position of music in the cultural life of later antiquity and the Middle Ages.

The beginnings of Greek music were mythical even to the Greeks. Mount Olympus, in the northern part of Greece, was the seat of the nine Muses, who gave music its name. From the north also came the cult of Dionysus to Greece, and this cult gave music an extraordinary importance. From Pieria, near Mount Olympus, came Orpheus, the incomparable singer, the peerless master of the cithara, the lyre or guitar, which became the favorite instrument of the Greek people. To these northern influences, culminating in the singing and cithara playing of Orpheus, were added influences from the southeast, from Asia Minor. The Phrygian aulos, or pipe, was imported into Greece in early times and became, like the cithara, a national instrument. These two instruments represent two different features of Greek music. The cithara was the favorite instrument of Apollo and had its noblest part in the cult of the god. From this cult is derived what even yet is called the Apollonian side of Greek art — the wonderful sense of proportion, the crystal-clear form, the serene beauty and unmarred purity, the perfect equilibrium that distinguish the manifestations of all classical Greek art. To the refined intellectualism and the superior moderation attributed to Apollo, the divine patron of art and science, is opposed a very different element: Dionysian ecstasy, passion, frenzy, sensuality. The aulos, the Phrygian pipe, was the favorite instrument of the cult of the god Dionysus, and in music it came to represent the dark, unbridled, passionate side of Greek art, its romantic upheavals, its sensual outbursts. This separation of the Apollonian and Dionysian elements in art has come down from antiquity as a precious legacy of the Greek understanding of the psychology of art, as an expression of the Greek awareness of the profound mysteries of the human soul.

Greek music passes beyond the mythological stage about the eighth century before Christ. The epic poems of Homer and Hesiod, which were in existence at that time, contain occasional references to music. It is certain, moreover, that Greek epic poetry was not read, nor recited aloud, but sung. What sort of music was applied to Homer's *Odyssey* and *Iliad* we do not know; probably it was chanted by a bard, who perhaps accompanied himself in a primitive manner on the cithara, or was accompanied by an assistant. One may perhaps assume with some probability that certain traditional melodies, manners of musical recitation, were applied, and that these melodies, adapted to the metrical line, fitted the words at every point and could therefore be repeated at liberty as often as seemed necessary. A similar practice was in use in the thirteenth century of our era, when French narrative poetry, like the story of Aucassin and Nicolette, was sung to certain tunes repeated over and over.

At any rate, from the start Greek music had the closest connection with poetry. As Greek poetry in the course of time developed an astoundingly subtle, complicated, and varied metrical scheme, so Greek music, inseparable from its poetic models, laid especial stress on rhythmical problems. The probability is that in its rhythmical aspect Greek music was far ahead of any later European music, including our own, but that on the other hand it lacked certain qualities indispensable in modern times. Thus the Greeks had no conception of harmony, the sounding together of various tones, and consequently they could not produce polyphonic music, which is based on the idea of harmony. In all the Greek treatises on the theory of music, however detailed, we find not a single hint of anything resembling what we call harmony, part-writing, polyphony. This may seem strange, but we must not forget that until as late as the twentieth century the idea of harmony, counterpoint, polyphony, was entirely foreign not only to all Oriental and exotic music (including that of the Far East, the Hebrews, the Arabs, the Egyptians, and primitive negro tribes) but also to that of the American Indians and the people inhabiting the Arctic circles. Harmony and counterpoint originated in central Europe about a thousand years later than Greek music and have always remained characteristic of European music alone. Even now the Oriental nations have not made harmony and counterpoint a part of their own music, and when they introduce European music, as, for instance, in Japan, the imported art is kept strictly separate from the old native music. These facts will help us to understand the apparently strange fact that Greek music was always meant as one-part music, and that chords, harmony, and counterpoint did not exist at all in ancient times.

It has sometimes been assumed that faint traces of polyphony are manifest now and then in later Greek music. In accompanying the vocal melody with an instrument, Greek musicians sometimes employed a kind of ornamental variation, dissolving the melodic line into florid instrumental passage-work that resulted occasionally in an accidental clash with the voice, a passing discord, a primitive counterpoint. But this "heterophony" is in reality not polyphony at all; it is only a variation of one-voice writing. Moreover, it was never treated systematically by the Greek theorists; whenever it occurs it appears as an accidental, improvised feature, an effect based upon chance rather than upon an artistic system of any kind.

What has affected later music, even modern music, more than anything else taken over from ancient music, is the system of intervals, scales, or modes discovered and perfected in Greek music. Pythagoras, the great mathematician, laid the indispensable acoustic and mathematical foundation of music. His investigations of the nature and qualities of musical tones and intervals have acquired a classical rank and are not yet antiquated. He has the immortal distinction of having been the first to formulate clearly the laws of proportion in music — that is, to explain how changing the length of a sounding string affects the interval. He found the elementary ratios of the intervals to be as follows:

$$\text{octave} = 1:2$$
$$\text{fifth} = 2:3$$
$$\text{fourth} = 3:4$$
$$\text{twelfth} = 1:3$$
$$\text{double octave} = 1:4$$

At a later epoch were added, among others:

$$\text{major third} = 4:5$$
$$\text{minor third} = 5:6$$

Every violinist constantly applies these elementary ratios, and the art of building and playing the stringed instruments could not have been developed at all without the knowledge of these basic facts of practical acoustics. Just as one cannot build the most insignificant house without an acquaintance with the laws of statics, mechanics, and equilibrium, so one cannot write a piece of music, however insignificant, without a knowledge of the system of intervals, scales, tonality. All these elementary conceptions of music were formulated with a high degree of exactness by Pythagoras and his successors. They evolved a system of scales which, with some modifications, was useful for at least fifteen hundred years and which even in our time has not lost very much of its validity. To Pythagoras not only Greek music but all subsequent music owes its systematic, practical, in fact, indispensable theoretical basis. Even before Pythagoras, mythical reports tell us of a scale on a pentatonic basis, i.e., a scale of five tones instead of the later seven tones, a scale omitting two notes, skipping over the interval of a third in two places. This fragmentary pentatonic system is quite universal in the infancy of music. It is found everywhere in primitive and exotic music; the Chinese, the American Indians, the Scotch, the Norse, the Celts, the Egyptians, and the Siamese all based their music on a pentatonic scale of some kind. Pythagoras is credited by later Greek writers with having filled in the holes in the older Greek scales and with having introduced the seven-tone scale which was universally adopted and has ever since been retained in European music. The Greek conception of the seven-tone scale — or eight-tone scale, if one adds the octave, repeating the first tone as a finishing touch — was a little different from ours. In thinking of the scale we have a visual image of the seven or eight keys of the clavier, organ, or piano, and our entire tone system is a multiplication of this space of seven or eight tones. The Greeks had no claviers, and their visual image of the scale was founded on the strings of the lyre or cithara. Their tone system was not, like ours, divided off into spaces of octaves but into groups of four notes, called tetrachords, and these tetrachords may have had their origin in the idea of four fingers playing on the strings.

In addition to this system of intervals medieval music, and in a modified sense modern music as well, inherited from Greece its scheme of rhythmical modes and of scales. The rhythmical modes or prosodic laws of medieval music are derived from the metrical refinements and the complexities of Greek poetry. Our conception of regular measure goes back to the musical interpretation of the meters used in the Pindaric hymns and in the plays of the great Greek tragedians. From Greek music Christian church music of the first millennium took over the Ionic, Dorian, Phrygian, Lydian, Mixolydian, and Aeolian scales — the church modes, as they came to be known — with their various derivations, transpositions, etc. And though this medieval system of the ecclesiastic modes was abandoned in the seventeenth century in favor of the modern major and minor modes, yet the old modal system is still alive and has been revived and applied again as a special refinement and spice, of melody as well as harmony, by artists like Brahms, the modern Russians, César Franck, Debussy, Respighi, and a number of others.

Though the names of the medieval church modes are identical with the names of the classical Greek scales, the meaning of these names is not the same in both epochs. What in Greek music was called Dorian had the name Phrygian in medieval music, and the ancient Lydian and Ionian scales were later confounded in a similar manner. This confusion arose a thousand years after the decline of classical Greek music, when only faint traces of ancient Greek art, science, and scholarship were left, and though these errors of interpretation have been corrected we have retained in modern music the medieval names of the church modes. The error has become so deeply rooted through a thousand years of constant tradition that an attempt at correcting it would serve only to increase the confusion.

Besides the names of the church modes modern music has inherited from Greece a number of terms like "diatonic," "chromatic," and "enharmonic." The meaning of these terms has also changed in more recent times, as in the case of the ancient scales and the medieval church modes.

The diatonic system is the original order of the various tetrachords throughout the compass of the two octaves employed in Greek music. The chromatic and enharmonic genders are obtained by artificial variations of the original diatonic tetrachords. What we call a chromatic scale is a scale in half-tones: C, C♯, D, D♯, E, F, F♯, G, G♯, A, A♯, B, C. The Greek chromatic scale was obtained by lowering the third tone in every diatonic tetrachord a half-tone. Thus, for instance, from the diatonic tetrachord B, C, D, E was derived the chromatic tetrachord B, C, C♯, E. The modern chromatic figure would be B, C, C♯, D. In the Greek chromatic tetrachord there is not a constant succession of half-tones, but a leap of a minor third, from C♯ to E, at the close. Thus the entire Greek chromatic scale is as follows: A, B, C, C♯, E, F, F♯, A — very different from our modern chromatic scale in structure and in effect.

"Enharmonic" change in modern music means calling the same tone by either of two names; for instance, C sharp as equivalent to D flat is enharmonic change in the modern sense. The Greek term enharmonic has a totally different meaning. An enharmonic tetrachord was obtained by introducing a quarter-tone once in every tetrachord at the second note. For instance, the diatonic tetrachord E, F, G, A in the enharmonic gender becomes E, E + 1/4, F, A. Thus we find quarter-tone intervals, for which we have no name in modern music and which, in many cases, we cannot even produce. It is impossible, for example, to play the Greek enharmonic scale on the piano, for the piano does not possess these small intervals. One might possibly sing an enharmonic tetrachord, if one had a voice flexible enough and ears sensitive enough to perceive the minute intervals. Until recently this enharmonic music of the Greeks was quite enigmatic, but of late we have gained a different view of this strange matter, thanks to modern research on exotic and primitive music, thanks also to some radical tendencies of ultramodern music. Comparative musicology has made us acquainted with the fact that quarter-tone intervals, unknown in European music, are still being used extensively in Arabic, Japanese, Chinese, Indian, and Siamese music, and we have learned that by constant application a sensitive ear can be trained to distinguish these minute intervals and to find in them a new attractiveness, a new excitement. The consequence has been that several modern composers have made a specialty of quarter-tone music, and are trying to enrich the vocabulary of music by curious and remarkable effects of sound derived from the systematic study of quarter-tones. After such experiences the

Greek enharmonic system appears less fantastic. An enharmonic tetrachord would have, for instance, the tones:

$$B, B + 1/4, C, E$$

$$\underbrace{}_{1/4} \underbrace{}_{1/4} \underbrace{}_{8/4}$$

The distances from one tone of this tetrachord to the next, in terms of quarter-tones, would be: $1/4 + 1/4 + 8/4$. A very strange proportion of sounds: two quarter-tones, followed by the leap of a major third $(C - E)$, equal to two whole tones or eight quarter-tones.

How the chromatic and enharmonic tetrachords were employed in practical composition we cannot tell, because the few remnants of Greek music do not give us information on this matter. Quite probably these enharmonic subtleties were a part of the later virtuoso instrumental music more often than of vocal music. For obtaining these chromatic and enharmonic genders the rule was that the initial and final tones of a tetrachord should always remain constant, should not be changed under any circumstances. The intermediate tones, however, the second and third, could be varied and replaced by other intervals. In instrumental practice the chromatic and enharmonic genders could easily be obtained through shortening certain strings of the cithara by means of little hooks and thus tuning those strings correspondingly higher.

Perhaps the most important discovery in Greek music was the invention of musical notation. It was demonstrated in ancient Greece for the first time in Europe that one did not have to rely exclusively on oral tradition in handing down music to posterity. Powers of memory, talent in imitation, long-continued practice and industry, until then solely responsible for the tradition of music, were one day divested of their old dignity, and were even considered with some mistrust, when some speculative Greek mind was struck by the idea that it might be possible to designate by clear symbols the tones of the singing voice, just as ages before it had been possible to invent a system of symbols in writing to indicate clearly the sounds of vocal utterance in speech. Quite logically this unknown inventor applied to music the letters of the Greek alphabet, which had already shown their usefulness so brilliantly in Greek literature. Possibly a similar idea may have been applied to music in the remote Asiatic centers of the oldest culture, in China and India. Our knowledge of the early stages of Asiatic music is still too vague to give us certainty on this point. It is possible, however, that the Greeks took over musical notation from Asia, just as they adopted the Phoenician alphabet. (Of late a little fragment of Babylonian music has been found and even deciphered.) But even if the idea was borrowed, the Greek achievement would lose little of its value for the future growth of the art of music. For all later music, down to the year 1900, those Oriental systems of notation — assuming that they existed — had no meaning at all; it is only in the last few years that modern musicological scholarship has begun to explore ancient Chinese and Indian theory of music, and the practice of European music for the last two thousand years has been built almost exclusively on the foundations laid by the Greeks. Furthermore, the Greek power of logical clearness, orderliness, and enlightened grasp of essentials is revealed in the manner in which Greek musicians interpreted, developed, and applied the idea of musical notation, whether it was their own or borrowed from Asia. Let us never forget the all-important fact that a literature of music can be accumulated and evolved only with the aid of a practical system of notation, that musical literature is impossible without this aid to memory and convenience for later study. It is true that the Greek notation seems primitive to us after two thousand years, but without it European music as it is could not have come into existence at all.

After all, the few relics we possess of ancient Greek music reveal clearly the fact that the Greek notation amply sufficed for the particular needs of this musical style. More cannot be said in praise of any later system, and it is at least an open question whether our complicated modern notation is as well adapted to the highly differentiated harmony and involved constructive problems of our music as the Greek notation was to the much simpler needs of Greek music.

It would seem advisable, therefore, to present here in brief form the ingenious principles of Greek notation, which set a model for all further endeavors in the field. Two German classi-

cal scholars, Heinrich Bellermann and Karl Fortlage, toward 1850
succeeded in finding the key to Greek musical notation, which
until then had always been falsely interpreted. Thanks to the
teaching of these two scholars and to more recent research we
are now in a position to read correctly whatever may still be
discovered of Greek music. An instrumental notation existed
in very early times. The various tones were designated by the
letters of the antique Dorian alphabet, which resembled the
Phoenician, and to some extent the Hebrew, letters. Chromatic
and enharmonic alterations were shown by inverting the original
letter for a rise of a half-tone and placing it sideways for a quarter-
tone. Thus, for instance, B was indicated by the Greek letter ꓘ;
B♯ by ꓵ; and B + 1/4 by ꓥ

The vocal notation is younger. In it were used the letters of
the later Ionian alphabet, the Greek alphabet as we know it. In
this system the letters from alpha to omega were used to de-
note a complete octave in quarter-tones, three successive letters
for every half-tone, with an intermediate quarter-tone, so that we
get 3 × 8 = 24 letters for 3 × 8 quarter-tones in the octave.
A, B, Γ, for instance, means F, E + 1/4, E. Δ, E, Z means E,
D♯ + 1/4, D♯. Contrary to modern use, the successive letters
of the Greek alphabet refer to the descending scale. We use the
letters of the alphabet in connection with the ascending scale.

From the subtleties of Greek musical theory we may logically
infer a very considerable refinement of Greek music, especially
rhythmically, just as we may infer from a highly involved and
flexible grammar the high culture of a language. We must be
very careful, however, to remember that our few fragmentary
relics of Greek music do not indicate in the least the real nature
of the Athenian art of music in the fourth and fifth centuries.

Though the Greeks inherited the elements of their music
from older nations, what they achieved with these foreign elements was something unique. Hebrew music had already em-
phasized the emotional power of the art. In the Bible music and
medicine, the art of healing sickness, are closely connected by
mysterious magical ties; music has the power of calming as well
as of exciting the passions. The Greeks intensified and system-
atized this doctrine by basing on it their entire system of public

education. In his famous book on the State, Plato most ex-
plicitly expounded this doctrine of the educational value of
music. Rhythm and melody, according to Plato, enter into the
soul of the well-instructed youth and produce there a certain
mental harmony hardly obtainable in any other way. Certain
keys, tonalities, and melodic formulas fortify the human character; others may weaken it. In some Greek districts constant
occupation with music was prescribed by law for everybody up
to the age of thirty years. Every Greek was sufficiently trained
in music to participate in any musical function. Choral singing
accompanied every solemn act of state; it was part of religion, art,
even gymnastics. The Pythian plays in Delphi were for a long
time dedicated exclusively to music and poetry, and gymnastics
were added only much later.

Considering this passionate and intensive culture of music in
Greece, we need not be surprised to find not only that the practice of music flourished to an extent far surpassing that of any
other nation, but also that musical theory and the philosophy of
music achieved incomparable precision, thoroughness, and depth.
Fate has decreed that the products of Greek musical art should
be lost to us almost entirely, but of Greek theory we still possess
an admirably well preserved mass of writings, especially from
the period of decline in artistic production.

It remains to indicate very briefly a sort of table of contents
of the entire history of Greek music. This sketch is gathered
from many sources in Greek literature, poetical, historical, philosophical, and theoretical. One of the chief sources is Plutarch's
De Musica, or "Essay on Music."

About 1400 B.C. Olen invented hexameter verse, the two-part
measure in which the Homeric poems are written. He was the
originator of the musical cult of Apollo, and the oldest writer of
Apollonian hymns in Delos. About the same time the first victor
in the musical contest at Delphi is mentioned, Chrysothemis from
the Isle of Crete, whose son Philammon, also a victor at Delphi,
is considered to be the originator of cithara hymns. Another
famous early musician was Linus, originator of plaintive, funeral
music, inventor of the lyre with three strings, and master of
folk song. A generation later lived Thamyris, son and grandson

of the Delphic musicians Chrysothemis and Philammon, who is credited with having invented lyre music without song. From his pupil Hymenaeus the name of the wedding song, "hymenaion," is derived. About this time, also, Pierus, son of Linus, brought the cult of the Muses from Thrace to Greece. The farfamed Orpheus was a grandson of Pierus. Thus early in ancient Greece we find those dynasties of musicians which have been so interesting a feature of all the history of music. The Homeric poems, dating about 1200, give evidence of considerable musical culture based on the Dorian tonality. The oldest of the extant fragments of Greek music is a Homeric hymn to Demeter, perhaps one of those short melodic phrases often repeated in singing the Homeric verses. This fragment was discovered about 1720 by the celebrated Venetian composer, Benedetto Marcello. Hexameter verse can well be sung to such a tune.

About 800 B.C. the Phrygian scale (D-d) was introduced by Hyagnis, who is also credited with having fixed the diatonic system for the aulos, or flute. His son Marsyas made further improvements in flute construction and music. In Greek mythology there is a familiar story that Marsyas aroused the jealousy of Apollo by his proficiency and was flayed by the god. Marsyas' son Olympus (733) is considered to be the first master of the historical epoch of Greek music. He introduced the Lydian scale (C-c) and created the classical form of Greek instrumental music for the aulos, the "nomos," a kind of sonata in five sections. His contemporary, Terpander, founded in Sparta another classical form of Greek music, the "kitharoidic nomos," a sort of cantata with cithara accompaniment. He also is credited with introducing the Aeolian scale.

During the next century the rise of lyric poetry with its abundance of complicated meters gives new rhythmical problems to music. Callinus is called the inventor of the elegy; Archilochus conquered new ground by the invention of melodramatic music through the novel connection of even and uneven, two- and three-part measure. Alcman's lyric choral music in Sparta, his maidens' songs, became famous all over the country; choral cantatas were cultivated by Stesichorus; the dithyrambic style is attributed to Arion.

About 600 a new style arose in Sparta, at that time the center of Greek music — the aulodic style, which consisted of singing with flute accompaniment. Thaletas of Crete was the chief master of this style. Sacadas of Argos became famous through his "nomos Pythios," which treats the fight of Apollo with the Pythian dragon, and is called the earliest specimen of program music. Polymnastus developed the enharmonic system and is also credited with having established the first system of notation. About this time, also, the great mathematician, Pythagoras, gave its acoustic, physical basis to Greek music. Other famous names of this epoch are the masters of Aeolian music on the island of Lesbos, Alcaeus and the poetess Sappho. The Alcaic and Sapphic odes in poetry recall their names even now, and so recent a composer as Brahms has written a "Sapphic Ode." Anacreon, the poet of enjoyment, was also a famous musician. His drinking songs he accompanied on the Lydian magadis with twenty strings.

The great classical epoch of Greek music starts about 525. Athens now becomes predominant in music. Lasus, the first celebrity of whom we hear, made a sensation by his bold orchestral use of instrumental accompaniment, and Pindar added to the accompanying wind instruments the lyre or phorminx. The music of the first Pythian ode of Pindar exists in a fragment that was discovered by the erudite Jesuit father, Athanasius Kircher, in the year 1650.

The height of the classical epoch of Greek music was reached by the great dramatic poets, Aeschylus, Sophocles, Euripides. They were not only poets but also composers who supplied their tragedies extensively with music, of which, unfortunately, nothing has survived except a fragment from Euripides' drama *Orestes*, performed in the year 408 at Athens. It was discovered in a papyrus manuscript at Vienna in 1892. The modern transcription can give only an approximate idea of it, partly because of the impossibility of writing the frequent quarter-tones in our notation and partly because of many little holes in the papyrus. Yet one distinctly perceives the tragic note of agitation in this noble piece of recitative. It is well known how great a part was allotted to music in Greek drama in the comedies of Aristophanes as well as in the tragedies of other poets. Even now a performance of a Greek drama without music is considered quite impossible, and modern composers have written new choral, orchestral, and solo music to Greek dramas. Greek scholars study so assiduously all the refinements of Greek poetry, with its wonderful versification, its rhythmical and metrical wealth, its alternation of chorus and solo, its fine dialogue, that it is all the more regrettable that nothing of the original music has survived.

Immediately after the time of the great tragedians Greek music begins to decline. Two hymns to Apollo, of the second century B.C., were found in 1893 in the French excavations at Delphi. The music had been carved on stone, on a wall of the Athenian treasure house of Delphi, and as much of it as can still be deciphered has been translated into modern notation. This "Paean of Kleochares" is a choral ode of Athenian artists and artisans to Apollo, the god of the Delphic oracle, written in 5/8 time. A very interesting inscription referring to this hymn was also found in Delphi. It reads:

"Resolution of the City of Delphi. Since the Athenian song-composer Kleochares, son of Bion, has written for our god Apollo a prosodium, paean, and hymn for the use of the boys' choir at the sacrificial festivities, the city council has resolved that the municipal conductor of the choir shall study these songs and perform them every year. And in order to show how the city honors those who write something worthy of the God, Kleochares shall be praised for his piety and for his devotion to the city, and he shall be crowned with a laurel wreath, as is the custom at Delphi. He shall also be an honored guest of the city, and he and his descendants shall have the right of presiding at the oracle and court of justice; he shall enjoy special privileges, like asylum, full exemption from taxes, and other rights due to the guest-friends and benefactors of the city. Signed: Mayor Patrondas, City Councilors Lyson, Nikias, Dion, Gnosilas, Enthydikos."

Certainly an interesting document. A short time before, in 280, Delphi had been attacked by the Gauls, who were expelled by earthquakes and landslides, ascribed to Apollo, and Kleochares dedicated his hymns to Apollo as a token of thanks.

The next few of the relics left to us are dated a couple of centuries later. In the vicinity of the town of Tralles in Asia Minor, a tombstone was found in 1889 by the English scholar Ramsey, with the following inscription: "I am tombstone and symbol at the same time. Seikilos placed me here as a permanent sign of eternal memory. Seikilos to his Euterpe." Below these words is inscribed a little song, with quite distinct musical notation, a precise indication of metrical and rhythmical values. This tombstone erected in the first century after Christ by Seikilos to his wife Euterpe is a touching monument, and at the same time records an unpretentious little tune, surviving from the remote days of antiquity, which shows us that plain melodious song of a popular type nearly two thousand years ago was not very much different from what it is now. The text of this Anacreontic little song contains a popular philosophy of life: "As long as you live, be cheerful; do not grieve much and toil too much, for the span of life is short and death reaches you soon." The only feature of the melody reminding us of its ancient origin is the scale used. We should call it G major with F natural instead of F sharp; this is the scale which in the theory of Gregorian chant is called Mixolydian; the Greeks called it Hypophrygian or Hyperlydian.

Finally we must mention three hymns of Mesomedes of Crete, who lived in the second century of our era; he was a favorite of the Emperor Hadrian and was a famous musician in his time. Even three hundred years later his songs were still known, as is testified by various references to him in the writings of the early Christian patriarchs. Another sign of his fame is that the three hymns in question have been preserved in a number of manuscripts, six of which, in Naples, Paris, Munich, and Florence, are still known. Vincenzo Galilei, father of the great astronomer, a musician of rank in his time, discovered these hymns of Mesomedes in 1581. He was not able to read the notation, however, and only in the nineteenth century were these precious little pieces correctly deciphered. The first hymn of Mesomedes is an invocation to the Muse, a very noble, impressive, and beautiful melody, even according to modern standards, in pure Dorian tonality: A, B♭, C, D, E, F, G, A. The second hymn of Mesomedes, to Helios, the sun god, and Selene, the goddess of the moon, is also written in the Dorian scale. It is a very effective vocal piece, with a fine climax and a very expressive rendering of the text in anapaestic rhythm. The third hymn of Mesomedes, to Nemesis and Dike, an ode to justice in the Ionian scale, is also a valuable piece of music, in style quite similar to its companions.

Though these remnants of Greek music are extremely few, yet by a freak of good fortune we have at least one small sample of each of the principal epochs. The Homeric hymn shows us the archaic style; Pindar's ode represents the earlier classical style and the Euripides fragment the later classical style; the Delphian hymn to Apollo comes from the Alexandrian age; the Seikilos tune is a product of Hellenistic culture in the early Augustan age; and the hymns of Mesomedes represent the final phase of Greek music, in the time of the Roman emperors Hadrian and Antoninus.

CHAPTER TWO

GREGORIAN CHANT AND ROMANESQUE ART

-》》-》》-》》-》》 ❖ 《《-《《-《《-《《-

I N THE preceding chapter it has been pointed out to what extent folklore, poetry, drama, philosophy, and mathematics contributed to giving music its elevated position in the cultural life of the Greeks. When we approach the new world slowly rising from the shattered ruins of antique culture in the Middle Ages, we find a great change in the conditions on which music and other arts depend for their prosperous advance. Poetry and drama, philosophy and mathematics have lost their independent existence as arts and sciences; they have come under the powerful control of the new Christian Church, which has extended its dominion to some degree over all political, social, cultural, and artistic events. All activities of life are now inseparably connected with the one supreme new ecclesiastical power which in a thousand years was to give an entirely new aspect to everything in Europe. One cannot comprehend the development of the art of music in the Middle Ages without a closer acquaintance with the rise, growth, and propagation of the Christian faith all over Europe, for music in those times had as its sole patroness — and a powerful one — the Christian Church.

Yet this new Christian music was tied with a thousand roots to the past, to pagan antiquity and the Jewish motherland from which the young faith was striving with all its power to emancipate itself. In general it may be said that early Christian medieval music took its form and liturgical order from the Jewish temple service, its theoretical basis and musical system from Greek models. Its musical material, melodic and rhythmical, was derived both from Jewish-Oriental and from Greco-Roman sources. The influences from the converted countries — Gaul, the Germanic countries, England, and Ireland — manifest themselves only a thousand years later.[1] It was not until the twentieth century that these matters were clearly understood, and recent researches on these problems constitute a considerable advance in our knowledge of the art in its earlier historical aspects.

At the time of Jesus Christ the Roman empire was dominated spiritually by Hellenistic culture; Greece had become a province of the Roman empire, but Greek culture, art, literature, philosophy — even the Greek language — had retained their dominant influence all over the Roman world. Just as in the seventeenth and eighteenth centuries the language, literature, and culture of France were considered the highest type of their kind all over Europe and were zealously studied and imitated by the higher classes of society, so in the time of the Roman emperors Greek culture was considered quite generally to be superior to every other culture, even Roman. The New Testament was originally written in Greek, not in Hebrew, but also not in Latin. The Latin translation of the Bible, the Vulgate, which later became the basis of the Roman Catholic church service, was written considerably later, after Christianity had outgrown the little district of Palestine and had become an ever-growing power in the Roman world in Europe. In Palestine, the country of the Jews, where the Christian religion had its origin, this Greco-Roman or Hellenistic culture was mixed with the still older Jewish-Oriental culture. Consequently, it is quite natural that the later Christian art of music should have retained so much of its two original components.

In the early Christian Church, music was the only art admitted at the service. This is partly because Jesus Christ and his Apostles are nowhere occupied with anything like architecture, sculpture, or painting, partly because, following the precepts of the Old Testament (Exod. 20:4,5), the Christian even comes to abhor the pictorial arts: "Thou shalt not make unto thee any graven

[1] On the curious problem of northern folklore and its part in medieval music the end of this chapter dwells somewhat more closely.

image, or any likeness of any thing that is in heaven above or that is in the earth beneath, or that is in the water under the earth." When St. Paul sees the countless statues in the Greek temples he is seized with wrath. In the Acts of the Apostles (17:16–17, 23–24, 29) we read:

"Now while Paul waited for them at Athens his spirit was stirred in him, when he saw the city wholly given to idolatry. Therefore disputed he in the synagogue with the Jews, and with the devout persons, and in the market daily with them that met with him. . . . Then Paul . . . said, Ye men of Athens, I perceive that in all things ye are too superstitious. For as I . . . beheld your devotions, I found an altar with this inscription: To the unknown God. Whom therefore ye ignorantly worship, him I declare unto you. God that made the world and all things therein, seeing that he is Lord of heaven and earth, dwelleth not in temples made with hands. . . . Forasmuch then as we are the offspring of God, we ought not to think that the Godhead is like unto gold, or silver, or stone, graven by art and man's device."

The early Christians had no magnificent cathedrals as places of worship; through their pious and devout attitude the humblest abode was changed into a temple. Wherever they prayed, they were, according to Jesus' own words, spiritually in the presence of Christ. But from the very beginning music was considered an indispensable part of the Christian divine service. As the first Christians were Jews, it is quite natural that they should have brought into the new religion a good deal of what they possessed and had been accustomed to in the Jewish divine service, and we know from the Bible what an important part music had in the Jewish divine service in Palestine.

Starting with the seventeenth century a whole literature might be cited of books devoted to music in the Bible. German Protestant theological writers and Dutch scholars, especially, contributed to this literature bulky volumes that are now forgotten. In 1692 a Dutch writer, Salomon van Til, published in Dordrecht a book, *Degt-, Sang- en Speelkonst* . . . , i.e., "Poetry, the Art of Singing and Playing of the Hebrew People." Friedrich August Pfeiffer, professor at the University of Erlangen, in 1779 wrote a volume, *Über die Musik der alten Hebräer* ("On the Music of the Ancient Hebrews"). In a learned *Entwurf der hebraeischen Altertümer* ("Sketch of the Hebrew Antiquities," Weimar, 1794) Heinrich Warnekros collected all the references to Hebrew music he could find in profane writings. The book most easily accessible to English readers, however, is Carl Engel's *The Music of the Most Ancient Nations, Particularly of the Assyrians, Egyptians and Hebrews*, which appeared in London in 1864 and was reprinted as late as 1929. The materials discovered in Oriental excavations, especially the sculptures in the British Museum pertaining to musical subjects, have been treated in this valuable book. Sir John Stainer's *The Music of the Bible* (new edition by F. W. Galpin, London, 1914) also deserves attention, as does a book by the German theologian, H. Gressmann, *Musik und Musikinstrumente im alten Testament* ("Music and Musical Instruments in the Old Testament," 1903).

All these books, interesting and valuable as they may be, still give us no answer to the main question: What was the music of the Hebrew divine service like? Unfortunately, no direct evidence has been found; no monuments of genuine Hebrew music have survived. Nevertheless, modern research has succeeded in giving us at least a partial answer. There is no doubt that the singing of the psalms of David formed the chief part of Hebrew temple music and that the earliest Christians took psalmody, the chanting of the psalms, over into Christian worship. Philo, the Jewish philosopher of the first century of our era, describing the singing of the new Christian congregations, expressly tells us that their chanting was the same as that of several Jewish sects. It is known that in the Jewish service the psalms were sung in both responsorial and antiphonic style. Both these styles were taken over into the Christian service and have been in use down to the present time.

Psalmody accompanied the Christian congregations to Rome and to other European countries later, and the Roman Catholic Church has preserved it to the present day. The traditional music of the Catholic Church is called Gregorian chant, and until recently it was quite generally believed that Gregorian chant was invented and written down by Roman musicians of the early Middle Ages. Recent discoveries, however, necessitate a revision of this belief. In many years of patient research throughout the Oriental countries in Asia Minor and North Africa, A. Z. Idelsohn, for years a resident of America, has collected the traditional melodies of the Jews in Palestine, Syria, the Yeminite countries, Egypt, Tunis, Morocco, Arabia, and Persia, and the melodies of the so-called Sephardic Jews in southern Europe. There cannot be any doubt as to the extreme age of many of these melodies. In accordance with the incredibly conservative mode of life of these Oriental people, it seems extremely probable that their traditional tunes, entirely unknown in Europe before Idelsohn's numerous publications, go back to antiquity. Closer study of these Jewish melodies has now revealed the surprising fact that numerous melodic formulas of Gregorian chant and even entire melodies are closely akin to, in part identical with, Jewish tunes. From this relationship we are fully justified in concluding that a considerable portion of what is now called Gregorian chant represents remnants of ancient Hebrew temple music, inherited by the Catholic Church. Thus it happens that, indirectly at least, a part of ancient Jewish music has been preserved in the guise of Catholic music.

In still another respect Jewish temple music is tied up with Gregorian chant. In many Hebrew Bibles, both old and modern, curious little signs, hooks of various shapes and twists, composite figures, are printed along with the Hebrew text. They represent a system of melodic recitation formulas. Invented in the first centuries of the Christian era, probably in Syria or Alexandria, they had the purpose of fixing in the Diaspora, or exile, the traditional Jewish mode of chanting and reciting the Bible. For centuries back these chants must have been transmitted merely by oral tradition, since the ancient Hebrews possessed no system of musical notation. As long as the Jewish national life in Palestine was fairly intact, this oral tradition sufficed. But after the Romans had made Judea a province of the empire, after the Jewish people had begun its perpetual life of exile, had set forth on its "eternal road" of migration, the tradition of the sacred chants must have seemed to be endangered. Hence the necessity arose of devising some system of musical notation to prevent the old chants from being forgotten. The unknown inventors of the cantillation accents may very probably have taken their cue from Greek musical notation, though in detail the two systems differed considerably. The new signs of cantillation fulfilled their aim excellently for at least fifteen hundred years. The tradition was safeguarded by them, and yet the old habit of retaining long stretches of music in the memory has remained alive in the Jewish divine service. For the parchment scrolls with the text of the five books of Moses used in the synagogues, the words must be written by hand in the traditional manner, without any vowel signs and musical symbols. In orthodox Jewish synagogues all over the world even now Jewish cantors sing by memory large portions of the five books of Moses according to musical symbols which they have learned by heart in advance, generally in their early youth. This chanting has never been written down in modern musical notation, which would be clumsy and wasteful of space in comparison with the minute symbols that appear below the Hebrew words without disturbing the appearance of the script in the least.

A strange similarity exists between the Jewish cantillation accents and what are called neumes, the original musical notation of medieval Christian music. So far nothing certain is known about the respective age of the two systems. Thus one might assume that the Jewish system is an imitation of the Christian neumes. But all probability points to the opposite view. As old Jewish melodies have been discovered in disguise in Gregorian chant, so it seems probable that the Christian neumes are an adaptation of the Jewish accents. The idea of vowel accents in Hebrew is certainly very old, and from vowel accents to musical accents is not a long step. The curious hooks, twists, and curves of the neumes, formerly compared with hieroglyphics, have of late lost much of their mysterious aspect. The key which deciphers them with fair accuracy was found in our own day, and the similarity between the ideas governing the two forms of notation is now even more evident than before.

But it is not only remnants of ancient Jewish temple music that are hidden in Gregorian chant. There are also many relics of ancient Greek musical art. To what extent genuine Greek melodies are actually contained in Gregorian chant is a question that has not yet been adequately studied and answered by musical research. But it is quite certain that Greek musical theory, at least, was a powerful factor in shaping Gregorian chant. The ancient Greek modes, the Dorian, Phrygian, Lydian, Mixolydian, and Aeolian scales or tonalities, were taken over by medieval Catholic music, though not without some curious mistakes and odd misunderstandings.

And now a third question arises: How was ancient Greek music related to ancient Hebrew music? Did Judea learn from Greece or Greece from Judea, or did both learn from the still older Egyptian music? What part have Babylon and Assyria, Persia and Phoenicia, in this old music? Fascinating questions, which so far have not been answered satisfactorily! One is free to make more or less fantastic conjectures. Thus it may have been that in very early times Greece imported musical ideas from Egypt and the Orient; that later, however, toward the beginning of the Christian era, Greek spiritual culture, now dominating Rome as well as Egypt and Asia Minor, influenced Hebrew music in its turn. And India, the mysterious old land of wonders, certainly contributed something to ancient music, especially after it came into direct touch with Europe through the domain of Alexander the Great of Macedonia. Shall we ever be able to answer fascinating but highly problematic questions like these in any really satisfactory manner?

When we center our attention on Gregorian chant and what preceded it, we return from the unsafe ground of hypothesis and fancy to the safer, though narrower ground of historical fact. In rough outline, at least, we may attempt here to reconstruct the history of Gregorian chant and to answer the question of what music meant in the hieratic world of the Christian nations in medieval times.

The earliest notices we possess go back to a few rather indefinite allusions to music in the apostolic books of the New Testament. More comprehensive information can be derived from St. Augustine's book, *De musica*, which in the main contains relics of Greek metrical art, and a good many musical notices are scattered through the *Confessions* of the same saint. Augustine also tells us that music in the western European church was

organized by Ambrosius, the great bishop of Milan, who introduced the use of hymns into the church service.

The term "hymn" goes back to antiquity. St. Paul speaks of a
new kind of singing in the earliest Christian conventions (Eph.
5:19, Col. 3:16), and he mentions as distinct species psalms,
hymns, and what he calls ωδαι πνευματικαι, a term somewhat
puzzling to the interpreters, which the English Bible translates
simply as "spiritual songs." Historians of music, of course, need
a more precise interpretation. The word "pneumatikai" has been
connected with "neuma," and the meaning seems to be odes,
chanted according to that system of conducting by hand from
which the "neumes," the signs used in medieval notation, were
later derived. Whatever explanation of this one may accept, it is
very probable that the hymns introduced a new popular, worldly
element into the divine service that differed from the solemn
chanting of the psalms. In the fourth century the hymns of the
Syrian Ephraem were particularly famous. The Oriental hymns
were brought to western Europe by Bishop Hilarius of Poitiers,
in France, and only a generation after Hilarius the Milanese
Bishop Ambrosius found the final, perfect form of church hymn.

These Ambrosian hymns are not fragments taken from the
Bible or the Gospels, but are new ecclesiastic poetry, Latin
verses written by Ambrosius and set to music by him and others.
Augustine mentions four world-famous hymns: "Deus creator
omnium," "Iam surgit hora tertia," "Aeterne rerum conditor,"
"Veni redemptor gentium." Aurelius Cassiodorus, one of the
few far-famed medieval authorities on music, adds to these the
hardly less admired hymns, "Illuxit orbi" and "Aeterne Christi
munera," as authentic Ambrosian hymns, and other writers attrib-
ute to Ambrosius also the hymns "O lux beata Trinitas," "Hic
est dies verus Dei," and "Splendor paternae gloriae." All these,
Latin poetry as well as melodies, are still alive in Catholic church
music; a number of them were taken over into the Protestant
Church by Luther and other reformers, and in German versions
they even now form part of the treasury of German chorales.

F. A. Gevaert, the distinguished Belgian scholar and former
director of the Brussels Conservatory, has laid the foundations
for the scientific treatment of many questions concerning the

earliest church music in his weighty book, *La Mélopée antique dans le chant de l'église latine* (Brussels, 1905), and in other works. The most recent research on these problems is presented with the greatest authority in the three volumes of Peter Wagner's unsurpassed work, *Einführung in die gregorianischen Melodien*, partly available also in English translation.

A particularly significant feature of the Ambrosian hymns is their treatment of word accent. Though they apply the prosodic meters of ancient Greek and Latin poetry, they differ from it in accent. Ancient poetry differs from modern European poetry in that the accent of prose language is often disregarded in the former, and the words in their accent are subjected to the laws of poetic meter. Thus the ancient languages have two kinds of accent, prose accent and poetic accent. In modern languages words retain the same accent in both prose and poetry. This modern system of accent is applied for the first time in the Latin Ambrosian hymns. It has also been observed that ancient Hebrew poetry does not conform to the double accent system of classical Greek and Roman poetry, but applies the method of unchangeable accent. Consequently, it would seem that the Hebrew principle taken over by the Syrian poets of the first centuries of our era came in as a part of the earliest Christian liturgy, which is older than the Roman liturgy. St. Augustine tells us that Ambrosius had hymns and psalms sung "secundum morum orientalium partium," and this explains his novel treatment of Latin accent, so different from the classical tradition. Thus Ambrosian chant revives the plain, popular melody of ancient secular song, and combines it with a new metrical order derived from the Hebrew-Syrian system of accent. The Ambrosian hymns echo Greek music, as well, by their use of the ancient modes, Dorian, Aeolian, Iastic, and Hypophrygian. They even provide for an accompaniment by the cithara, the classical Greek instrument. In their peculiar conglomerate of classical literary art with Oriental traits the Ambrosian hymns arrive at a new religious spirit. Compared with the unsymmetrical irregularity of psalmody, the jubilant Alleluia, their poetry as well as their melody has a new element of symmetry. The hymnic poem was divided into a number of similar stanzas, each containing four verses or lines. To each syllable the melody gave in general only one tone. The result was a plain, easily remembered tune, quite similar to the popular tunes of later antiquity. In short, the hymn may be called a spiritual folk song, and the Ambrosian hymn became a thousand years later the model for the chorale of the Protestant Church.

The wonderful impressiveness of the Ambrosian hymns called forth similar productions by other poets and musicians. St. Augustine, Paulinus, bishop of Nola, and Prudentius are also distinguished authors of hymns. A little later, in the fifth century, one of the most famous and beautiful Catholic hymns was written by Sedulius, "A solis ortus cardine," a melody which has also with certain variations found its way to the Protestant Church in Luther's chorale: "Christum wir sollen loben schon." Other famous authors of hymns were Venantius Fortunatus, Pope Gregory the Great, with the famous melody, "Conditor alme siderum," and Paulus Diaconus, with the melody, "Ut queant laxis," which later attained especial importance in the teaching of music. The famous teacher and theorist, Guido of Arezzo, used this tune to help beginners in remembering the complicated rules of his system of "solmization," a kind of musical spelling of which the Italian and French modern solfeggio is a last slight remnant. It seems strange, considering the success of these hymns, that Rome should not have permitted the use of hymns in the divine service until six hundred years later, in the twelfth century. St. Benedict, the founder of the Benedictine order, admitted hymns in his convent rules as early as the sixth century, and gradually they became a regular part of the divine service in most churches, except at Rome and a few other places. The reason given for this refusal of Rome is not without interest, because it served as a precedent almost a thousand years later in the Protestant Church. The Council of Laodicea had established the rule that in the church service only the words of the Bible should be admissible, and not new poetry like the hymns. A thousand years later the reformed churches of Switzerland and France maintained the same intolerant attitude toward everything not taken directly from the Bible.

The oldest part of Christian musical liturgy is the so-called *officium*, the service of the various hours. The nocturnal office called *vigiliae* (in German, *Mette*) is divided into three *horae nocturnae*, the first, second, and third nocturns. At daybreak the *laudes matutinae* (morning prayers), also called *gallicinium* (the chant of the cock), are sung. The daytime *horae* are *prima hora* (six o'clock), *tertia* (nine o'clock), *sexta* (twelve o'clock noon), *nona* (three o'clock in the afternoon), vespers (at sunset), and *completorium* (complin). The musical contents of the *officium* consists of psalms and *laudes* or *cantica*. It is useful to remember that a considerable part of the polyphonic ecclesiastical music written later, especially many motets, was destined for the *officium* of the various hours.

The psalms were chanted according to the old Jewish styles of responsorial and antiphonic singing. These terms, often misunderstood on account of their apparent identity, are essentially different in their meaning. As this difference has importance for the various forms and styles of medieval liturgical music and of composition down to modern times, some clearness on the sense of the two terms must be attained.

"Antiphonic" is applied to the dialogue, in alternation, of a double chorus. It is properly used only with reference to choral music. Much later, in the sixteenth century, the constructive idea of antiphony was most successfully revived in the double chorus and the polychoral style of the Venetian school, by Willaert, Gabrieli, and their successors in Venice and Rome. Antiphony in medieval music retained a rather plain, syllabic, declamatory manner. "Responsorial" is applied to the responses of a chorus to a solo singer. This responsorial manner brought into church music a virtuoso element, the soloist's elaborate and florid coloratura, which has remained to the present time the delight of Oriental singers, of Arabian, Persian, and Egyptian musicians, and of singers in Jewish temples. This florid style of the Oriental Church was introduced into Rome rather early. Toward the end of the fourth century Pope Damasus sanctioned the *jubilus*, the jubilant strains full of rapid, brilliant coloratura used for the Alleluia. Five hundred years later these jubilant alleluia coloraturas were transformed into a new and important form of church music, the sequence.

St. Augustine in a famous passage has given an aesthetic appreciation and justification, even glorification, of the jubilant alleluia music inherited directly from the Jewish service. What he says of this type of ornamental coloratura singing without words in his commentary on the Twenty-second Psalm might still help composers in the proper treatment of melismatic coloratura: "One who is jubilant does not utter words but sounds of joy without words. The voice of the soul overflowing with joy tries as much as possible to express its emotion, though without giving it a clear sense. A person full of great joy at first utters in his exultation a few inarticulate sounds, not words with a special meaning; afterwards, however, he proceeds to jubilant sounds without words, so that he appears to express joy with his voice, a joy so excessive that he cannot find words for it." In St. Augustine's commentary on the Thirty-second Psalm we read: "And for whom has this 'jubilatio' more propriety than for God, the unspeakable? Language is too poor to speak of God. And if language cannot help you and yet you do not like to be silent, what is left for you but to shout in jubilant strains, so that your heart may be glad without uttering words? The boundless width of joy cannot be comprised within the narrow limits of syllables." And it is in the jubilant alleluia strains of Gregorian chant that many genuine relics of antique Jewish temple music may have survived.

Next to the psalmody of the *officium*, the *cantica* made up the oldest liturgical repertory. These lyric episodes from the Old and New Testaments have retained their liturgical importance from the very beginning of the Christian religion to our day. The oldest known liturgical songbook, the Codex Alexandrinus of the fifth century in the British Museum, contains no less than thirteen *cantica*, among these such famous pieces as "Cantemus Domino gloriose enim," sung by Moses after the passage through the Red Sea; "Audite coeli, quae loquar," Moses' *canticum* before his death; the *canticum* of Isaiah, "Confitebor tibi Dominum"; the "Magnificat" from Luke 1:46; the *canticum* of Simon, "Nunc dimittis servum tuum." The *Canticum canticorum*, the canticle of Solomon, has in late times become especially dear to musicians.

The Biblical precept to "sing" the psalms, not merely recite them, was obeyed literally, as is testified by many statements in the writings of the saints. Pope Leo I, who lived about 450, expressly related that "the Psalms of David are piously sung everywhere in the Church." Only singing, however, and no playing of instruments, was permitted in the early Christian Church. In this respect the Jewish tradition was not continued. In the earlier Jewish temple service many instruments mentioned in the Bible had been used. But instrumental music had been thoroughly discredited in the meantime by the lascivious Greek and Roman virtuoso music of the later ages, and consequently it appeared unfit for the divine service. The aulos was held in especial abhorrence, whereas some indulgence was granted to the lyre and cithara, permitted by some saints at least for private worship, though not in church services. It is interesting to note that the later Jewish temple service has conformed to the early Christian practice and, contrary to Biblical tradition, has banned all instruments. Orthodox Jewish synagogues now object even to the use of the organ.

As to the power of song, an anonymous author of about A.D. 370 in a Greek treatise, "Questions and Answers to the Believers," has treated the matter with an eloquence and an inspired beauty of diction that is almost unequaled. After disapproving of "soulless instruments," he pleads for "pure singing." "Song," he writes, "awakens the soul to a glowing longing for what the song contains; song soothes the lusts of the flesh; it banishes wicked thoughts, aroused by invisible foes; it acts like dew to the soul, making it fertile for accomplishing good acts; it makes the pious warrior noble and strong in suffering terrible pain; it is a healing ointment for the wounds suffered in the battle of life; St. Paul calls song the 'sword of the spirit' because it protects the pious knight against the invisible enemy; for 'the Word of God' if sung in emotion has the power to expel demons. All this gives the soul the force to acquire the virtues of devotion and is brought to the pious by ecclesiastic songs."

Centuries later Thomas Aquinas, the greatest authority of scholasticism, discussing in his famous *Summa theologica* (Quaestio 91, Articulus II) some problems of ecclesiastical music, explains the superiority of singing in the following words: "Instrumental music as well as singing is mentioned in the Old Testament, but the Church has accepted only singing on account of its ethical value: instruments were rejected because they have a bodily shape (*figuralia sunt*) and keep the mind too busy, induce it even to carnal pleasure (*ad corporalem delectationem*). Therefore their use is unwise, and consequently the Church refrains from musical instruments in order that by the praise of God the congregation may be distracted from concern with bodily matters."

In the course of time the liturgy of the Church underwent considerable change. The celebration of the mass became the center of the entire liturgy, and the older *officium* was pushed into the background. The mass is not primarily a musical form but a liturgical complex in which music has a certain part, together with many other ceremonies, including not only a sermon, processions, and the bodily worship of kneeling and rising, but also the splendor of the costumes of the clergy, the impressive architecture of cathedrals, the art of great painters and sculptors, even the smell of incense. The Catholic mass is, in fact, a powerful appeal not only to the religious emotions but also to the senses by many means, of which music is only one. In the course of fifteen hundred years the mass has also become a musical form, but its present parts, Kyrie, Gloria, Credo, Sanctus, Benedictus, Agnus Dei, have not always had the absolute authority they now possess, and were introduced only slowly and gradually.

Two types of prayers made up the mass: (1) the *proprium missae*, which comprises the Introit, the Gradual, the Alleluia, the Tract, the Offertory, and the Communion with varying text and varying music according to the peculiar character of each single celebration; (2) the *ordinarium missae*, with fixed words and melodies comprising what is now generally called a mass from the musical point of view, the Kyrie, the Gloria, the Credo, the Sanctus, the Benedictus, and the Agnus Dei.

In the Gregorian mass, after it had reached its final stage about the twelfth century, the chants of the *proprium* and the *ordinarium* were combined in a well-established order. The music all through the celebration, without exception, is purely vocal (whether solo or choral) one-part music, without harmony or counterpoint, which are achievements of a much later age. The Gradual, the Alleluia, and the Tract were taken over directly from the Jewish service, and it is in these portions of Gregorian chant that one might reasonably expect to discover genuine remnants of old Jewish music. In their style these pieces, sung between readings from the Bible, represent the solo psalmody of the cantor with responses by the congregation, in later times by the *schola cantorum*, or choir of professional singers.

Ten pieces of music normally were needed for the solemn mass, five each from the *proprium* and the *ordinarium*: (1) The Introit, liturgical choir-singing accompanying the entrance of the priests. (2) The Kyrie eleison, sung by the people, a confession of sins and a prayer for pardon. (3) The Gloria in excelsis, sung by the priest, continued by the choir. (4) The Gradual, sung by the cantor and the *schola* after prayers and readings from the Bible. It got its name from the steps (*gradus*) on the platform (*ambo*) on which the singers stood. It is followed by the jubilant Alleluia. On days of mourning the Gradual is replaced by the wailing Tract, sung in one long-drawn-out (*trahere*) strain. In the book of the prophet Jeremiah and in the penitential psalms the Jewish liturgy had abundant material for these characteristically Jewish chants of wailing, which have retained their validity all through the ages in the Jewish synagogue. (5) The Credo, which is sung after a reading from the Bible and the sermon. (6) The *Offertorium* (Offertory), which accompanies and follows the benediction of bread and wine. (7) A prayer of thanks, and the Sanctus. (8) Silent prayers, procession; the Pater Noster, and, after the breaking of the Host, the Agnus Dei. (9) The chanting of the Communion, after the Holy Sacrament. (10) Final prayers, benediction, and the dismissal of the congregation, "Ite, missa est."

Even this dry enumeration will show what wonderful possibilities for music are presented in that unexcelled liturgical work of art called the mass.

The Introit, the Offertory, and the Communion make use of the antiphonic style and are meant to be sung in dialogue by a double chorus, whereas the Gradual, the Alleluia, and the Tract are responsorial pieces, sung by a soloist with responses from the people or the *schola*.

The Kyrie, the Gloria, the Credo, the Sanctus, and the Agnus Dei originally had much less importance than they have now. As the choir of professional singers became more and more dominant in the liturgical service, these simple forms, previously left to the common people, were taken over by the trained singers; they slowly gained in importance until the eleventh century, when the mass reached its final form, which in the main it still preserves, in text and liturgical order.

The Kyrie is one of the oldest liturgical forms, and, as its name indicates, it has a Greek origin and is in Greek, whereas all the other parts of the mass have Latin words. The Christe eleison was adopted only about the sixth century. The Sanctus, used as early as the second century, also belongs to the oldest sections of the mass. Like the psalms, it was certainly taken over from the Jewish temple service. Even now the Jewish liturgy has a very solemn prayer, "Kadosh, kadosh, kadosh adonai Sabaoth hamamlakim"; "Sanctus, sanctus, sanctus Deus Sabaoth" is the literal Latin translation of the Hebrew words, and the Hebrew word "Sabaoth" in the midst of the Latin text points plainly to the Jewish origin of this prayer.

The question in what manner and by what roads the music of the early Christians spread over Europe is as important as the inquiry into the origin and the sources of Christian music. We take it for granted that, as the Christian religion spread, the music attached to it was propagated. But this primitive explanation cannot possibly suffice if we take into consideration the immense magnitude, weight, and extension of the Christian movement.

One must distinguish between the Christian religious idea and the Christian Church. The Christian religion was for some time a purely spiritual movement. Its chief aim was preparation for the hereafter, for the eternal life of the soul after bodily death; its kingdom was indeed not of this world. The gradual growth of the Christian idea, as it spread its moral, spiritual power further and further, forbade, however, the strict maintenance of the axiom "not of this world." To keep itself alive through long ages

of persecution, the Christian idea needed a fixed organization.
It had to take into consideration earthly, as well as heavenly life.
The pious religious exaltation of the Apostles and a number of
the saints might have sufficed for a few individuals, a few religious
fanatics, ready to accept any suffering for their religious con-
victions. But as soon as larger masses of people had to be taken
into consideration, the Christian religion had to be changed into
the Christian Church. The Church is, so to speak, the executive
office of the Christian religious idea. It is concerned with spreading this idea all over the world, with setting up an order, fit to
stabilize the Christian idea, to maintain and constantly increase its
power, an institution modeled after the system of political government, the state. Like the state it set up a system of laws, a certain
social order, a well-ordered financial system, a large body of efficiently trained officers and employees. In this state-like organization music had a most important part. It helped the Church most
efficiently by its unique power of impressing the feelings. On
the other hand it in turn was benefited by the patronage of the
Church, and by and by received an impetus greater than ever
before, even in the golden age of Greece. The Christian idea,
Christian religious feeling in its merely spiritual aspect, might
have inspired many an artistic mind individually to inventing
music imbued with a specifically Christian spirit. But all these
scattered productions would have remained solitary, exceptional
attainments, without the power of spreading, forming a school,
or creating a continuing style of art. To the Christian Church
with its powerful, orderly, and extensive organization music
owes its organization, its system, order, form, and authority,
its outward frame and support, its power of forming schools and
establishing definite styles.

   Although in early Christian times, as we have seen, music was
the only art admitted at the divine service, within a few centuries
architecture, poetry, the plastic arts, and painting had become
integral parts of the Christian service. To further its far-looking
plans the Church, once formed, had to make a compromise with
Greco-Roman culture. Moreover, many remnants of paganism
found their way into the Christian Church, at least into the Christian communities, indulgently admitted and overlooked by a

wide-awake, prudent church government, highly expert in turning to profitable use human weaknesses, indestructible superstitions, inherited beliefs, and cherished habits. Otherwise the Church could not have won over as it did millions of pagans in all provinces of the Roman empire. The severe, austere, Puritan attitude of the Bible toward the arts could no longer be strictly maintained, and so the arts were modified in order to make them suitable to the Church. Music, equally allied to the Church and to the arts, participated in this slow process of assimilation and thus gained many an impetus toward the evolution which we call growth and change of style.

In architecture the Church took over the constructive idea of the old basilica, gradually shaping it in a particular manner, giving it certain characteristic aspects, and thus finally forming out of Greco-Roman elements something specifically Christian in aspect and idea. The Christian basilica later became the constant architectural basis of all cathedral architecture, as distinguished from Oriental styles, and its form has been retained by all subsequent styles of church architecture. We see its formal idea essentially preserved in the Romanesque, Gothic, Renaissance, and baroque styles of architecture, however different they may appear superficially. As this Christian basilica became the almost exclusive home of artistic music for nearly a thousand years, some knowledge of it would help musicians to understand many a characteristic detail of church music, which without such knowledge must always remain obscure. Later in this chapter it will be shown that Romanesque basilica architecture and Gregorian chant are emanations in different directions of the same underlying attitude of mind.

The best idea of the appearance of an early Christian basilica can at present be obtained from two little churches in Rome. San Clemente goes back to the fourth century. Its present state, a reconstruction of the eleventh century, still shows the original ground plan and many of the original furnishings, notably the altar, the marble screens enclosing the choir in the middle of the nave, the pulpits used for the reading of the Gospels, and the old mosaic decoration. The venerable Roman church, Santa Maria in Cosmedin, dedicated in 380 and rebuilt in the seventh century, has many remnants of the original structure still intact — the flat roof, the choir, the pulpits, and the marble floor. As in San Clemente there is a court or cloister in front of the basilica proper where the catechumens and penitents stood, since they were not admitted within the church and had to be content with looking on and listening to the service from a distance. The chorus of singers generally had its place in the choir, fenced in by a marble or metal frame in the middle of the nave, not far from the place for the clergy and the altar. The Gradual of the Roman Catholic Church gets its name from the steps (*gradus*) which the soloist mounts to the ambo, the pulpit, from which he sings or recites. The two old churches just mentioned still retain the original ambo with the steps.

The Christian abhorrence of pictorial and sculptural ornament was overcome rather early. For the abundance of mosaics and wall paintings the excuse was given that they served as "a Bible of the Illiterate"; the common people, unable to read the Bible, thus could at least see the Biblical stories depicted.

As the power and extent of the Church's influence increased, the question of the language of the service acquired importance. Hebrew, or rather Aramaic, the native tongue of the first Christians, was limited to a small district of Asia Minor. Greek, the language of the New Testament, was for centuries the universal language of cultivated people in the Roman empire. When, however, masses of the lower classes, who did not understand Greek, were converted to Christianity, the vernacular Latin was preferred by the Church. Later, as a great many countries with many different languages became Christian, Latin was retained in the Church, because it was the only truly international language. To this day Latin has remained the language of the Catholic Church all over the world, and thus the Latin language has assumed great importance for everything connected with church music particularly that of the Catholic Church.

Toward the fourth century the imperial Roman power had suffered so much from the long-continued onslaught of the barbaric northern tribes that the Emperor Constantine sought an alliance with Christianity, though he did not suppress paganism. To revive the imperial power he thought fit to leave Rome, with its pagan memories, its shattered ideals. He took up his residence in the old city of Byzantium on the Bosphorus, Christianized it, and renamed it Constantinople. There he hoped to build up a new Rome as a stronghold, a powerful citadel of Christianity, where he would be looked upon by all Christians as their protector. In this year of the birth of Constantinople, A.D. 330, the division of the Roman empire into an eastern and a western sphere was actually commenced, though nominally there was still only one emperor. Rome's ancient glory could not be destroyed, however, by the departure of the emperor. On the contrary, the Roman bishop, who at the Council of Sardica in 347 had had precedence granted him, now acquired greater power and influence than before. The papal power was born on the day on which the imperial power left Rome, and the fifth century, which marks the constant decline of the imperial power, brought a corresponding increase of power to the Roman Church.

This division of the Roman empire into an eastern and a western part is reflected in a strange manner in the history of music. While we can trace in Rome and the western countries a slow but constant rise of church music, culminating in the glorious and monumental Gregorian chant, the musical history of the Byzantine empire has until very recently been one of the darkest stretches in our science. We know a good deal of Byzantine architecture, sculpture, painting, but of Byzantine music very little was known before the twentieth century. It is probable that many documents of Byzantine Christian music were destroyed by the Turks in their fanatical hatred of Christianity. In the last thirty years research on Byzantine sources has made considerable progress, and scholars of many nations are occupied at present with their proper interpretation. The melodic substance of Byzantine ecclesiastical music is of particular interest. As these melodies are even older than the Roman chant, they may some day reveal still more of the ancient Jewish music, but they are also significant as the source of the later Russian and Armenian music. There cannot be any doubt that even in later medieval times Oriental music came, by way of Byzantium, into manifold touch with Roman and western European music.

Even earlier professional convent schools for music had been founded in the Near East, at first in Syria, Antioch, and Egypt. Rome followed their example in the fifth century. In the time of Pope Sixtus a convent community was founded for the practice of psalmody, by day and by night, and Pope Leo the Great (440–461) established the Convent of St. John and St. Paul. To the latter was afterwards annexed the celebrated Schola Cantorum, the papal school of singing, which through later centuries became outstandingly important both for the papal chapel at St. Peter's cathedral and for church music throughout the realm of the Roman Church.

From about 450 until about 850 there is a large gap as regards musical documents. We find ourselves here in one of the darkest of dark ages. Until the fifth century a pale echo of Greek culture and art is still noticeable. Now, however, the shaky foundations of ancient culture and learning are overthrown, together with the Roman empire, by the violent assaults of the northern barbarians, the Teutons, Germans, Franks, and later by the Mongolian Huns and Vandals. The *Völkerwanderung*, the migrations of entire tribes from one country to the other and their attacks upon the people whom they found resident there, had for consequence the almost complete destruction of the glorious architecture and sculpture of antiquity, the burning of great libraries, the loss of precious literary works, the overturning of older social institutions, states, and governments. No wonder that in these turbulent centuries, full of barbaric cruelty, of endless war and destruction, music hid its face. What happened in music in these four hundred years we do not know.

The old Greek system of notation fell into utter oblivion, and the people who had to do with music in those times had no skill to write down what they imagined and invented. St. Augustine does not mention musical notation, and a fifth-century treatise by Gaudentius says that the art of writing down music had been entirely lost. Isidore of Seville, who lived until 636, mentions expressly that the only means of acquiring a knowledge of music was to listen attentively with the ear and learn to sing the tunes by heart. How could one expect the art of music to prosper in so barbaric an age?

As far as history is concerned the whole musical activity of these four barren centuries is reduced to the names of four men, who for a thousand years to come retained a quite unique celebrity. Two of them, Boethius and Cassiodorus, are concerned with studies of classical Greek music; the other two, Pope Gregory the Great and St. Benedict, point forward to new aims in the art of music. All were active in Italy in the sixth century. Boethius and Cassiodorus are connected with Ravenna and King Theodoric the Great, the founder of the Ostrogothic kingdom in Italy; Pope Gregory and St. Benedict were active in Rome.

The old city of Ravenna, on the eastern side of Italy, is not generally visited by the great crowd of travelers. Yet Ravenna, once the residence of Theodoric, the city where Dante found a refuge, has unique sights to offer in the mausoleum of Theodoric and old Byzantine chapels with incomparably fantastic and gorgeous mosaic work. Boethius, a far-famed authority in medieval musical matters, and one of Theodoric's ministers, was put to death by Theodoric for political reasons in 525. His five books, *De musica*, however, and his philosophical writings have kept his name alive and admired for a thousand years.

To Cassiodorus, the descendant of a noble Syrian family that settled in Italy, culture owes a considerable debt for having restored education and learning in an age full of destruction and barbarism. After a long political career at the court of Ravenna as minister to Theodoric, he retired from public life and founded a kind of monastery on his estate, his aim being to save whatever he could of ancient culture, which was already fast disappearing. He collected precious old manuscripts and wrote a number of books, a history of the Gothic kings and treatises on the liberal arts and on music.

His great contemporary, St. Benedict, also deserves a place of honor in the history of music, though he had little to do with music itself. St. Benedict was the founder of the Benedictine order, one of the most justly renowned institutions of the Catholic Church, which, after thirteen hundred years, is still alive and active in the service of its great ideals. These ideals were at first quite generally directed toward the salvation of learning by Christianity, without special reference to music. In the course of time, however, music became one of the chief concerns of the learned Benedictine monks; research on Gregorian chant, especially, owes almost everything to the Benedictine order. In his original rules, formulated in 544, St. Benedict mentions the Ambrosian hymns, expressly admitting them to the divine service. From the start the center of the Benedictine order has been the monastery at Monte Cassino in the Apennines, on the route from Rome to Naples; this venerable old building is still one of the great sights, and scholars from many countries work constantly in its rich library. The monumental publication of the French Benedictines of Solesmes in the twentieth century entitled *La Paléographie musicale* certainly is one of the weightiest attainments in the entire compass of musicology, of prime importance for our knowledge of Gregorian chant.

The fourth great name in the sixth century is that of Pope Gregory I (590–604), who succeeded in obtaining for the papacy the real leadership in all Italian national affairs, and in gaining more and more independence from the imperial power. One of the greatest of musical achievements is connected for all time with Gregory — Gregorian chant, the basis of Catholic church music ever since. In recent times Gregory has been deprived of a part of the credit formerly attributed to him so lavishly. But it can hardly be denied that music owes to him the systematic beginnings, at least, of Gregorian chant. From his time on, music became more important in the church service and was cultivated more intensively in the convents.

When Rome started about this time a grand system of religious colonization, it sent its music along with its missionaries to help in Christianizing the northern barbarians. The Catholic Church was established first in England, and there the conquest of the Church was so complete that this country henceforth helped the mother church in spreading the gospel among the heathen. English missionaries brought Christianity to Germany: Willibrord (or Willibrod) to Friesland, and Winfrid to Franconia and Thuringia. From that time church music found a home in Germany as well. In the city of Wesel and in other Rhenish towns Willibrodi churches have kept alive the name of the English missionary in Germany. Winfrid received from Pope Gregory II the name of *Bonifacius*, and posterity has given him the title of "Apostle of the Germans." He became archbishop of Mayence and organized the German Church.

Not until the ninth century do we hear of any advance in musical art. In the meantime a certain consolidation had taken place in Europe. The Frankish empire, established for several centuries, had at last reached a certain cultural height. With Charlemagne, who about 800 had obtained a power comparable to that of the old Roman empire, was born the ideal of the Holy Roman Empire, which until the Reformation was an active power of the first magnitude in the world. Charlemagne's predecessor, Pepin, had introduced Roman ecclesiastical singing into the Frankish empire, and now the Holy Roman Empire, so closely allied with the Holy Roman Church, became of prime importance for music. Under the shelter of these two greatest powers of the world music flourished for many centuries; it had no other home for a long time to come. In his eagerness for the advancement of culture in his vast empire, embracing what today is called France, Germany, the Netherlands, Austria, and a part of Italy, Charlemagne erected churches, convents, and schools. He adopted the Roman form of the mass, propagated the study of Roman chanting, and invited Italian authorities on science and art to teach in his countries. The so-called Carolingian renaissance in arts, sciences, and literature testifies to his cultural efforts.

But Rome was not the only source of this Carolingian renaissance, which became the foundation of the great French civilization. The Celtic influence also helped considerably in shaping it, for Ireland in the fifth century was almost the only country in Europe not devastated by the attacks of the barbarians. Through all these turbulent ages the Irish preserved an old European art, the neolithic art of La Tène. St. Patrick, the apostle of the Irish, converted them from their ancient druidic religion, and as early as the sixth and seventh centuries Ireland was an asylum of the Latin Church; her convents, daughters of the famous Monte Cassino monastery founded by St. Benedict, were seats of learning and of art at a time when France and Germany had hardly any higher culture at all. The Venerable Bede, the Anglo-Saxon scholar, was the greatest authority of his age in all Europe, as eminent in Greek and Latin scholarship as in theology, grammar, rhetoric, and music. There can hardly be any doubt that Ireland contributed considerably to the growth of the art of music, but the details have not yet been sufficiently explored. Charlemagne called Irish monks to his court to help him in his efforts in advancing culture, and Alcuin, the great Celtic scholar, the former director of the famous York cathedral school, became his adviser. Alcuin founded the model school of St. Martin at Tours and directed the highest school of the empire, the court academy. In one of his musical treatises he gives us information concerning the use of the ancient modes, continuing the teaching of Boethius three hundred years before. There is no doubt that Alcuin's interest in music became important in the various schools founded by him.

Einhard, Charlemagne's biographer, tells us that the emperor was fond of listening "at meals to music or reading." It was hardly the solemn Gregorian chant which the emperor desired to hear while he partook of a hearty meal. It must rather have been some kind of secular music played on instruments, or sung with or without instrumental accompaniment. Perhaps he preferred the popular songs and dance tunes of the Frankish and Germanic people. The famous collection of German songs and tales made for him by his scholars was unhappily destroyed by his successor, the pious Louis, for whom these songs were too full of pagan traits. Such a collection of old German songs, had it been preserved, would have been one of the most precious documents of music and poetry. As it is, we know next to nothing of medieval secular music, owing to the fact that the Church did not care to propagate and to preserve this music on account of its pagan character. Or perhaps Charlemagne listened at his banquets to the skillful Irish musicians, whose music was certainly altogether different from Gregorian chant and Ambrosian hymns. Perhaps he even took a fancy to the two-part music of the northern Celtic and Scandinavian tribes. The celebrated Irish philosopher, Scotus Erigena, who lived about this time, tells us of two-part singing in his country, and in the twelfth century another northern writer, Giraldus Cambrensis, tells us that for many centuries the people in Wales, northern England, and Ireland had sung in several parts. As early as 609 we hear of a Celtic stringed instrument, the chrotta, the ancestor of the later vielle. viola da gamba, and violin, an instrument permitting a melody to be played simultaneously with a primitive harmony of bourdon character, similar in effect to the Scotch bagpipe.

Of all the extensive activities in the arts and sciences during the Carolingian renaissance very little is left to us; even the architecture has disappeared for the most part. The church of Germigny des Près is the only existent monument in France, though at least one of the great structures built by Charlemagne is still intact in Germany, the cathedral of Aachen (Aix-la-Chapelle), in which the great ruler is entombed. Here the beginnings of the Romanesque style of architecture, that style so strangely related to Gregorian chant, are manifest.

What we call the history of medieval music proper starts for us in the ninth century; at least, the earliest documents surviving date from this time, a generation after Charlemagne. But it is to this great ruler that the organization of the various centers of art and science is due in the main. For about three centuries the art of music remains a monopoly of the famous convents in France, Germany, and Italy, and all that we know of medieval music is transmitted to us by a number of manuscripts written by learned monks. The empire of Charlemagne could not be maintained in its immense extension by his successors, and it was divided into three parts by his heirs, but this weakening of the imperial power could not affect materially the normal growth of music in the now separate kingdoms of France, Burgundy, and Germany. The French monastery of St. Amand becomes the cradle of polyphony. Here taught Hucbald, who is called the inventor of the organum, the first crude attempt at polyphonic writing. In Germany Walafrid Strabo, the abbot of Reichenau, who died in 849, becomes a famous protector of art; he ranks in the history of literature as the first Swabian poet. Hermannus Contractus, a monk of Reichenau, is the author of several of the most important and instructive musical treatises of the Middle Ages. Hrabanus Maurus, abbot of Fulda and archbishop of Mayence, becomes the far-famed *praeceptor Germaniae*, the teacher of Germany. The study of music becomes a specialty of the famous convent of St. Gall in Switzerland,

near the Lake of Constance. Two St. Gall monks, Notker Balbulus and Totilo, are famous inventors of new forms of ecclesiastic music, which combine lyric poetry with music. Notker
Balbulus creates the sequence, Totilo creates the trope, two
species of ecclesiastic music that retained their importance for
centuries. The library of St. Gall even now contains priceless
manuscripts of Gregorian chant. Book illustration and miniature
painting were also practiced a good deal in these convents for
at least five hundred years, until the art of woodcut illustration
in printed books became popular; they are often an important
source of information in musical matters, a source far from
being exhausted so far.

About the year 1100 we see religious music dividing into two
branches. Polyphony had already started on its way. It was,
however, very crude in its first immature stages, no safe possession as yet, but rather a doubtful speculation for the future. But
the other branch of music — Gregorian chant — had been growing and maturing for five hundred years; it had become a
firmly established art, of a strength, clearness, expressiveness, and
mastery of construction beyond comparison. Whatever in earlier
medieval ideas on music had been sound and fertile found its
final and proper place here, and the monumental structure of
Gregorian chant is not only the most perfect expression of religious feeling in its time but one of the greatest achievements in
music. Nothing in contemporaneous European literature, philosophy, painting, or sculpture can stand comparison with it; only
Romanesque architecture from about 900 to 1200 is equal to it
as a monument of ecclesiastic art. Gregorian chant comprises
an immense number of melodies, thousands of pieces, a vast collection of compositions. All this music is conceived for one voice
only, without harmony, without instrumental accompaniment.
The entire attention and interest are centered, therefore, in the
construction and expression of the melody in its relation to the
words, in its rhythmical diction. The solemn tranquillity of
Gregorian chant, its wonderfully sensitive and appropriate proportions, its broad and noble melodic contours, its restraint even
in agitation, its highly ingenious and interesting construction, its
apparent simplicity, its basis on the plane: all these traits are musi-

cal parallels to the architectural ideas of the Romanesque style. Anyone with an eye and a feeling for architectural beauty who has leisurely and frequently observed Romanesque cathedrals will easily understand the striking similarity of the attitude expressed in terms of these two different arts. Structures like the wonderful cathedrals of Naumburg and Bamberg, the splendid church of St. Michael of Hildesheim, the cathedral of Mayence, the magnificent Romanesque churches (older than the cathedral) in Cologne, the French Romanesque cathedrals at Toulouse, Angoulême, Nevers, Arles, the cathedral in Pisa, and San Zeno in Verona, all these have the quiet solemnity of Gregorian chant, their unsurpassed spatial rhythms, their harmonious proportions reminding us strikingly of the music that rang through them. They are Gregorian chant translated into terms of architectural construction, and the spirit of the solemn and intensely religious chants animates their wide levels, their admirably proportioned walls, their rectangular forms, and their straight lines softened in their rigidity by rounded arches. In looking at these Romanesque edifices one has the feeling, to use musical terms, of unison and octave, not of harmony and counterpoint. The complication of the constructive idea is not displayed, as in the Gothic style, but hidden. As in Gregorian chant, everything gives an impression of great simplicity, although both Gregorian chant and Romanesque architecture are far from simple at bottom. In both cases a great and highly refined constructive art is reduced to the simplest possible terms, which yet are adequate to give proper expression to its spiritual contents. There is much less display of the intricate, the fantastic, the ecstatic than in later polyphonic music and in Gothic architecture. Yet all these more exciting and passionate traits exist in Romanesque and Gregorian art; they merely are not allowed to preponderate. They are kept in an undercurrent, so to speak; they remain in shadow and, if they appear at all, are only hinted at. The Latin and Oriental traditions together produced the Romanesque style, and the same combination of origins shaped Gregorian chant.

The age that saw the completion of two such magnificent monuments of ecclesiastical art had reached heights of perfection beyond which it was impossible to go. New tendencies sprang up about 1200, a new system of art and thought that opened what is known as the Gothic period. Its musical equivalent, polyphony, marks the beginning of one of the richest chapters in the entire history of music.

CHAPTER THREE

THE GOTHIC PERIOD

T HE most important of all the changes experienced by music
is without question the rise and growth of polyphony, which,
beginning rather crudely about the year 1000, transformed the
art of music, giving it an entirely new aspect and opening for it
new possibilities of fantastic compass that are still effective. If
we ask ourselves what kind of mind could have devised and developed these incomparably fertile and far-reaching musical
ideas, we are led to an examination of the spiritual forces active
from about 1100 to 1400, to a consideration of the political problems of the epoch and its achievements in theology, philosophy,
literature, and art. Possibly the fundamental idea of polyphony,
the idea of singing or playing several different sounds simultaneously, came from the pagan nations of northern Europe,
the Scandinavians, Germans, and Britons, and the Celts of England and Ireland. But the credit for having perceived the possibilities in this primitive conception of harmony is due to the
Christian scholars and artists of the Benedictine monasteries in
France, England, and Germany. Polyphony as a principle of
art is inseparably connected not only with the music of the Catholic Church but also with the ecclesiastic spirit in its various manifestations, artistic and otherwise.

The analogy of Romanesque architecture with Gregorian
chant has been pointed out in the preceding chapter. Gregorian
chant, like Romanesque architecture, represents the first phase
of the great medieval art of construction. Musical polyphony

in its spiritual basis corresponds to the second phase of medieval constructive art, to the Gothic style. The art of polyphony could only have been invented in an age capable of conceiving the fantastic magnificence of Gothic structure. Both Gothic art and polyphony are emanations of the scholastic spirit which dominated the theology, philosophy, and poetry of the later Middle Ages. The imposing Gothic cathedrals of Rheims, Rouen, Amiens, Cologne, the bold polyphonic structures of the Parisian school of Leoninus and Perotinus in the thirteenth century and later of the early English and Dutch schools, the scholastic theology and philosophy of Thomas Aquinas, Albertus Magnus, Bonaventura, Duns Scotus, the German mysticism of Meister Eckhart, the magnificent poetic conception of Dante's *Divina Commedia:* all these different achievements are outgrowths of the same quality of mind. Compared with the monumental character of the Gothic cathedral, or scholastic philosophy, or Dante's profound transcendental poetry, the polyphonic music of this epoch seems immature and even crude. It could not be otherwise, for music was a new and very young art, taking its first steps on an unknown road, whereas philosophy, poetry, and architecture were old, filled with a rich inheritance from antiquity. Nevertheless, the scholastic spirit is as evident in the immature conceptions of the early French motet, the first great achievement of the new polyphonic art, as in the accomplished and ingenious music of the great Dutch masters two hundred and fifty years later.

Before discussing the musical expression of the scholastic spirit, however, it seems proper to ascertain what attitude this scholastic spirit had toward the study of music.

Medieval education and learning were comprised of the seven liberal arts. Four of these, the so-called quadrivium, were put under the head of mathematics: arithmetic, geometry, astronomy, music. Music was considered a part of mathematics, a very strange conception for us. Yet there is a certain truth in it, though ordinarily the close connection of music and mathematics is not apparent. It is revealed only after penetrating studies in acoustics, as well as in musical composition and form. Boethius is responsible for the doctrine that science is far superior to art

as a mental achievement, and his great authority contributed
largely to the scholastic conception of music as a mathematical
science. To us this attitude seems to lessen the significance of
music, but in medieval times it was a distinction that helped
music to be deemed worthy of serious study. It also explains
the considerable number of medieval theoretical treatises in comparison with the almost total absence of actual musical documents other than Gregorian chant and hymns. Though he
considered music a part of mathematics, Boethius still attributed
to it a special aim. While the other disciplines of mathematics are
concerned with the search for truth, music has in addition an ethical tendency, a striving toward the Good. Boethius also teaches
that the human body and human mind are shaped by nature in
proportions analogous to the proportions that dominate music.

When Clovis, king of the Franks, desired to have in his
service a musician who could both sing and play on the cither
(a "kitharoidos") in the Italian style, he applied to the Gothic
king Theodoric in Ravenna. Theodoric sent the request to the
greatest musical authority in his vicinity, Boethius. The letter
written to Boethius by Cassiodorus in Theodoric's name, which
is to be found in Cassiodorus' writings, contains a rather complete enumeration of the moral powers of music, its exhilarating
and pacifying effects, and an interesting aesthetic evaluation of
the five ancient modes of music: "The Dorian mode effects
chastity and pudicity. The Phrygian stirs to fighting and engenders wrath, whereas the Aeolian mode calms the tempests of
the soul and lulls the calmed soul into sleep; the Iastic mode
sharpens dull insight and directs the profane mind toward
heavenly aspirations; the Lydian mode soothes the heavy cares
of the soul and expels vexation by pleasant entertainment."
Here music reaches decidedly beyond the confines of mathematics, moving in the direction of emotional impression, even
though it is not yet ready for precise expression of feeling. Yet
all these powerful emotional effects are due to the mathematical
order in music. We perceive here that strange coupling of the
fantastic with a strict, cool constructive faculty so characteristic
of the later medieval, especially the Gothic, mind. These two
opposing traits do not always manifest themselves in the same

person. Some authors represent the scholastic type, others the mystic type. But there is hardly a theologian of rank, a philosopher, politician, historian, poet, who does not consider it his duty to speculate on the nature of music in his writings.

One of the great problems of the art of music, the emotional problem, is solved here by Cassiodorus in an elementary way by means of a readymade prescription, a certain scale being assigned to each of the varying sentiments. Later ages devised more highly differentiated systems of emotional expression. By and by, all the constituents of composition are called upon for aid. In the later Italian madrigal picturesque word-associations are sought through melodic and rhythmical means. Monteverdi looks for support to declamatory accent and colorful chromatic harmony; tempo, melodic cut, rhythm are exploited in the symbolical formulas or motives of Bach and Handel; harmony, tonal color, symphonic complication are added to the expression of the various *affetti*, till a climax of emotional expression is reached in Beethoven. Wagner and the modern romantic composers exercise their inventive ingenuity in more and more subtle and differentiated "expression," until in the twentieth century "impressionism" and "expressionism," up to that time almost identical, are evolved as separate styles.

All through the Middle Ages, as late as the fifteenth century, the great universities of Paris, Oxford, Bologna, Padua, Prague, expressly prescribe the study of music, not only for professional musicians but for every candidate for the degree of *magister artium*. Music is here considered an art in the scholastic sense (that is, a science), not an art in the modern sense.

There are, however, various trends even in scholastic speculation on music: a rationalistic tendency on a Greek basis; an emotional, irrational tendency on an Oriental basis. These two attitudes are represented musically in Christian church music by the strictly measured "closed" form, the symmetrical melody of the Ambrosian hymns, and the "open" style of the jubilant coloraturas, with their almost formless melodies. Both tendencies were later combined in a highly ingenious manner in the Dutch polyphony of the fifteenth century. But even within the rationalistic Greek theory there are distinct classifications. The

Pythagorean doctrine of numbers and proportions was interpreted in two different manners in later Greek philosophy: the
Platonic idealistic harmony of the spheres is denied by Aristotle's
doctrine, based on a realistic empiricism. The earlier centuries
of the Middle Ages rather favor the Platonic conception of
music, whereas the later ones are influenced by the philosophy
of Aristotle as interpreted by Arabian scholars. Through the
Crusades and the Moorish domain in Spain, Arabic speculation
had come into close touch with occidental philosophy. Adelard
of Bath, the most celebrated English scholar before Robert
Grosseteste and Roger Bacon, was a pioneer in the study of Arabic science and philosophy in the twelfth century. He wrote a
commentary on the Arabic *Liber ysagogarum Alchorismi in
artem astronomicam*, in which, according to the medieval academic practice, music is also treated.

Roger Bacon, the founder of modern philosophy, studied in
Paris at the time of the great Parisian school of Perotinus. In his
Opus majus is included an essay on music, in which he treats not
only sound but also gesture, and couples elocution with vocal
music. He also studied the effect of music on the health and the
temper of men and animals. Michael Scotus, the astrologer of the
Emperor Frederick II in Palermo, gives in his *Physionomia seu de
secretis naturae* a compendium of the occult sciences, including
the music of the spheres, followed by a "notitia totius artis
musice," with discussion of the doctrines of Boethius and Guido
Aretinus: "The number seven rules the world . . . for seven
is the number of the planets, of the metals, the arts, the colors,
the tones of music, the odors."

Medieval Jewish philosophy also believes in the mysterious
power of the sacred numbers seven, ten, and twelve. Neumark
in his *Geschichte der jüdischen Philosophie des Mittelalters* sum-
marizes these tendencies as follows: "The insight into this eternal
principle of number and measure is also the essence of prophecy,
and thus the connecting link between prophecy and music. The
prophetic mood is evoked by music because the principle of number and measure is the same in both forms of utterance of human
emotion: The law of proportion, valid in music and in color combinations, is the law of world-creation."

From these mysterious regions the distance is not very far
to the occult conceptions of the Jewish cabala, speculations in-
dulged in earlier in ancient China, Egypt, and Arabia. In
scholastic musical theory there is a reflection of these mystic
doctrines. One Elias Salomonis (1274) makes fantastic sketches
of the solmization syllables of Guido of Arezzo to show their
mysterious symbolism and hidden meaning. The eight church
modes for him are descendants of the mystic primeval *tonus*;
his "son" is the first church mode, the others are brothers, grand-
sons, companions, etc. Aribo Scholasticus shows in strange
drawings the analogy between the various tetrachords and the
life of Christ, from the lowest tetrachord (Christ's humble life
in poverty) to the highest (Christ's ascension). Johannes de
Muris, the great musical scholar of the University of Paris,
a man of European celebrity, explains that the entire structure
of music is based on the number four, in conformity with the
structure of the world, the macrocosm, and of the human body,
the microcosm. There are four elements: warm fire, moist air,
dry earth, cold water. These elements build up the entire world,
but by the varying proportions of their mixture they also produce the four temperaments: the choleric, the sanguine, the
phlegmatic, and the melancholy. There are four seasons, four
weeks in the month, four divisions of the day. The four final
notes of the authentic modes, D, E, F, G, are built on top of
each other, just as the four elements are: earth at the bottom,
water above the earth, air above both, and fire still higher, in
the empyrean. The relative position of the authentic and plagal
modes de Muris very cleverly connects with the main and secondary properties of each element. Water, for instance, is cold,
but also moist, like air; earth is dry, but sometimes also wet, like
water. In his great work *Speculum musices* Jacobus of Liège describes a whole cosmology of music, one of the most fantastic and
grandiose attempts of this kind, akin in smaller proportions to
Dante's *Divina Commedia*; the Church, Heaven, human life, the
virtues, the Last Judgment, and many more ideas are here
brought into direct relation with the laws of music. And the
great Dante himself thought much about music, observed its
effects, formulated its laws. In his poetry he is mainly concerned

with the beautiful and touching effect of singing; in his prose writings, however, the scholastic spirit induces him to systematic investigations of the nature of music. It would not be difficult to collect from Dante's poetry a little musical anthology, and from his prose-writings a very professional-looking extract of a thoughtful and speculative character.

After such glances into the extensive medieval theory of music we shall be better prepared to understand and to appreciate the mental attitude of the famous Parisian school which in the twelfth and thirteenth centuries created the strange Gothic form of the French motet, with its scholastic traits. This rather complicated form is surprisingly bold and fantastic. Its idea consists in building two entirely different and independent melodies on top of a third one, whose theme is a *cantus firmus* from Gregorian chant. The scholastic trait is found in the peculiar treatment of this *cantus firmus*. It is not plainly stated, according to the common practice in similar cases, but is subjected to an academic prescription. The form demands that this *cantus firmus* should be arranged, in one of half a dozen different modes, in a rhythmical order conforming to one of the ancient classical prosodic systems. The *cantus* had to follow from beginning to end either iambic, spondaic, trochaic, dactylic, or anapestic meter, with rests between the sections, without any regard to the natural rhythm of the melody. Here one sees scholastic law and orderly system enforced. It is immaterial whether the system suits the melody or not; the *cantus firmus* has to conform and is forcibly cut up accordingly. Along with this rigid, dry scholastic system, however, the bold Gothic spirit of complication comes into play. Against the strict order and regularity of the *cantus* in the lowest part are written two higher voices, or counterparts, without any apparent connection with each other or with the *cantus*. Three totally different melodies are forcibly welded together; in general, also, three different texts are sung simultaneously, very often in different languages: dance melody and amorous song against solemn Gregorian chant, 3/4 against 6/8 time, French words against Latin words. This fantastic play of the imagination delighted the people who reveled in those grotesque heads of animals and demons, in those curiously distorted human faces carved in stone which are so strange an ornament of the Gothic cathedrals. The boldness and novelty of the musical conception is apparent at once, but its immaturity is equally apparent, for in the thirteenth century music was far from having acquired sufficient technical mastery to cope with constructive problems of such great complexity and difficulty.

Yet at times this music of the Parisian *ars antiqua* rose to high summits. When the now nonexistent International Society of Music celebrated its last festival in Paris in June 1914, shortly before the outbreak of the World War, a sensational impression was produced by French motets of the thirteenth century, heard for the first time, probably, since the Middle Ages. The Sainte-Chapelle, a gem of Gothic architecture, was exactly the right place for this memorable performance; seven hundred years ago Leoninus and Perotinus, the two far-famed heads of the Parisian school of composition, may have performed their motets in this very same chapel. Some of Perotinus' most powerful works have recently been published both in books and in records, and it is now possible to get a clear impression of this remarkable music. Its almost barbaric strength, its utter disregard of beauty of sound, its constant use of piercing dissonances, and its ingenious polyphonic structure give it a curious resemblance to some of the ultramodern music of the Schönberg type.

It is in the music of the great Dutch masters, however, that the Gothic spirit, with its grandeur and with its scholastic subtlety of speculation, finds its finest and most adequate expression. To reach this summit nearly three hundred years were needed, and in order to understand the nature of such a progressive development it is necessary now to turn to some of the other roads pointing toward the still distant summits. So far we have dealt exclusively with ecclesiastical music, inspired by Christian religious feeling, written for the needs of the church service by composers who were almost always priests. The motet of the *ars antiqua* is an attempt to combine the old ecclesiastic severity with an entirely new feature, the charm of the love songs and dance melodies of chivalry.

Toward the year 1200 a new kind of music made its appearance, a secular music whch did not originate in the convents and did not enjoy the protection of the Church: the songs of the troubadours in France and Italy, of the minnesingers in Germany. We possess many thousands of these melodies, often very attractive and even beautiful, full of a lyric charm, a youthful freshness altogether different from the solemn strains of Gregorian chant. This new lyrical amorous music is the product of a new culture, a new class of society; it is the music of the age of chivalry. Until about the eleventh century higher education and learning were a monopoly of the clerical orders; slowly, however, the privileged nobles acquired some intellectual culture. After centuries of barbaric warfare they gained an interest in the gentler arts of peace. About 1200 poetry sprang up in profusion in all the European countries; a rich literature of romance and song was accumulated, and at the same time a new style of music made its appearance.

The easiest access to the spirit of medieval chivalric society and culture is to be found, however, not in the parchment manuscripts of the twelfth century and in the vast modern literature devoted to them, but in the music-dramas of Richard Wagner: *Tannhäuser* and *Lohengrin*, *Tristan und Isolde*, and *Parsifal*. With the insight of genius Wagner knows how to animate the soul of this distant epoch, even without the aid of an antiquarian spirit in his music. Though as a dramatist he does not aim at historical exactness, though he always speaks of myth as the proper subject matter for music-drama, yet myth can reveal historical truth by reviving the atmosphere and spiritual attitude of a certain epoch, and it is through this visionary power of revival that Wagner aids the student of the history of culture and of music.

This chivalric society is quite distinct from the Church. It represents the worldly power and the splendor of the imperial court. The entire history of the years 900 to 1200 is filled with one recurring theme in a hundred variations: the unceasing struggle for supremacy between Pope and Emperor. The Roman Church had evolved its music, the Gregorian chant; the imperial state likewise produced its poetry and music, very different from the music of the church in style and spirit. This new music of the troubadours, with its delight in melody, may be characterized as ennobled folk song. So far the music of the people had been considered too vulgar and insignificant to be worthy of recording; we do not, in fact, possess a single collection of popular tunes prior to 1200. This does not mean that such tunes did not exist earlier. The people had always had some sort of popular music, but the Church had no desire to encourage or propagate it, and it was entirely ignored in the centers of learning and education, the famous convent schools. When, however, the constant struggle between the papal power and the imperial power made the knights more and more antagonistic toward the Church, more and more independent of it, they ceased to go to it for the satisfaction of all their cultural needs, and turned to the people, whose popular style of singing they adapted to their more refined taste. The result is a great treasure of lyric poetry and music from about 1200 to nearly 1400. Thibaut, king of Navarre, Le Châtelain de Coucy, Wizlaw, prince of Rügen, Walther von der Vogelweide, Gottfried von Strassburg, Wolfram von Eschenbach — these are some of the outstanding names of men who were noblemen, knights, poets, and composers at the same time. In this literature we cherish the earliest blossom of lyric love song, and one of the most precious products of early music. The songs of the troubadours have lost almost none of their fragrance and freshness, their melodic charm, even after seven hundred years. The high perfection of lyric style in this literature cannot, of course, have sprung into existence suddenly; the troubadours must have had a long chain of predecessors, of whom nothing is recorded as yet in the annals of history.

In the culture and literature of chivalry we see for the first time since antiquity the rise of a romantic spirit, as opposed to the classical spirit of the Gregorian art. It is a common — but erroneous — notion that romanticism is a modern trait which first appears in the nineteenth century. Classical and romantic tendencies are as old as art, and even ancient art has its romantic features. The history of art shows a constant swing from the classical to the romantic and back again, with all varieties of intermediate stages. The classical and the romantic are like the north and south poles, certain sections of art being for generations under the influence of one and then for generations under the influence of the other. The romantic spirit is one of the chief elements of Gothic architecture, with its play of light and shade, its fantastic lines, its mystic qualities, its high-soaring pillars and spires leading the eye and the spirit upwards, heavenwards, away from the dullness of everyday life. It also animates the great epic poetry of the Middle Ages, the romance of Tristan and Isolde, the mystic piety of the Parsifal legend, great parts of the *Nibelungenlied*; and in lesser degree it permeates the songs of the troubadours, whose lyric poetry has as its central point the erotic theme, the glorification of the beloved mistress by the young knight. For the first time since antiquity woman makes her appearance in lyric song and music, and the eternal mystery of the two sexes comes within the confines of art. Imagination is set in play; profound instincts are excited and let loose; in short, the romantic element is introduced. One may even go as far as to say that the erotic problem in art is perhaps the central point of all romanticism.

Even the realm of medieval religious spirit is not free from this romantic atmosphere. The austere piety of early Christianity, the sublime severity of Byzantine art, the unfriendly, almost repulsive looks of the images of Christ and the Apostles, so characteristic of early mosaic work and Byzantine art — all these are changed in the twelfth century. It is the age of the Crusades. That all Christianity should unite in a vast campaign against the infidels and make great expeditions overseas into unknown foreign countries in order to liberate the holy seats of Jerusalem, expel the Moslems, and make Jerusalem the capital of Christianity is an idea so fantastic that it could have originated and been realized only in a romantic age. The old fanatical religious austerity is now softened, too, by the introduction of the feminine ideal. It was in these ages of the Crusades that the Marianic cult sprang up. Mary, the mother of Christ, the immaculate virgin queen of heaven, the mild, compassionate, forgiving, consoling spirit, the bright evening star, is the idealization of all womanly virtues. If anything is romantic, this new passionate cult of the Virgin Mary is romantic, and Mary herself is altogether different from the austere Christ, the stern judge of the world, depicted in Byzantine art. Marianic poetry is lyric and romantic and musical at the same time. It was St. Francis of

Assisi who discovered this bright new light of humanity, and if he had accomplished no more than this it would suffice to make his name immortal. One of the most cherished themes of spiritual poetry, painting, and music all through the ages, down to our own time, originates in this Franciscan conception: the queen of heaven, soaring above the heavenly hosts, surrounded by the choir of the angels, and, below, unfortunate mortals yearning for peace of soul and praying to her with deeply felt, passionate outcry. A reflection of this new idealization of womanhood animates even the erotic poetry and music of the troubadours, minstrels, and minnesingers.

Thus far music had been serious, fervent, austere, even ecstatic. Now a new quality is added of sweetness, grace, tenderness, delicacy; in short, a womanly note. Music, until now exclusively masculine in character, is transformed by the addition of new lyric, romantic, and erotic tones. A new world of expressiveness is discovered. Though these troubadours' songs, taken singly, are brief and unpretentious in bearing, the new possibilities opened up by their fresh spirit are immense; they have not yet been exhausted, and the art of music is immensely indebted to them even now.

This new lyric music is a reaction against contrapuntal church music; it asserts the right of the individual against the control, frequently tyrannical, exercised by the Church. Supremacy and universality were the aspirations of the Church; it demanded obedience and complete subjugation from the people and stood firm against manifestations of individualism.

The youthful romantic spirit of the twelfth century marks the dawn of the Italian Renaissance. It is the immediate precursor of this great movement. The Franciscan spirit rejuvenates the Church, brings it closer to man, gives a friendlier, more humane aspect to religion, and reconciles to a certain extent the ecclesiastical and worldly interests so hostile to each other in these ages. Music, too, gains from this new lyric and romantic spirit its first springtime, full of budding blossoms, of fresh young green, of mild air and bright sunshine. Secular art has now gained a place; it has asserted its power and remains as a force in art forever. The history of music henceforth has to deal with a new problem of prime importance: ecclesiastical music and secu-lar music in their antagonism and their mutual relations.

By and by this new romantic and lyric spirit in music goes beyond its original confines of solo song with a very primitive instrumental accompaniment. Polyphony, or counterpoint, so far almost exclusively the domain of church music, is gradually adapted to the new lyric style. This combination proved very fertile indeed, and its descendants may be traced down to the twentieth century. The first remarkable results of the mixture of polyphony and secular melody appear in what is known as the *ars nova* in the fourteenth century. This "new art" fills the gap between the older Gothic style of the great school of Paris in the twelfth century and the beginning of the Dutch school early in the fifteenth century. An immensely interesting litera-ture of this music, mainly Italian, between 1300 and 1450 has been explored only recently and constitutes one of the chief discoveries in the field of musicology.

In its aesthetic tendency the Florentine *ars nova* is closely in touch with the rise of poetry and fiction in the early Italian Renaissance, with the beginning of humanistic studies. The rapid rise of culture in the numerous Italian city-republics and princely courts had as a consequence a growing demand for a more refined and elegant type of music, fit for the social enter-tainment of artistically minded people. Musicians were not slow in recognizing the possibilities for musical treatment that were offered by the new poetry, starting with Dante's *La Vita nuova* and continued by the many minor poets around Dante, whose sonnets Dante Gabriel Rossetti has translated into English so beautifully. Petrarch's famous sonnets and *canzone* to his adored Laura were for centuries favorite texts for musical settings. In Boccacio's *Decameron* and other collections of amusing, though not always very chaste and moral stories, music is frequently mentioned and musical scenes are occasionally de-scribed. The peculiar slender grace and refined elegance of the new Italian madrigals, *ballate*, and *caccie* (for one or two solo voices with instrumental accompaniment) is perfectly in keeping with the painting of Botticelli and other early masters. Reading the poetry chosen by these Italian madrigal composers we find ourselves in the atmosphere of cultivated Italian society between 1300 and 1400; through the music we catch glimpses of the delightful scenes that appear in so many of the frescoes painted on the walls of Italian palaces, city houses, and cathedrals in the fourteenth century. As an example we may take a *caccia* (i.e., a catch, a canon) for two voices, with a free third part for an accompanying instrument, by Nicolaus Praepositus de Perugia, who lived in the fourteenth century.[1] The poem describes a company of girls walking in the blooming meadows and woods of spring, gathering flowers and herbs, chatting with each other. One of them exclaims with pleasure as she perceives an especially pretty flower; another suddenly cries aloud, having wounded her finger by touching a thorn. A grasshopper is admired; mushrooms are picked. Then the vesper bell sounds. The sky darkens; there are distant thunder and threatening clouds, but the nightingale begins singing beautifully. Suddenly torrents of rain come down, and everybody hastens home as quickly as possible. One might search the entire art of music back to antiquity without finding anywhere a single piece of music that attempts to describe a scene of this character.

With these innovations entirely new problems spring up in music. Looking at the style of composition in these early Italian madrigals we perceive that at first they continue the style of the French motet, with a *cantus firmus* as basis and two independent parts above it. But there is a very remarkable progress in harmonic feeling. The powerful but almost barbaric groundtone of the old French motet is changed to a graceful play of rhythms and melodic phrases. A little later, about 1350–1400, the Italian masters advance a step further. Solo singing, as found in the troubadours' songs, is used again, but instead of the former improvised instrumental accompaniment, which was never written out, we find an elaborate polyphonic accompaniment. The voices of solo instruments, flutes, little violas, lutes, harps, little organs or psalteriums, most artistically intertwined, provide an elaborate, graceful, and fantastic figuration, especially in the interludes between the single vocal phrases.

---

[1] This charming piece is accessible in Professor Johannes Wolf's valuable collection of old masterpieces, *Sing- und Spielmusik aus älterer Zeit*.

One of the most impressive creations of early Renaissance art is that striking wall painting in the famous *campo santo*, the cemetery at Pisa, representing the Triumph of Death. This monumental painting, generally ascribed to the master Orcagna, includes in its tragic scenes one delightful and touching little episode, a musical scene. We see a gathering of young ladies and gentlemen, fastidiously dressed in the newest, most splendid fashion, playing and singing, while grim Death, waiting in a corner, is just raising his huge scythe to fell his victims. Here is a very realistic representation of the practice of the *ars nova:* one gentleman is playing the viola; a young lady has in her lap a little psaltery, a tiny clavier, such as we often see in old pictures, worn on a silk ribbon around the neck by elegant ladies.

This new madrigal style with florid instrumental accompaniment spread from Italy to France, to the Netherlands, and to England. A representative northern composer in this style is Guillaume de Machault (1300–1377), the leading master of the French *ars nova*.[2] A fine example of Machault's art is to be found in the three-part motet, "De souspirant cuer," remarkable for its rhythmical freedom as well as for its surprisingly advanced harmony.[3] The satirical "Roman de Fauvel," well known in early French literature, contains (at least in the splendidly illustrated Parisian manuscript, fonds français 146, published in facsimile by Pierre Aubry) many motets, ballads, rondeaux, and lais, in a style similar to Machault's, as musical illustrations. These pieces have a special significance for the connection of music with literature and with miniature painting, all three arts being combined in this precious manuscript, which is dated about 1310.

Quick tempo, lively rhythms, elaborate instrumental figuration are especially characteristic marks of many of these Italian and French pieces of the fourteenth century. In Italy this extremely original, vivid, and picturesque art comes to a surprisingly abrupt end at the beginning of the quattrocento, about 1425. The cause probably lies in political changes, which brought with them corresponding changes in art. The most flourishing

---

[2] A complete edition of his music (edited by Professor F. Ludwig) is in course of publication in Germany.

[3] Included in Johannes Wolf's *Sing- und Spielmusik aus älterer Zeit.*

period of the Italian madrigal, *ballata*, and *caccia* coincides almost exactly with the removal of the papal residence from Rome to Avignon, in southern France. During the years of this Avignon residence Rome lost a good deal of its ecclesiastic power, and Italian music in this period was much less occupied with church music than with secular song.

As early as 1324 Pope Johannes XXII sent forth from Avignon a famous decree against figurated music in the Church, anticipating the charges brought against contrapuntal music at the Council of Trent more than two hundred years later, in the time of Palestrina. Pope Johannes attacks the abuse of polyphony in church music, aiming mainly at the artificial motets of the *ars antiqua*. Composers, writes the Pope, "cut the melody into pieces with *hoquet* (an effect of sobbing, sighing), enervate it by descant and *tripla* (counterpoints), and sometimes even add secular motets. Thus they show a lack of respect for the basis of church music, are ignorant of its laws, do not know the church modes, and do not distinguish them from each other, but rather confuse them. . . . Thus their tones run about restlessly, intoxicate the ear without calming it, falsify expression, and disturb the worship of the congregation instead of awakening it; they favor lasciviousness instead of dispelling it."

The scandalous state of the papacy in the fourteenth century could hardly have a good effect on church music. In 1378, one year after Pope Urban VI had returned to Rome, one of the most shameful episodes of papal history had its beginning. An antipope, Clement VII, was elected by an opposing party of cardinals, and while Urban, just returned from Avignon, took up his residence in the Lateran Palace in Rome, his adversary, Pope Clement, took possession of the newly vacated papal palace in Avignon. This Great Schism, the simultaneous rule of two hostile popes, divided Christianity into two opposed camps. This miserable state lasted from 1378 to 1417, and its influence on music is seen in the fact that the period is barren of good church music, while the secular Italian *ars nova* continues to flourish. The old ecclesiastic motet had been debased more and more through the use of erotic songs and dance melodies, and during the period of papal depression and schism Italian composers lost all taste in church music. It was not until 1417 that the Schism was brought to a definite close by the exciting Council of Constance, when the papal power showed all nations that it had regained its strength. The Dominican Inquisition, begun in the thirteenth century, was let loose against reformers of faith, like the already deceased Wycliffe, translator of the Bible into English, whose bones were burnt, and John Huss, the Bohemian reformer, who was burnt alive at Constance.

The immediate consequence of the restored power of the papacy under Martin V is soon perceived in a new rise of ecclesiastic music in the period starting about 1425. After two hundred and fifty years the famous old Paris school of counterpoint and the French motet had lost their vitality. The successor of the French school in leadership is the school of Cambrai, in the Netherlands, which dominated the entire musical world for more than a century. The age of the great Dutch music now has its beginning.

At the time of the *ars nova*, in the fourteenth century, a new and simpler style of polyphony began in England and later spread to France and the Netherlands. French contrapuntal complexity is replaced by a more harmonic style of writing; euphonious triads are preferred to the former fierce discords. Three great names represent this transition to the new Dutch style of Cambrai, those of John Dunstable, the greatest English composer of his age, and the Dutch masters, Binchois and Dufay. The three are contemporaries. Dunstable, famous both as musician and astronomer, died in 1453 in London, where one can still see his tomb in St. Stephen's Church; Dufay lived in Cambrai after 1450 and died there in 1474; Binchois died in 1460. The reorganized papal power in Rome soon made use of this rising Dutch music, for which the Avignon popes had a marked predilection. During its sojourn in Avignon the papal see had come into closer contact with French and Dutch music, at that time nearly identical, and, native talent for ecclesiastic music being scarcely available in Italy after a hundred years of erotic madrigals and ballads, the papal chapel now turned to Dutch singers and composers. Thus from about 1450 there was an invasion of Dutch musicians into Italy which for a hundred and fifty years to come established the predominance of Dutch music throughout Europe. We have come to the start of a most important new chapter in the history of music.

Everybody speaks of Dutch music and Dutch painting. Few people, however, are aware of the fact that in the fifteenth century, at least, Dutch music and painting were at home in Burgundy. This once rich and powerful country disappeared from the map of Europe completely four hundred years ago, and for most people the famous Burgundy wine is the only reminder of the existence of one of the most flourishing of European countries. The territory of Burgundy, now divided between Belgium, France, Luxembourg, Switzerland, and Germany, comprised a broad corridor starting at the Dutch seacoast at the entrance of the English Channel and extending southward as far as the Lake of Geneva. It reached the height of its power and wealth under the rule of its dukes Philippe le Beau and, especially, Charles the Bold, who came to the throne in 1467. The court of Philippe and of Charles in Brussels was one of the most luxurious of the European courts. Both dukes were extremely cultivated and great lovers of art. Their immense wealth, the general prosperity of the country, the great commerce of cities like Brussels, Antwerp, Bruges, and Ghent, and the natural talent of the Flemish for music, painting, and architecture all helped to make this country the most cultivated region of Europe, the only rival of Italy, which was just entering on the artistically rich period of the Renaissance.

Charles the Bold was a liberal protector of artists. Great painters like Jan and Hubert van Eyck of Ghent, Rogier van der Weyden, and Hans Memlinck were in his service, and a whole galaxy of great Dutch masters of music embellished with their unrivaled art the splendor of the brilliant and luxurious Burgundian court. Gilles Binchois, Anton Busnois, Pierre de la Rue, Alexander Agricola, shining lights of the first Dutch school, were active for many years at the Brussels court, and their new style of music, their brilliant achievements in performance carried the fame of Dutch music all over Europe. Charles was himself an accomplished musician, a composer of motets and chansons. The splendor of the tournaments and festivities at his court was unparalleled, save here and there in Italy, and his court chapel at that time hardly found an equal anywhere in Europe. In the incomparably charming old town of Bruges the magnificent bronze monument erected over the tomb of this warrior and lover of the arts is still one of the great sights.

The town of Cambrai in Burgundy was the seat of the most celebrated school of music of the fifteenth century, and in Cambrai most of the great Dutch masters of music were educated. It was to the school of Cambrai cathedral that the papal court and the royal courts of Europe turned to secure able musicians for their chapels. Nowhere could one find composers, conductors, singers, and players comparable to these Dutch-Burgundian artists. We shall meet them everywhere in our rapid survey of the artistic state, in Italy, France, Germany, Spain, and even such smaller countries as Poland.

While the music of Burgundy and the Netherlands filled all Europe with its fame, history is singularly silent as regards great musical accomplishments in France during the fifteenth century. A glance at French history will explain why Paris, for centuries the greatest metropolis of music, enjoying absolute supremacy and authority over all Europe, should have sunk into insignificance toward 1400. France had reached one of the most unfortunate eras of her history. What is known as the Hundred Years' War with England raged, with a few intermissions, from 1337 to 1453. This long-drawn-out struggle has gained a romantic glamour through the heroic and marvelous feat of the peasant girl, Joan of Arc, who brought about the defeat of the English army besieging Orléans in 1430. These hundred years of warfare utterly exhausted France, and it was fifty years before the country recovered sufficiently to show results of weight in art and science. Scarcely had peace been established between France and England when the new king of France, Louis XI (1461–1483), filled out another quarter of a century fighting his most powerful neighbor and adversary, Charles the Bold of Burgundy, and a number of other powerful French princes, with the final result of a transition from feudalism to monarchy in France. He finally succeeded in his political aim of subduing all France to the royal power of the Valois dynasty, but the price paid for this victory was the poverty and cultural ruin of the French people, who had to endure a rule of terror under a despotic, cruel, almost insane king.

One of the most remarkable and interesting historical documents we possess is a description of the state of Europe about 1450 written by the papal legate, Aeneas Sylvius, later Pope Pius II, who in those years traveled about on diplomatic missions in many countries. This cool, shrewd, and highly cultivated observer tells us of the low state of culture and prosperity in France as compared with the great artistic accomplishments of the wealthy and flourishing cities of Burgundy. Charles of Burgundy had great political plans. He aspired to erect a great Rhenish empire, to add to his countries the rich Rhenish provinces, so that the great river Rhine, from its source high up in the Swiss Alps, on its course through Switzerland and Germany, to its mouth in the Netherlands, should be entirely controlled by Burgundy, adding immensely to the wealth of the country by its incomparable commercial utility. But the jealousy of France and the independent spirit of Switzerland frustrated this great Rhenish enterprise. In murderous battles with the Swiss and the French Charles was defeated; he fell in battle near Nancy on the fourth of January, 1477. Louis of France had got rid of his most formidable rival. His aim now was to get as much as possible of the immensely rich Burgundian country. Charles's daughter and heiress, Mary of Burgundy, the richest princess of Europe, he planned to make the wife of his son, Charles VIII, hoping thus to secure Burgundy to France by inheritance, without long wars and endless troubles. But Mary of Burgundy, we need not be surprised to find, had no less than seven suitors from the princely families of many countries, and she finally chose young Maximilian of Habsburg, later the German emperor Maximilian I, of whom we shall have more to say as one of the greatest patrons of music. Louis of France, enraged at Mary's refusal to become his daughter-in-law, did not give up his desire of possessing the Burgundian countries. A war with Maximilian was the consequence. Finally in 1482 peace was made, and Burgundy was divided between Germany and France. In this same year Mary of Burgundy, wife of Maximilian, lost her life by an accident, and a year later her relentless enemy, Louis of France, died after a vicious life full of cruelty, destruction, and war. At the time of his death France was still the real lowland of Europe in cultural respects, much inferior to the Burgundian Netherlands, to Italy, and even to Germany. This state of affairs explains why we hear next to nothing of music in France during the entire fifteenth century, when Dutch music had begun to win renown throughout Europe.

The Dutch music of the fifteenth century represents the final expression of the Gothic spirit in terms of musical composition. Extending from about 1450 to nearly 1600, from Dufay to Orlando di Lasso and Jan Pieterzon Sweelinck, it is not uniform in style throughout the course of its vigorous life of a hundred and fifty years. Only its first half, from about 1450 to 1530, belongs to Gothic art proper; its later productions add features that are more or less in the spirit of the Italian Renaissance. Most of the great Dutch musicians — Dufay, Okeghem, Josquin de Près, Heinrich Isaak, Pierre de la Rue, Obrecht, Alexander Agricola, Adrian Willaert — were internationally famous artists, traveling constantly from one country to another, in eager demand at the imperial court at Vienna or Innsbruck and at the French royal court at Paris, sought by the kings of Bohemia and Poland, by numerous dukes and princes in Italy, and especially by the papal chapel in Rome. Dutch music, with its peculiar complication, joined to an ecclesiastic character of great impressiveness, appealed to all the European countries as the perfect musical expression of the dominant spirit of their age. As Gothic architecture spread throughout Europe and reached to England and the Scandinavian countries, the complex Netherlandish art of music followed. And just as Gothic architecture was modified more in Italy than in any other country, so the Netherlandish art of music, practiced by the great Dutch masters themselves, was not fully assimilated by Italian artists. It is extremely interesting to observe the way in which, after about 1530, Italian composers who were pupils of the Dutch masters asserted their national traits against the powerful influence of the imported Dutch art. The final outcome of this struggle we see in Palestrina and his school, in the two Gabrielis in Venice, in the Italian madrigal, where the spirit of the Italian Renaissance asserts itself victoriously. More detailed treatment of this phase of development, however, belongs in the chapter on the Renaissance.

A closer inspection of Dutch music at its climax, with Josquin de Près as the dominating figure, reveals the traits which justify us in calling it closely akin in spirit to Gothic architecture. The art of counterpoint had attained a virtuosity of treatment, a mastery of complication, an organic, logical development hardly ever paralleled in later styles, except by Bach in certain aspects of his art, which revives the Gothic spirit to some extent. In the Dutch motets and masses the piling up of several voices on top of each other, the complex subtleties of canonic treatment, the fantastically curved melodic lines running parallel, obliquely, contrary to each other, intermixed with pauses, with strange, adventurous coloratura — these are like a reflection of the pointed Gothic arches, the slender spires, the lofty pillars, the complex play of lines in the Gothic cathedrals. An ecstatic piety and the play of a fantastic imagination are combined in a unique manner with the strictest, most severe, and most complex plan of construction, a union of apparently irreconcilable elements that characterizes the Gothic style of architecture as well. The *conditio sine qua non* of this music is polyphony. A strictly linear style of writing is here carried to its final consequences.

Thus the Gothic spirit, that peculiar combination of the strictest, coolest logic, the most rigid law, with the fantastic flight of the imagination, led to the discovery of possibilities in music undreamt of before — to the rise of lyric and romantic music as we find it in the songs of the troubadours and in the fascinating amorous music of the Italian *ars nova* in the fourteenth century, and to the marvelous structure of Dutch polyphony, the application of architectural ideas to music on the grandest scale, full of daring feats of musical engineering, yet of the most strictly logical development. Both these accomplishments, polyphonic construction and the introduction of the romantic spirit, are like new continents discovered in music, comparable in their artistic importance to the discovery of America by Christopher Columbus. They have not had a merely local and temporary importance; they have become the lasting property of the art of music. They have been varied a thousandfold, changing their proportions, their mutual relations, in every age, but since their first appearance they have never been absent from music, and they have enriched it beyond measure. Modern music owes an immense debt to the Gothic spirit, for its characteristic traits, transposed into music, are the very elements and foundations of symphonic music. No later influence is comparable in lastingness and vitality, and all later artistic revolutions and innovations, fascinating as they may be, dwindle into comparative insignificance beside the enormous sustaining power of these Gothic contributions to the art of music.

CHAPTER FOUR

THE RENAISSANCE

THE epoch from about 1300 to 1600 is generally known as the Italian Renaissance. It is one of the most brilliant periods in the entire history of the human race, and one whose equal, at least in artistic achievement, the world had not seen since the Periclean Age of Athens, nearly two thousand years earlier. For music, as for the other arts, the Renaissance was extremely fertile, and some of its ideas still govern our spiritual and artistic life.

"Renaissance," in the narrow literal sense of the term, means rebirth, revival. The aim was originally the revival of classical antiquity in the arts and sciences, but in the pursuit of this aim the term Renaissance acquired a new meaning, wider and much more important. It had for its ideal the rebirth, the rejuvenation of the human spirit and intellect. For the future, its most striking trait was the discovery of the individual and his powers. Medieval culture had not acknowledged individualism; the Church, undisputed ruler in all spiritual matters, demanded belief in its dogmas, obedience to its rules; philosophy, science, and art were admitted only within strict confines. During the Renaissance art broke away from this bondage to a considerable extent. The impersonality of the epic and a desire to express the feelings of a people or a class were no longer at the bottom of art; the lyric expression of the personal feelings of the individual artist now for the first time since antiquity became of prime importance. What this attitude means for music hardly needs explanation. The whole modern idea of music as an art is based on a recognition of the value and significance of the individual, on personal expression, and for this fundamental aesthetic point of view we owe a huge debt to the Italian Renaissance.

This attitude made a marked and lasting impression upon music during the Renaissance itself, though in curiously intertwined ways. Naturally it affected secular music more than church music, but Italian church music was also profoundly influenced and changed by it. Its earliest reflection is seen in the Italian *ars nova* of the fourteenth century, already described in some of its main characteristics. From about 1450 to 1550, however, the development of this musical type was disturbed and diverted by the introduction into Italy of Dutch music, which in its contents and technique, its expression and style, is much more akin to the Gothic spirit than to that of the Renaissance.

The entire sixteenth century is an unusually interesting one, for it marks the transformation of musical art under the mutual influence of northern and southern traits, Dutch and Italian, Gothic and Renaissance. This antagonism is comparable not so much to a battle, a fight for life, as to a wrestling match. At the end neither of the two combatants is defeated; both are sound, but they are different from what they were before. Or one might say that the music of the sixteenth century is the offspring of Dutch-Italian parentage, and that its features resemble those of both parents. As the year 1600 draws near, it may seem to a superficial observer that the Renaissance spirit is the final victor in the long contest. Looking more closely, however, we find that the solid Dutch basis had become indispensable to later Italian music, and that Dutch polyphonic art and constructive skill are manifest in whatever of later Italian Renaissance music became deeply rooted and fertile for the future. Italian music in the seventeenth century could have eliminated the Dutch basic features only at the risk of losing its vitality, its permanent artistic value. Several bold attempts at the complete overthrow of the Dutch artistic attitude were made in Italy, but they were all short-lived and ended by drying up like rivers in a desert. One of the most fascinating problems of modern research on style is concerned with the various phases of this phenomenal process of transformation in Italy between 1450 and 1600.

For about one hundred years, up to 1450, Florence was the center of the new Italian *ars nova*, but after the restoration of the papal power, church music took the lead again, the papal chapel in Rome became the musical center, and for another century Florence, with its *ballate*, its *caccie*, its amorous and elegant madrigals, is lost from sight, regaining predominance only for a quarter of a century, from about 1580 to 1605, when monody and opera were created. Dutch musicians make their appearance in Italy from about 1420, and the lists of the papal chapel show Dutch names from about 1425. One of the earliest of these Dutch guests in Italy is the great master Guillaume Dufay, from Cambrai. As a boy of sixteen years he found a position at the court of the Duke of Urbino in Pesaro, a little town that later was not of much importance musically, except for the fact that Rossini was born there in 1792. Dufay spent nearly ten years (1428–1437) at the papal chapel in Rome, and it was he who was most influential in establishing the predominance of the Dutch art in Italy. Compared with his superior mastery of composition, the efforts of the native Italian musicians must have appeared insignificant, especially in church music. A generation later the great Josquin de Près spent years as singer in the papal chapel, and around these two superior artists a great many other Dutch musicians of more or less fame are grouped.

A few significant dates from the fifteenth century may help to give a clearer and more lifelike aspect to the rather dry enumeration of names of old Dutch masters. What was happening in the world at the time when the celebrated music school of the Flemish cathedral of Cambrai was sending forth artists of international fame to all the European countries? In 1430 the peasant girl, Joan of Arc, accomplished the marvelous and heroic feat of expelling from France the invading English army besieging Orléans. In 1453 Constantinople was finally captured by the Turks; the last shadow of the Byzantine empire vanished forever, and the Turkish power became for centuries a menace to Europe. The latter event had eminent importance not only for subsequent European political affairs but also for the growth of culture, particularly in Italy. The spiritual tendencies of the Renaissance were considerably strengthened by the expulsion of Christian scholars and artists from Constantinople. These scholars and artists sought a refuge in the western countries, especially Italy, and brought with them priceless manuscripts that helped to propagate the study of Greek language and literature in western Europe. In the history of music it has not yet been determined precisely in what way this influx of Byzantine science and art left its imprint, for the entire history of Byzantine music is still dark. But it seems unquestionable that there was a Byzantine influence upon music in the fifteenth century, and to discover its nature remains an important problem for future research in musical history. Another extremely important event in the later fifteenth century has already been mentioned briefly in the preceding chapter — the victory of the French king, Louis XI, over Charles the Bold of Burgundy in 1477. France henceforth becomes a centralized monarchy and after about 1500 rouses from her long exhaustion. Paris, between 1200 and 1300 the center of the musical world, was entirely insignificant during the entire fifteenth century; it was not until the sixteenth century that the French Renaissance once more made it an able competitor, and not until the seventeenth, in the classical epoch of Louis XIV, that it once more became a leader.

The year 1492 is a particularly interesting one. It is generally considered to mark the beginning of the modern era of history, the close of medieval times. Its rights to this claim are derived from Columbus' discovery of America, which, however, has almost no bearing on musical matters for centuries later. The same year marks the close of the Moorish reign in Spain; the Moorish capital, Granada, is captured by the Spanish and the pious king Ferdinand and the bigot queen Isabella, under the influence of the fanatical Inquisition and its grand master Torquemada, expel the Jews from Spain. From this time on Spain, thus far of almost no importance in the history of music, becomes a country of musical activity in the European sense. What the centuries of Moorish and Jewish residence in Spain mean for music is an attractive problem as yet unsolved.

In the same year occurred the death of Lorenzo de' Medici, the great protector of the arts in Florence. Under his rule Florence had risen to the very first rank, to undisputed leadership in art, and to this day the sight of the city is an incomparable experience to all lovers of noble art. In specifically musical matters the supremacy of Florence was past, Rome having taken the leadership. Nevertheless, Lorenzo was also a great lover of music, and many famous musicians enjoyed his protection. Squarcialupi, the greatest organist of his time, was for many years the leading musician at Lorenzo's court. After Squarcialupi's death, Lorenzo called the celebrated Dutch musician, Heinrich Isaak, to Florence.

This great master offers a striking example of the mixture of Dutch and Italian traits after 1500, for he brought to Italy his magnificent mastery of the art of polyphony, of which he later gave to the world a truly monumental specimen in his *Choralis Constantinus*. This huge work is the first polyphonic treatment of the entire collection of Gregorian chants that make up the *Graduale*, i.e., pieces added to the ordinary parts of the mass, according to the liturgy of the entire year. Other very characteristic specimens of Isaak's work are two glorious six-part motets, which are among the greatest masterpieces in this form. Isaak here does homage to the two great powers of the world, the Pope and the Emperor. The first motet, "Optime pastor," is dedicated to Pope Leo X, whom Isaak knew personally at Florence while the future pope was still a young Medici prince and probably one of Isaak's pupils, along with the other Medici children. The second, "Virgo prudentissima," glorifies the imperial power and is dedicated to the Emperor Maximilian I. In later years Isaak was made court conductor at Maximilian's imperial court. While all these works show Isaak as an unsurpassed master of Dutch polyphonic art, he was influenced somewhat by the Italian *ballate* in Florence. He was one of the chief musical collaborators of Lorenzo de' Medici at the yearly carnivals in Florence, those gorgeous pageants and masquerades in which all the people of Florence, all the trades, all the arts, participated. Lorenzo himself wrote many a poem for these pageants, and Heinrich Isaak composed a great number of those gay and witty songs in Italian style known as *canti carnascialeschi*. While at Florence Heinrich Isaak met his countryman, Jacob Obrecht, also one of the greatest of Dutch musicians. Obrecht had been sent by the Emperor Maximilian as diplomatic agent to Florence, with a special mission to Lorenzo. Nowadays one can hardly imagine a musician as ambassador on important political missions. Yet the age of the Renaissance shows us quite a number of great musicians, painters, and architects as ambassadors of kings, popes, princes, who in turn displayed the wide range of cultural interests that is characteristic of the Renaissance mind. Obrecht spent his last years at Maximilian's court at the head of the imperial chapel, where the great Josquin de Près was his colleague, and Heinrich Isaak and Ludwig Senfl his successors. Obrecht died in 1505 in Ferrara, a victim of the great plague that devastated Italy at that time.

Technical inventions as well as historical events have more than once brought about considerable change in the musical life of the various countries. To take familiar examples, what a change has been brought about in our day by the phonograph, the radio, and the sound film! A similar revolution was effected about seventy-five years ago when steamships, railroads, and the telegraph were universally introduced, when traveling to foreign countries was made quick and easy, and when musical culture was spread, though often much diluted, to countries far from the European home of music. The influence of these modern inventions on music seems slight, however, in comparison with the significance of the invention of printing for the progress and propagation of the arts. When the first books were printed, about 1450, science and art, thus far accessible only to a select few, were, so to speak, socialized. The cause of education made an immense stride forward as soon as books became cheaply procurable in large numbers. Up to 1450 books had been a costly possession; they were written by hand on parchment in hours of patient labor by professional scribes, often great artists in their line, and only a few exceptionally wealthy persons could afford the luxury of a large library. But in the sixteenth century books came within the reach of the middle class, of fairly well-to-do citizens all over Europe. Music felt the benefit of printing and publication very soon. The great Dutch masters were immensely lucky in being the first to profit from the new invention, for they could not have obtained so rapid, complete, and sweeping a victory without the invaluable aid of printing. The printing of music, begun about the year 1500, was first an Italian specialty. Unlike most of the other practical arts, the art of printing has not been gradually improved after insignificant beginnings. The oldest books, the incunabula, printed before 1500, have never been surpassed for exquisite beauty of workmanship and durability and excellence of paper. With the *Odhecaton*, a collection of about a hundred pieces by various composers, the first printed collection of part music, published in Venice in the year 1501,[1] the greatest master of music printing, Ottaviano Petrucci, commenced his career as publisher. The thirty publications of his press are now the incomparable treasures of a few of the greatest libraries of the world, and immense prices are paid for them. These Italian publications acquainted the entire musical world with the new works of the famous Dutch masters: Josquin de Près, Jacob Obrecht, Heinrich Isaak, Ghiselin, Brumel, Japart, Ockeghem, Pierre de la Rue, and many others. Before long the sensational Petrucci publications were imitated by other printers, and about 1525 we see music publishing well established as a flourishing trade, not only in Venice but also in Rome, Florence, Paris, Antwerp, Nuremberg, Augsburg, and other places. An important consequence of music printing was that the works of the masters were now performed not only in great cathedrals and in the palaces of cardinals and princes but also in the houses of the citizens, in the churches and schools of smaller towns and even villages. Musical culture, in short, was spread in a measure formerly impossible. And as the work of the great artists helped the business of the publishing houses, the artists themselves were spurred on by their success and their growing fame to create fresh works that would surprise the ardent lovers of music with ingenious and beautiful new effects.

The wonderful rise of Italian music in the sixteenth century reveals just one phase of the great spiritual and cultural achievements of the Italian Renaissance. Music is inseparably connected with poetry and with the culture of social life. This last-named

---

[1] See the article by Gustav Reese in *Musical Quarterly* (New York), January 1934, on the *Odhecaton*.

topic is finely illustrated by a book famous in Italian literature of the cinquecento, Baldassare Castiglione's *Libro del cortegiano* ("The Courtier"), published in 1528. The author, himself a member of the best Italian society, describes in detail what accomplishments were generally expected of a "cortegiano," a nobleman of the court society, and gives us a most interesting and complete account of the life and manners of the court. The book was translated into English by Sir Thomas Hoby in 1561, and from this English nobleman's translation a few paragraphs relative to our subject may be quoted here. Enumerating the accomplishments of a gentlewoman, Castiglione speaks of dancing and music. It is becoming to a gentlewoman:

"Not to use swift measures in her daunsinge.

"Not to use in singinge or playinge upon instrumentes to muche devision and busy pointes, that declare more cunning then sweetnesse.

"To come to daunce, or to showe her musicke with suffringe herself to be first prayed somewhat and drawen to it."

Speaking of a gentleman's social accomplishments, Castiglione says it is appropriate for a gentleman:

"To daunce well without over nimble footinges or to busie tricks.

"To singe well upon the booke.

"To play upon the Lute, and singe to it with a ditty.

"To play upon the Vyole and all other instruments with freates."

Castiglione, very much a man of the Renaissance, also points out one important reason why music was practiced so much and so skillfully by cultivated amateurs in his time. He says: "And princypally in Courtes, where (beside the refreshing of vexacyons that musicke bringeth unto eche man) many thynges are taken in hande to please women withal, whose tender and soft breastes are soone perced with melody and fylled with sweetnesse. Therefore no marvaile that in the olde times and nowe a dayes they have always bene enclined to musitiens, and counted this a moste acceptable foode of the mynde."

Here we perceive plainly the erotic origin of the Italian madrigal, in fact, of all Italian chamber music, sung, played, danced, or presented theatrically. Modern song and chamber music is to a certain extent erotic in character, but not nearly so exclusively erotic as Italian Renaissance music. Living constantly in an artistic atmosphere of great distinction, women of the higher classes of society had become so fastidious in their tastes that a young gentleman intent on winning the favor of his lady had to be an expert and skillful musician; a blundering amateur would have appeared ridiculous in that society.

Although Rome was the stronghold of Dutch ecclesiastical music in Italy until about 1550, Venice transforms this Dutch polyphony in a characteristically Italian manner. The strictly linear music of the Dutch masters, with its relationship to Gothic architecture, was not by any means either natural or agreeable to Italian musicians. They learned the technique of counterpoint very thoroughly from their Dutch masters, but their innate sense for melody, for pictorial effect, for clearness of construction, made them add a characteristically Italian melody and color. In the case of Palestrina in Rome later we see a wonderfully harmonious blending of Dutch linear design and subtlety of construction with Italian beauty of sound and melodic sense, but Venetian composers attacked the problem differently. In Venice the central place of musical activity had been St. Mark's. We are not very well informed on the masters active there in the fifteenth century, and we first meet with a name of great celebrity when the famous Dutch composer, Adrian Willaert, is appointed chief conductor at St. Mark's in 1527. From this year dates the Venetian school, which within about sixty years was universally acknowledged throughout Europe and acted as a sort of counterbalance to the older Dutch system.

The Venetian style of composition is based on the Dutch technique of construction, but new features are added that to some extent crowd into the background the strictly linear contrapuntal Dutch construction, which is comparable to a sketch in black and white. This linear design and the finely balanced play of three or four single voices now receive much less attention than the general acoustic effect. The Venetian masters are fascinated by the ideal of a full, rich, brilliantly colored sound. Experimenting with a view to obtaining this quality, they succeed in mastering to an amazing degree a new art of rich sound-color. No doubt the native genius of Venice had impressed itself profoundly on those susceptible Dutch artists, Adrian Willaert and his Dutch disciples. Wherever they looked in Venice, they must have been struck by the eminently picturesque effect of the scene. There was the large luxurious city built almost entirely over water, with canals instead of streets, gondolas and boats instead of horses and carriages. There was the fantastic architecture of the glorious church of St. Mark, with its Oriental splendor, its cupolas so unlike the Gothic spires, and its rich ornament of mosaic. Next to it stood the hardly less picturesque palace of the doges, looking out on the Adriatic Sea, and before it the wonderfully harmonious Piazza of San Marco. Here started the Grand Canal, lined with the palaces of the nobility in which hung masterpieces of the Venetian school of painting between 1500 and 1600, with their glowing colors, their brilliant and picturesque contrasts of light and shade. When Master Willaert came to Venice in 1527, Venetian painting had reached its greatest height. Giovanni Bellini was dead, but such masters as Titian, Palma Vecchio, Paolo Veronese, Tintoretto, and Giorgione created marvels of pictorial art very different in the character of their coloring, in the broad brushing of their paint, from the clean contours, the correct and splendid draftsmanship of the painting of Raphael and the Florentine and Roman artists. Color is predominant here, as opposed to the purity of design and contour of Florence and Rome. These new marvels of color express the characteristic genius of Venice, and we find them reflected in Venetian music. Willaert went to Venice at the height of his artistic powers, after having served the courts of Paris, Rome, Ferrara, and Hungary with great distinction, and the colorful art of Venice must have impressed him deeply. Very soon we see him transforming his finely wrought Dutch design into those broad levels of color so characteristic of Venetian painting. The elaborate contrapuntal writing becomes much plainer; a new harmonic chord effect is introduced, full of strange and picturesque sound, broad level stretches of tone, impressive dialogue effects, and contrasting tone colors.

Willaert also created the new style of *chori spezzati*, in which two distinct choral bodies answer each other in dialogue and are finally combined in powerful climax. For this, the peculiar architecture of St. Mark's, with its two choirs and two organ lofts at a distance from each other, gave him his first impetus. A primitive use of double chorus had been made for a thousand years in the venerable antiphony of the Gregorian chant of the Catholic church service. The new Venetian technique, however, went considerably beyond the old impression of mere dialogue, adding striking effects of sound-color and a characteristic emotional expressiveness. This writing for double chorus was later extended to three and even four choruses and became the Venetian specialty for nearly a century. It reached its final perfection in the works of Andrea Gabrieli and his nephew Giovanni Gabrieli, successors of Willaert's at St. Mark's. In their choral works for eight, twelve, sixteen, even twenty voices, a choir of low voices often opposed to one of high voices, we see the musical parallel to the Venetian painting of Titian, Paolo Veronese, and Tintoretto. In a comparatively short time the Dutch music of Willaert had been thoroughly acclimatized and was imbued with the spirit of the brilliant Venetian art, a wonderfully fertile assimilation and transformation of style.

The year 1527, which has been mentioned as the birth year of the great Venetian music, was memorable in many other respects as well, but chiefly for the dreadful *sacco di Roma*. Once more, as so often in medieval times, the northern barbarians invaded the sacred city of Rome; once more France and Germany fought each other on Italian soil, and the dreaded German and Swiss *Landsknechte*, or mercenary soldiers, under General Frondsberg attacked Pope Leo X, the friend of France. Rome was plundered by the grim *Landsknechte* after a carnage, many houses were burnt, and priceless treasures of art were carried off or destroyed. This disaster is often considered the end of the Italian Renaissance, at least in Rome. Difficult times followed in Italy. As the news of the plundering of Rome spread, a French army invaded Italy, captured Genoa, and marched toward Naples, expecting to meet its German enemies there. Only the outbreak of a pestilence saved Naples from being plundered like Rome. In the same year the Medici family was expelled from

Florence for a second time, and the great historian of Florence, the proponent of the unsentimental, unscrupulous politics of the Renaissance, Machiavelli, died.

The alarming news that had come to the papacy in recent years from Germany and Switzerland, where Protestantism under the vigorous leadership of Luther and Zwingli endangered the authority of the Catholic Church more and more, was given fresh significance by the sack of Rome, and the first measures of the long-drawn-out Counter Reformation were taken in consequence. The part of music in the Counter Reformation was an important one. The genius destined to be its most glorious protagonist was born in 1526 in the little country town of Palestrina that lies between Rome and Naples.

When the spirit of the Italian Renaissance is being discussed, Palestrina cannot be passed over lightly, for his music shows some of the most characteristic aspects of Renaissance art in their purest form. He spent his entire artistic career at Rome in the service of the Catholic Church, most of the time at the famous papal chapel of St. Peter's, though he was absent from it for about seventeen years. This absence illustrates very forcibly the tendencies of the Roman Counter Reformation. In 1555 Pope Paul IV set up an iron rule. He pursued with the greatest severity everything and everybody likely to injure the Catholic Church in the eyes of the world. Michelangelo's glorious fresco paintings in the Sistine Chapel were offensive to him because of the nude bodies that were represented, and he ordered the painter Daniel da Volterra to supply them with appropriate clothing. This fact alone makes it manifest that the half-pagan Renaissance spirit, with its delight in reminiscences of antiquity, was vanishing, that a severe new bent of mind had become dominant. Another of Paul's reforms was the removal of all married singers from the papal chapel, in order to enforce celibacy and accentuate the clerical character of all the institutions of the Catholic Church. Palestrina had to quit his post and was called back only years later, when another pope of less severity occupied the papal throne. Palestrina's music does not manifest in any way the characteristic traits of the spirit of the Counter Reformation, which becomes evident only a generation later in the music of the baroque age. Yet the astonishing fact remains — one might call it an irony of fate — that this music of Palestrina's, so full of the Renaissance spirit, so traditional in its general aspects, so unsensational in a propagandistic sense, was destined to become the most powerful musical ally of the Catholic Church in its combat with Protestantism. To this very day Palestrina's music is justly admired as the most comprehensive, convincing, and successful interpretation of the true Catholic spirit, not only in music proper but in all the world of art.

In the music of Palestrina a student expert in problems of style can find summed up the entire process of transformation which the Dutch style underwent in Italy. Palestrina had learned his art from Dutch masters, and he himself finally mastered the Dutch technique of counterpoint and construction to perfection. Yet his music would not have meant much to posterity had it remained only a copy, however skillful, of the Dutch manner. What makes it unique and incomparable is the fact that this master alone knew how to apply to the severe and complex Dutch art of design and construction the Italian melodic bent, sense of color and proportion, the Italian accent, voice, and soul. The broad stream of these characteristic traits of the Italian Renaissance carries along with it as smaller tributaries all the traditional Dutch traits. Palestrina is not in the least a revolutionary artist, bent on forcibly overthrowing a former state of things; his music shows us a classical paradigm of evolution, of gradual and legitimate transformation.

It is the general fate of revolutionary art to represent a new start which is bound to be superseded by subsequent progress, whereas great evolutionary art means not a beginning but a conclusion, a climax, an arrival at perfection. And Palestrina, like Orlando di Lasso, like Bach, Mozart, Beethoven, Verdi, and Wagner, belongs among the great names of evolutionary art.

The lasting value of Palestrina's art is based upon two essential qualities: purity of style, and the coupling of ideal contents with ideal form. Though Palestrina's music is narrower in scope than that of other masters of the first magnitude — Bach, Mozart, Beethoven — yet within its limits it must be called one of the most sublime achievements of all art. It is the ideal ecclesiastical music, superior even to Bach's church music. The Catholic spirit certainly has never found a more congenial or more convincing artistic expression. As regards its form, attention must be called to the perfect equilibrium that is maintained between the logical construction of its contrapuntal design and its wonderfully rich effects of sound, full of color, light, and shade. Only in Mozart's music do we meet with a similar equilibrium, though on a very different plane. Works like Palestrina's *Missa assumpta es*, *Missa Papae Marcelli*, *Stabat Mater*, and motets from the *Canticle of Solomon* and the *Improperia*, show us characteristic aspects of his art in various directions and prove the immense range of his religious music, its peculiar combination of seraphic mildness and exuberant brilliance, of ravishing beauty and passionate outcry, of soaring heights of ecstasy and profound seriousness of meditation.

Palestrina's motets and masses are the musical counterparts of the paintings of Perugino, Leonardo da Vinci, Raphael, and of the great Florentine painters, Filippo Lippi, Fra Bartolomeo, and Andrea del Sarto. In certain seraphic sounds in Palestrina's motets and masses we perceive a spirit akin to that of the touching and adorable Fra Angelico da Fiesole, a century earlier, whose frescoes in the convent of San Marco in Florence are unique in their purity and childlike confidence. Whoever has felt the mysterious power of Raphael's Sistine Madonna in the Dresden Gallery, its inexplicable purity, grace, and simplicity coupled with a sublime religious emotion, will also be touched profoundly by Palestrina's music, which is so similar in effect. The art of sculptors like Donatello and Luca della Robbia also has its musical reflection in the clearness, the wonderful precision and beauty of Palestrina's plastic design, and such great Renaissance architects as Palladio, Alberti, and Bramante helped Palestrina to acquire his wonderful sense of harmonious proportion and of rhythmical and graceful construction.

Ruskin, discussing the "division of arts" in his *Aratra Pentelici*, speaks at length, with reference to painting, sculpture, and architecture, of the "musical or harmonic element in every art." According to Ruskin, "the science of colour is, in the Greek sense, the more musical, being one of the divisions of the Apolline power." He also explains that "the second musical science, which belongs peculiarly to sculpture (and to painting so far as it represents form), consists in the disposition of beautiful masses. That is to say, beautiful surfaces limited by beautiful lines." Sculpture is defined by Ruskin as "the art which, by the musical disposition of masses, imitates anything of which the imitation is justly pleasant to us; and does so in accordance with structural laws having due reference to the materials employed." All these observations of Ruskin's lose nothing of their significance or validity if we change the observer's point of view and look at the problems primarily from the angle of music. With very slight modifications those mutual relations can be beautifully exemplified by Palestrina's music.

Perhaps the most striking and brilliant artist of this brilliant Renaissance epoch was Orlando di Lasso, who is generally coupled with Palestrina, just as Bach is coupled with Handel. It may be left out of consideration here how far this comparison of two essentially different artists, merely on the ground that they happened to be contemporaries, is appropriate at all. Both Palestrina and Orlando di Lasso are incarnations of the Renaissance spirit, but they represent different aspects of this dominant spirit. Orlando di Lasso represents the cosmopolitan versatility of the Renaissance. From his music alone one could not tell with any degree of certainty whether he was Dutch, Italian, French, or German. Yet it has none of that vague, colorless and uncharacteristic international aspect which is so tiresome in the ultramodern music of the present day. Hearing the masses and motets of Orlando di Lasso, one would take him for a genuine Dutch artist, a successor of Josquin de Près. But one can also see in him a companion of Palestrina of Rome, a cousin of Andrea Gabrieli of Venice. In his Italian madrigals he appears as genuinely Italian as any one of the great Italian madrigalists of his time. If one looks at his wonderfully clever and vivid French chansons, one might believe that a native French artist had written them, and in his German songs he is a thoroughly German musician, with all the exuberant German humor and rough jollity, wearing a broad grin. The words of his music are written in five languages: Latin, Italian, Dutch,

German, French. He was equally at home in many countries, having spent his youth in the Netherlands and Italy, his earlier manhood in Paris, and his later years in Munich, where he died in 1594, in the same year as Palestrina.

Di Lasso is unique artistically in that he mastered with the same facility three different styles. He sums up once more the characteristic traits of Dutch polyphony, which in his work reaches an end that is like a glorious sunset. At the same time he has a full command of all the resources of Italian Renaissance art, with its wonderfully harmonious proportions, its elegance and refinement of taste, its exquisite appropriateness of coloring, its perfect blending of design and color. But this stupendous achievement does not exhaust his powers. He is likewise a great master of the baroque style (to be discussed in one of the following chapters). This baroque tendency is especially evident in his motets, which crown the form in its history of seven hundred years. To speak of the motet without adequate knowledge of Orlando di Lasso's achievements would be like discussing the cantata without a close acquaintance with Bach's two hundred cantatas.[2] One does not risk the charge of exaggeration when one ranks Orlando di Lasso in the fullness of his magnificent production even higher than the great Palestrina. He may justly be likened to such painters of the first magnitude as Michelangelo and Rubens; he may certainly be called one of the greatest musical geniuses of the entire history of music. Yet his work is hardly known at present, even to otherwise highly cultivated musicians. Without great difficulty one could fill a dozen concert programs with di Lasso motets and madrigals that would amaze a cultivated modern audience by their wonderful expressiveness, their passionate style, their picturesque details, their noble and truly poetic bearing.

Palestrina has achieved public favor through being regarded

[2] When many years ago I wrote my *History of the Motet* I had to study about six hundred di Lasso motets — only six hundred, because at that time no more were available in score. For the second English edition of the *History of the Motet*, which is in preparation, I shall have to take into consideration about three hundred more di Lasso motets. In the meantime the complete edition of di Lasso's works, commenced in Germany about 1900, has made progress, though owing to the World War and to other international troubles the estimated seventy volumes are still far from completion.

as the prince and even the savior of Catholic church music, as the musical incarnation of Catholic religious feeling, wearing a gloriole around his head as the greatest master of papal Rome. To be sure, people generally are satisfied with this label and leave the thirty-three volumes of his music on the shelves of the great libraries. As yet Orlando di Lasso has no such label to bring his name, not to mention his music, into public favor. But such giants of art as Palestrina and Orlando di Lasso can afford to wait another fifty or even a hundred years for the modern world to appreciate the religious feeling, the artistic excellence, the vital human traits, and the spiritual force that are essential qualities of their music.

Italian madrigal and the beginnings of opera, about 1600, are two other eminent products of the Renaissance spirit — the last emanations of this spirit, in fact, before its successor, the baroque style, became predominant. Italian church music of the sixteenth century never lost sight of its direct descent from Dutch music. If we look for a musical form of pure Italian stock which represents fully the characteristic traits of the Italian Renaissance, we must turn away from mass and motet and approach the Italian madrigal between 1550 and 1600. This is very different in character from the older Italian madrigal — for solo voice with instruments — of a hundred and fifty years earlier, in the time of the *ars nova*, but it is no less Italian in character. The earlier Italian madrigal has been characterized in a preceding chapter as a product of the early Renaissance spirit, akin to the art of the so-called "primitive" painters. Compared with the slender, youthful grace of the earlier madrigal, the new type of 1550 appears as the fully expanded flower of genuine Renaissance music. It represents the essence of the finest social culture and in its lyric elegance of manner reflects both the spirit of Italian poetry in its highest perfection and that of Renaissance architecture and painting.

Renaissance poetry, with its finely shaped, balanced forms, presents musicians with new problems of expression and construction. Petrarch, Torquato Tasso, and Sannazaro find their congenial composers, just as centuries later Goethe, Heine, and Eichendorff find their Schubert and Schumann. The polyphonic technique of the motet is still retained in the madrigal, but the severity of the form has disappeared. The strictly linear style is softened; new charms of melody, of chromatic harmony, suggestive of light and shade and of delicately tinged color, are added. The *cantus firmus*, the folk-song tune of the polyphonic German and Dutch part song, is given up entirely. The composer is no longer concerned with an interesting arrangement of a popular tune; he is intent on inventing for himself a melody appropriate to the lyric expression of the poem. Single words and phrases receive a most painstaking musical interpretation, with effects of tone color, declamation, and accent far beyond anything attempted in the older motet and part song. Hearing those wonderful madrigals by di Lasso, Gabrieli, Marenzio, Monteverdi, Gesualdo, prince of Venosa, and many others, one is strongly impressed by their striking similarity to the painting of the Renaissance. Hardly a trace is left of the old Gothic, Netherlandish style. The linear character, the severely complicated construction of Gothic architectural form have been replaced by a picturesque tendency; the sense of color, formerly half asleep in music, has been awakened. In their mental attitude these madrigalists are companions, cousins, of the great Florentine and Venetian painters, Perugino, Raphael, Andrea del Sarto, Bellini, Palma, Titian, Tintoretto, Veronese, Correggio. Yet their prevailing love and regard for color effects does not detract from their feeling for form. Proportion, contrast, symmetry, harmonious equilibrium acquire a new meaning in this music, a meaning that is derived from Renaissance architecture. Consequently, to acquire a feeling for such features of Renaissance architecture helps one to penetrate to the soul of Italian madrigal music.

The Italian madrigal comes to its perfection in Luca Marenzio. By his admiring contemporaries he was called "il più dolce cigno," the sweetest swan, a reference to one of the most celebrated madrigals of the entire century, Arcadelt's "Il bianco e dolce cigno cantando more" ("The sweet white swan dies singing"). In his exquisite lyric style, his polished elegance, his wonderful refinement, his sense for color and delicate shadings of tone, his emotional sensibility, Marenzio meant to the cultivated people of 1600 throughout Europe something like what Chopin means to us. Like Chopin, he died rather young, and he belongs to that romantic galaxy of youthful prodigies whose art reached an early perfection, but whose lives too came to an early end. Pergolesi, Mozart, Schubert, Chopin, Mendelssohn, Hugo Wolf, Shelley, Keats are thus akin to this enchanting singer, Luca Marenzio. His madrigals, of which there are more than six hundred, are one of the most precious treasures of lyric art.[3]

Marenzio, more than any other madrigal composer, set a model that was eagerly accepted and imitated, especially by the great English school of madrigalists in the Elizabethan period. In Germany such composers as Hans Leo Hassler and Johann Hermann Schein, like their English colleagues, successfully adapted the spirit of the Marenzio madrigal to the genius of the German language and to their national manner of emotional expression. Next to Marenzio, the great Claudio Monteverdi and the tragic Prince of Venosa led the Italian madrigal to its ultimate perfection and to its ultimate possibilities, thus bringing to a close this form of Renaissance music. Both Monteverdi and Venosa, however, have their center of gravity in the new baroque epoch of the seventeenth century; indeed, even Marenzio in his later works points distinctly toward the baroque style. The last period of the madrigal stands midway between the styles and marks the transition from the Renaissance to the baroque spirit.

A few years later, after the madrigal had reached its height, another aspect of the Renaissance spirit comes alive in music. As a result of the desire to revive ancient Greek drama, monody, recitative, a declamatory style that stresses dramatic expression, and the use of instrumental accompaniment become fashionable; in fact, opera comes into existence. This time the change is much more radical than in the lyric madrigals. Polyphony and canonic and fugal writing are declared old-fashioned and are replaced by a monodic recitative style. But while the idea of reviving the drama of classical antiquity is thoroughly in keeping with the Renaissance, the development of opera in the seventeenth century

[3] A complete edition of these wonderful pieces, which have never been generally accessible, was recently started in Germany, but the undertaking has been interrupted because its able editor, Dr. Alfred Einstein, a leading scholar in musical history, has been forced to leave Germany and all his work there.

quickly loses sight of the ideals and intentions of its Renaissance fathers, the highly cultivated aestheticians of the Florentine *camerata*, who about 1600 speculated on the nature of the old Greek music as it was applied to drama and made the first attempts at a declamatory style and operatic music. Baroque tendencies very quickly monopolized the new style, and opera became the most significant of baroque musical achievements.

Before going on to a more detailed treatment of the baroque spirit it seems advisable to characterize briefly the Renaissance spirit in music. Its chief novel feature was the lyric expression of erotic sentiment in a highly artistic form, and in the *ars nova* of the fourteenth century it produced the earliest manifestations of a truly Italian style of secular music. It is marked later by the contest between the Dutch and the Italian musical styles, and by the formation of a new Italian style in the sixteenth century, of which the outstanding representatives are Palestrina and the Roman school, and the two Gabrielis and the Venetian school. About this time it discovered color as a powerful new means of expression and produced in the later Italian madrigal the most highly refined product of Italian aristocratic culture. It met with striking success the new problems raised by the development of the humanistic spirit, by the invention of the art of printing, and by the mutual approaches of the various arts. Always it was sensitive to the influences of poetry, painting, and architecture, and all these leave their clear imprint upon it.

CHAPTER FIVE

THE REFORMATION

THE theme of the relation between Protestant music and the Reformation is one that for the most part concerns Germany. To understand it fully one must have some knowledge not only of the development of German music before the arrival of Luther but also of the cultural and social state of Germany toward 1500. And it is important that it should be understood, for the consequences of the Reformation are among the most vital and powerful of the factors that shape modern music.

Of all the important musical countries Germany is the latest to enter the international contest of art. Though German accomplishments in literature, architecture, painting, and sculpture were very considerable at an early date, until 1400 music was of little importance. Credit for its rise and development up to this time belongs to France, England, and the Netherlands; the *ars nova* was practiced chiefly in Italy, France, and Burgundy, and Germany's sole contributions of note were the melodies of the minnesingers. The earliest record we have of German polyphonic music is about 1400, though a number of earlier sources must have perished. Of one such case, at least, we know. In the Franco-Prussian War of 1870–1871, at the bombardment of Strassburg, a precious musical manuscript was destroyed which contained pieces by a number of early German composers, whose names we do not find anywhere else. But it is possible that fortunate discoveries will help musical research to clear up the rather dark history of early German polyphonic music. It is a strange and remarkable fact that in a period of only about seventy-five years (1450 to 1525) German music should have risen to a rank equal to that of the music of the Netherlands, France, England, and Italy. This quick awakening from a long slumber, this rapid growth, is one of the most astounding feats of the German musical genius. Its historical, cultural, and psychological reasons, however, have not yet been treated with the care that so singular and important an artistic event deserves.

Though German professional musicians did not contribute much to the advancement of their art in the fourteenth century, the German people at large accomplished through their folk song something that retained great importance for German music for centuries to come. Folk song is not a product of professional art, the work of individual composers, like the songs of the minstrels and troubadours. Nobody knows where it originated or who began it, but everywhere the people sang it, one person learning a song from another — words as well as music, for music and poetry were inseparable, rather like Siamese twins, in fact, grown together. This characteristic and beautiful folk song, which later becomes the basis for German art music, reveals the best and most lovable traits of the German people in a manner that, though primitive, is unsurpassable for emotional depth, youthful freshness, sturdiness, and melodic beauty. In his *Deutsches Leben im Volkslied*, a classic work, Rochus von Liliencron, one of the most cultivated German scholars of the last century, has described German life in the fourteenth century, and has shown how it is reflected in folk songs. They are not highly refined aesthetically; they do not show the hand of a scholarly poet; they are rather like wild flowers, growing in the fields and meadows, in the German forests, on high mountains, in valleys, on the banks of rivers. But it is not only nature and the German landscape that come alive in them; the German people also appear in their daily labor as peasants, artisans, tradesmen, soldiers, knights, magistrates, and princes. All classes of German society, high and low, men and women, old and young, honest men and rascals, in cities and in villages, have acting parts in these songs. For a hundred years, from about 1450 to 1550, German composers never tired of treating these popular tunes over and over again in their part songs, written in the Dutch contrapuntal manner.

The earliest document of the German polyphonic treatment of these folk songs known at present is the so-called *Lochheimer Liederbuch*. It is a manuscript containing about sixty compositions for several voices, by unknown composers. The date of its actual writing is about 1440, but some of the songs in it must be much older; on the whole, it gives us a survey of the average state of polyphonic writing in Germany from about 1300 to 1450. The purely artistic value of the single numbers differs very much, ranging from primitive, clumsy attempts to highly finished workmanship and profound expressiveness. As it is, the Lochheim Liederbuch is one of the most precious documents of early German music. Like most of the song manuscripts of its kind it was probably compiled and written by order of some wealthy and cultivated amateur.[1] The manuscript itself has been for centuries one of the most precious possessions of the famous library of the prince of Stolberg-Wernigerode, one of the magnates of the German empire. Many travelers have seen the castle of this princely family in the lovely medieval town of Wernigerode and have admired the beauty of its location, which commands a glorious view of the entire chain of Harz mountains with its magnificent dark forests, a region made famous by Goethe's "Harzreise im Winter" and by Brahms's choral rhapsody to parts of this poem. The library, one of the oldest and largest private libraries in Europe, was sold at auction in 1933, and the Lochheim Liederbuch came into the possession of the Berlin State Library.

A few decades after the completion of this Liederbuch, we find German part song established as an art of high rank. It was this type of music — folk song in a polyphonic setting — along with Dutch motets and masses, that Martin Luther heard first in his native town of Eisleben, later in the larger city of Erfurt in Thuringia, where he spent several years as a young monk, and still later on his many journeys through the German countries. From

[1] A very beautiful photographic reproduction of this costly manuscript recently appeared in Germany (Woelbing, Berlin, 1925).

these songs Luther got his ideas as to the proper character of Protestant church music.

The time about 1500, when Luther as a youth was preparing for his religious revolution, marks a climax in German life. Throughout the country the people are thrifty and busy. A high civilization animates life everywhere. The middle classes, the citizens, burghers, town folk, are now the real backbone of the nation. Commerce, trades, and the arts are flourishing. The life of this period was revived with admirable art by Richard Wagner in his glorious opera, *Die Meistersinger von Nürnberg*. Even today in cities like Nuremberg, Rothenburg, Augsburg, Danzig, Lübeck, Hildesheim, Braunschweig, and Erfurt the visitor can see the wonderful architectural frame of this old German life, and he can get a vivid picture of people, houses, furniture, and clothing from the paintings of great German masters like Altdorfer, Lucas Cranach, Albrecht Dürer, Grünewald, and Holbein.

In architecture and fine arts this period represents both the last phase of Gothic art and the transition toward the style of the Italian Renaissance. In the preceding century the revival of classical scholarship known as humanism had taken root in Germany. This new humanistic ideal had its origin in Italy toward 1400, and it received a powerful impetus from a disastrous event of great moment for later European history. In 1453 Constantinople finally succumbed to the attacks of the Turkish power. Moslem armies now invaded Europe at its east end, after having for centuries overrun the western edge of Europe, particularly Spain. The Byzantine empire was crushed. This disaster, however, had one good result in that it brought to western Europe the best of the old Byzantine learning and culture. Crowds of classical scholars fled westwards from their homes in Constantinople, taking with them their precious manuscripts, their old traditions and scholarship, their love for ancient literature and art. The Italian Renaissance was greatly enriched by this influx of scholarship from the East, and German culture soon profited from it also. The study of Latin — and often also of Greek — of mathematics, grammar, poetry, and music made up the regular curriculum of the higher schools or *gymnasia*. Even

before the Reformation, education had to a certain extent es-
caped from the control of the learned monks and the convent
schools of medieval times. The citizens themselves built up
schools for their children, and the influence of humanistic studies
was felt not only in the universities and higher academic schools
but also in elementary instruction.

What musical culture in Germany owes to these gymnasia in
every German town can hardly be overestimated. From 1500
to at least 1750 music was taught very thoroughly in them.
Though, of course, not every German schoolboy had musical
talent, he nevertheless learned enough about music to become
an appreciative listener, and many young people in all professions
were made fair amateurs, capable of playing various instruments
and of singing in part songs and motets. It is to be remembered
that, two hundred years after Luther, Johann Sebastian Bach
had to rely mainly on schoolboys from St. Thomas' School in
Leipzig and on students of the university for the performance
of his cantatas and his Passion music.

German literature of musical theory from 1500 to 1700 is
rich in treatises on singing, composition, and questions of practice and theory, books that were written for the pupils of the
gymnasia as textbooks. Many of these treatises we value very
highly at present, not only as sources of information but as
remarkable documents of musical culture. We should look
in vain for musical textbooks of a similar quality and artistic
tendency among our school books today. One of the chief
monuments of Protestant art shows by its title what the German school meant for the art of music. In 1544 the Wittenberg printer Georg Rhaw published a collection entitled *Newe
Deutsche Geistliche Gesenge fuer die gemeinen Schulen* ("New
German Spiritual Songs for the Ordinary Schools"). If we open
the book expecting to find simple pieces of juvenile scope and
character, we shall be disappointed. We find here a vast collection of motet-like pieces, mostly on the new Protestant chorale
melodies, written by the best German composers of the time, often
very pretentious pieces of great contrapuntal skill, full of difficulties of performance. A publication like this one, destined for the
use of the "common schools," would be impossible nowadays in

any country, even Germany. In Nuremberg the rector of St. Lorenz' School, Johann Cochlaeus, was the author of a musical school book entitled *Tetrachordum musices* which was reprinted no less than seven times between 1500 and 1526. Each year on the feast of St. Catherine the pupils of St. Lorenz' and two other Nuremberg schools had a public musical competition that was largely attended, in which, with their rector as conductor, they sang the mass.

It is characteristic of German music, especially with reference to later Protestant tendency, that there was a great liking for the organ and a highly developed skill in organ building. As early as 1450 Germany appears to be ahead of other nations in both organ playing and composition, and this predominance, accentuated in later Protestant music, reaches its climax in Bach's incomparable compositions for the organ. In 1475 we hear of Conrad Rosenberg of Nuremberg, who built organs with manuals and pedals for the Nuremberg church of the *Barfüsser* (barefoot friars) and for the cathedral in Bamberg. In 1483 Stephen Castendorfer from Breslau added the pedal to the cathedral organ in Erfurt. In 1499 Heinz Kranz built the great organ in the Brunswick cathedral. At the same time a fine instrument was ordered for the cathedral in Strassburg. Shortly after 1500 the organ pedal was introduced generally in Germany.

As early as 1450 the blind organist of St. Sebaldus' Church in Nuremberg, Conrad Paumann, enjoyed European celebrity. A guest at many courts, he was made a knight and received rich presents from the Emperor Frederick and the dukes of Mantua and Ferrara in Italy, and was appointed organist at the famous Frauenkirche in Munich, where he died in 1473. His *Fundamentum organisandi* carries its title justly, and has retained its historical importance as a fundamental treatise on organ playing to this very day. The Nuremberg poet, Hans Rosenplüt, wrote the following quaint but sincere verses in praise of the blind master Paumann:

> Noch ist ein maister in diesem gedicht,
> Der hat mangel an seinem gesicht,
> Der haist maister Conrad Pauman,
> Dem hat Got solche gnad gedan,

Dass er ein maister ob allen maister ist
Was er tregt yn seinem sinnen list
Dy Musica mit yrem suessen don.
Solt man durch kunst einen meister kron
Er trug wol auf von golt ain kron.

The difficulty of the task may excuse the clumsiness of the following attempt at an English translation:

Of another master will I write
Who has trouble with his sight,
His name is Conrad Paumann,
To him God so much grace has done,
That he made him greatest master of all
When he from his mind does call
Music with her sweetest sound:
Could one by art win a master's crown
He would surely get a golden crown.

Of Paul Hofheimer, the Emperor Maximilian's famous court organist, the poet Ottmar Nachtigall writes thus: "He is never wearisome through lengthiness, nor poor through brevity; wherever his mind and hand can reach he moves on with free, elastic gait. His most brilliant execution never interferes with the majestic stateliness of his modulations; he is never satisfied with producing something merely grand and solemn; it must always be also verdant and delightful. He is not only unsurpassed, but he has never been equalled." What artist would not be proud to be criticized in such eloquent and appreciative terms?

The romantic Emperor Maximilian, the last of the knights, as he liked to be called, maintained at Vienna and elsewhere one of the most luxurious courts in his luxurious age, and in it music had a prominent part. We possess several curious and highly interesting documents that give us a very distinct idea of the grand style of life at Maximilian's court. They are entitled *Der Theuerdank* and *Der Weiszkunig*, and were written by the Emperor himself. Together they form an account of the ideal education and courtship of a young prince. Many characteristic woodcuts illustrate these books. There also exists a magnificent pictorial work, dated about 1500, which represents the court of Maximilian in a large number of woodcuts executed by the best

German artists, mainly by Albrecht Dürer of Nuremberg, the greatest genius in German art of his time. In this *Triumphzug Kaiser Maximilians* ("Triumphal Procession of Maximilian") we see the Emperor demonstrating the splendor of his court by a festive procession in imitation of the custom of the ancient Roman emperors. Music has its place in the book, and in several of these splendid pages we see the imperial chapel with all its members, portrayed from life: sixteen boys and men, all singing from a single music book, two players of *trombone* and *cornetto* helping along. There is also a portrait of the famous court organist and composer, Paul Hofheimer, seated at the organ. Another of these fine woodcuts shows us the instrumental band and gives us an idea of the orchestra of those times. The emperor himself wrote a notice on this page, entitling it "Musica suesz Meledey," and he goes on to enumerate the various old-fashioned instruments in the quaint German of those days: "ain tamerlin, ain quintern, ain grosse lauten, ain rybeben, ain Fiedel, ein kleine Rauschpfeiffen, ain Harpfen, ain gross Rauschpfeiffen." Here are a flute and a little drum, played together by one performer; two chalumeaux (a sort of oboe), a guitar, a lute, a viola, a harp, and a viola da gamba.

Maximilian himself is commemorated by a monument erected on his tomb in the cathedral in Innsbruck, one of the most magnificent works of the German Renaissance, with bronze figures of the Emperor and all his ancestors, masterpieces of the greatest Nuremberg artists. Every visitor who spends a few hours in the charming mountain town, midway between Munich and the Italian border, stops to admire it.

Maximilian had himself proclaimed emperor in 1508, a memorable year for both art and church history. In this year Martin Luther was appointed professor of theology at the recently founded University of Wittenberg, where he commenced the religious reformation which was destined to shake all Europe down to its deepest foundations and which was incidentally of prime importance for music. In the same year Michelangelo began work on his monumental fresco paintings in the Sistine Chapel of the Vatican, Raphael was commissioned to ornament the Vatican rooms with his world-famous frescoes, and Titian painted one of his most admired paintings, "The Tribute Money," now a treasure of the Dresden Gallery.

These years of the growth of Luther's influence were exciting times in the history of political events, as well as of culture and the arts. It is a curious fact that at the beginning of the sixteenth century the fate of Europe lay in the hands of three youths. The Emperor Charles V, the grandson of Maximilian, was twenty years old when he ascended the throne in 1519. Francis I, king of France, Charles's lifelong opponent, began his political career and his reign in 1515 at the age of twenty-one years, and Henry VIII of England was only eighteen years of age when his rule began in 1509. The three most powerful rulers of Europe were antagonists whose political aims and warfare, together with Luther's religious revolt and the Pope's counteraction, gave the entire century its historical, political, and cultural contents and its significance for the future.

The political, religious, and artistic atmosphere of these portentous years, in which the Protestant spirit, the Protestant Church, and Protestant music were born, deserves to be sketched in briefly here.

In 1510 appears Ariosto's *Orlando Furioso*, one of the chief poetical works of Italian literature, and Titian paints his wonderful picture, "Sacred and Profane Love," still one of the great sights of Rome, in the Borghese palace. In 1511 Luther is sent to Rome to inquire into the state of Church affairs. In the same year a fundamental German instruction book on music appears in print: Sebastian Virdung's *Musica getutscht*. In 1512 the first of a series of very important collections of German part songs is published by the printer Oeglin in Nuremberg, and Heinrich Finck, one of the great German composers of this epoch, dies. In the same year Raphael paints his enchanting Galatea frescoes in the Villa Farnese in Rome. The great German painter, Holbein, settles in Basle. The Medici, expelled from Florence a few years before, capture Florence with the aid of a Spanish army, and henceforth the Florentine republic is abolished. Leo X, later the great adversary of Luther, is elected pope. In 1514 Bramante, the architect of St. Peter's, dies, and Corregio discovers the principle of chiaroscuro, that peculiar mixture of light and shade which became so important an element not only for painting but also for music in the brilliant tone color of the Venetian school, in the harmony and color effects of the Italian madrigals, and still later in the modern orchestra.

The next year, 1515, is interesting in cultural respects because of a number of literary productions that were extremely characteristic of the new mental attitudes which prepared the ground for the Reformation. Among them is the collection of stories relating the pranks of Till Eulenspiegel, that famous book of buffoonery, daring jokes, and hostility toward the established order of things, toward the placid inactivity of the comfortable and well-satisfied burghers. *Till Eulenspiegel* is known to musicians, if not in the original, at least through Richard Strauss's brilliant orchestral fantasy, but in connection with our present subject it is well to remember that this insolent and aggressive book represents a grotesque counterpart of the spirit which animated Martin Luther in higher spheres of the mind. Another publication of the same year has acquired great literary fame: the *Epistolae virorum obscurorum* ("Letters of Obscure Men"), a brilliant masterpiece of unsparing satire on the lives and morals of the monks in their monasteries. Its authors were some of the learned humanists who represented the highest cultural ideal found in Germany and who upheld liberal views and tolerance in matters of religious creed in a very intolerant and illiberal time. A persecution of the Jews had been started once more in Germany, and a baptized Jew by the name of Pfefferkorn tried to recommend himself to his Christian associates by accusing the Jewish sacred books of heresy and demanding that the Emperor Maximilian command all Hebrew books to be burned. Reuchlin, one of the great German humanists, the first German scholar interested in Hebrew language and literature, defended the Jewish writings. A violent quarrel arose between the liberal humanists and the narrowminded and intolerant theologians of Cologne, and the satire of the Obscure Men, full of sharp and spicy peppercorns, was the witty revenge of the humanists. Such occurrences as these indicate the tension of the mental atmosphere in Germany; a few years more and Martin Luther was to set all Europe afire.

But everywhere there was an abundance of nervous excitement in the world. In 1516 Francis, king of France, was engaged in bitter war with the Emperor Maximilian in Italy. In 1517 Luther nailed his portentous ninety-six theses to the door of the Wittenberg Schlosskirche. In the same year the great Dutch composer, Heinrich Isaak, died, followed in the next year by Pierre de la Rue, also a Dutch composer. In 1518 Luther challenged Rome by sending his theses to Pope Leo X, and Melanchthon, professor of Greek in Wittenberg University, became one of Luther's most valuable helpers by connecting the new movement of the Reformation with humanism. A year later Luther had his sensational dispute with the famous theologian, Johann Maier von Eck, at the University of Leipzig. Leonardo da Vinci, the greatest of Italian geniuses, died in this year, as did Maximilian, whose grandson, Charles V, succeeded him as German emperor. In 1520 England became involved in the Reformation, and Cardinal Wolsey burned Luther's books; Raphael died in Rome. In 1521 the greatest master of music, Josquin de Près, expired; King Henry VIII of England began his fight against Luther; and Luther began his translation of the Bible into German at the Wartburg in Eisenach.

This last point deserves a word of comment. The German Bible ranks among the highest accomplishments in German literature, and if Luther had done nothing else his magnificent German Bible would have sufficed to give him a place of honor in the history of both music and literature. For four hundred years this Bible text has inspired countless German composers of religious music, great and small. Works like Bach's cantatas and Passion music and Brahms's *Deutsches Requiem* would not be what they are without Luther's inspiring, powerful, and characteristic diction.

In 1524 Protestant church music had its birth. In that year Luther's musical collaborator, friend, and adviser, Johann Walther, published in Wittenberg the first monument of Protestant polyphonic art, the *Wittenbergisch-Gesangkbüchlein*, a collection of spiritual songs and motets for the use of the Protestant divine service. But for four centuries Luther's own contributions, his German chorales, have been much more important for

Protestant music. Luther had a perfectly clear conception of the kind of music he needed for the new Church. He wished to reach the common people, and for that neither the Latin language nor Gregorian chant were of use to him. To achieve his end he introduced German instead of the Latin of the Catholic service, and chose in place of the noble but complex melodic substance of Gregorian chant something much simpler, less pretentious, more akin to German folk song.

One of Luther's immortal accomplishments is the Protestant chorale, the new German spiritual folk song, so wonderfully adapted to the German people and to the spiritual nature of the Protestant Church. A number of these chorale melodies, especially "Ein' feste Burg ist unser Gott," have been attributed to Luther himself. Even though actual evidence is lacking concerning his activity as composer, he remains the originator of the idea, and he knew how to inspire artists of rank to write in a style adapted to the character of the Protestant creed. And there is no doubt that the words, at least, of some thirty of the finest German chorales were written by Luther. With these he takes his place at the head of all German spiritual and religious poetry. Since his intention was to make the common people in the churches sing the chorale tunes, he made them as plain and as popular as possible. At the same time he knew how to give them a dignified spiritual character, with no trace of vulgarity, of cheap popularity, emptiness, or insignificance. The most famous chorale attributed to him is "Ein' feste Burg ist unser Gott." It was written in 1528, when pestilence, at that time a frequent and dreadful guest in Europe, was approaching once more, and to a certain extent it is a poetic paraphrase of the Forty-sixth Psalm. But what a power of language, what a strong manly soul in these verses, what a consoling confidence in the help of God, what a courageous militant spirit against the evil in the world!

Most of Luther's chorales were written in the years 1523 and 1524. The melodies were new only in part; a number of them were taken over from the Ambrosian hymns of the Catholic Church, from medieval sequences, from Gregorian chant, and from German popular songs. Luther did not simply copy these old melodies; he changed them and adapted them to their new purposes with eminent insight and skill. In their simplicity and plastic clearness, in their powerful rhythm, their song-like character, and their melodic beauty these German Protestant chorale melodies are essentially different from the Latin Gregorian chants. The entire complex of German chorales was not, of course, created in Luther's time but extends over a period of almost two hundred years. Nevertheless, Luther created its form, gave it its soul and character. Through four centuries these Protestant chorale tunes have been the most precious material of German church music. Innumerable compositions have been written on them. One cannot imagine Bach's art without the *cantus firmus* of these glorious spiritual folk songs. No cantata, no Passion music, no Bach motet, no organ chorale prelude without these tunes. They are the center of all Bach's church music, its deepest and most solid foundation. Gregorian chant has a similar importance for Catholic church music, but there is a very marked difference between the Gregorian and the Lutheran *cantus firmus*. Gregorian chant in a polyphonic composition is rarely noticed by the ear; it acts rather like a hidden support, an invisible skeleton. The Lutheran *cantus firmus*, with its powerful rhythm, its vigorous, plain melody, dominates every composition into which it is interwoven; it is something like the tall, strong Gothic pillars, clearly visible to every eye.

The chorales, however, are used not only as a *cantus firmus* in more pretentious artistic compositions, not only as means to another end, but plainly and simply as ends in themselves. As they are sung by the congregation in the church, they are no longer accompanied on the organ in the elaborate contrapuntal style of Dutch origin, but in a plain harmonic, homophonic style that introduces to music perhaps for the first time in a systematic way what is called the common chord, or triad. With this harmonic-chord style a new chapter in music is started; the Protestant Reformation in Germany with its plain religious folk song ushers in a new age in music as in many other aspects of life.

The German part songs of the years 1520–1550 are extremely interesting as musical documents of the years of the Reformation. Being perhaps the most valuable musical productions of the age in Germany they deserve a little closer inspection. These songs, which give expression to all that made up the everyday life of the German people toward 1500, in the sixteenth century become the material of German art music. German polyphonic music, like Italian music, is a daughter of Dutch art. How Italy superimposed her own distinctive national qualities on this Dutch foundation has already been explained in the chapter on Renaissance music. Something similar happened in Germany. The ecclesiastical forms, motet and mass, in German music of the sixteenth century can hardly be distinguished from their Dutch models, but the characteristically German music of the period reached one of its summits in the polyphonic treatment of German folk song. In Nuremberg, the greatest commercial and art center of Germany, music printing flourished, and the famous publishing firms of Nuremberg sent out thousands of German part songs, written by a great number of German composers. Extensive collections of songs by various composers, the song books of the Nuremberg publishers Ott and Forster, were reprinted in Germany about 1900. Here we find them all — the valiant, manly, severe German masters of song, worthy colleagues of Albrecht Dürer, Hans Holbein, and Lucas Cranach, of the great Nuremberg sculptors and woodcutters, Veit Stoss, Adam Krafft, Tielman Riemenschneider.

These four-part songs have neither the fascinating elegance and refinement of the Italian madrigal nor the sparkling wit, the crystalline form of the French chansons, but they are filled to the brim with that peculiarly German emotion, the sincere, heartfelt, candid expression of sentiment and longing — *Sehnsucht* — which has ever since been the distinguishing feature of the best German music. They are German to the core and great works of art besides, and these two qualities assure immortality to the best specimens of this extensive literature. Only a fraction of it is at present accessible in printed scores. Professor Emil Bohn of Breslau has spent a whole lifetime in collecting and transcribing in score with his own hand about five thousand of these old German part songs. This precious Bohn collection, now in the Berlin State Library, gives a fairly adequate idea of the wealth and artistic value of this German song literature of the sixteenth century. The leading masters are Heinrich Finck,

Heinrich Isaak, Hofheimer, Thomas Stoltzer, and especially Ludwig Senfl. Heinrich Finck was for many years *Kapellmeister* at the royal court of Poland, in Cracow and Warsaw. Mention has already been made of Heinrich Isaak in connection with music at the court of Lorenzo de' Medici in Florence, and of Hofheimer, court organist of the Emperor Maximilian. Ludwig Senfl, born in Basle in Switzerland, the pupil of Heinrich Isaak, became his master's successor as *Kapellmeister* of the Emperor Maximilian in Innsbruck. Later he was active in Munich until 1555. In their particular style his German songs have never been surpassed, and only rarely equalled.[2]

Martin Luther was not only a great lover of music, a skillful amateur, to some extent even a composer, but he knew perfectly well what powerful aid music could bring to the cause of the new Protestant movement. The new Protestant Church favors only music, no other art. Of all masters of the epoch Luther admired Ludwig Senfl most, and in his writings many references can be found to music in general, to single composers, and to Senfl in particular.

All these German songs are what we should call arrangements of folk songs. Because the style in which they are written is particularly characteristic of German music at the time of the Reformation, it is necessary to go into some detail in discussing it. In this epoch it is never the composer's ambition to invent new melodies; almost invariably the popular melody is given to the tenor, with more or less florid ornamentation, and the composer's art becomes manifest only in counter melodies, in contrapuntal voices opposed to the tune. A peculiar, and to most people very puzzling, feature of this song style is its free rhythm, which is diametrically opposed to our present conception of rhythm regulated by bar lines. The polyphonic music of the fifteenth and sixteenth centuries is written wholly without bar lines; in fact, what we call regular time is almost entirely absent from these songs. They have a certain free rhythm, but it is so

[2] Years ago I published, through Breitkopf & Härtel in Leipzig, thirty-six part songs of this epoch in an arrangement for practical performance. Eight carefully chosen Senfl songs in this collection illustrate his admirable skill in counterpoint, his strong melodic inventiveness, his versatility, the great range of his expressive power, and a constructive art of the first rank.

foreign to later music that we cannot even indicate it clearly in our manner of writing in score. The time changes constantly in the single parts, and we find not only 3/4, 4/4, and 6/4 time, but frequently also 5/4 and 7/4 time, very rare guests in modern music. Often it happens that the four parts sing simultaneously in different times: for instance, soprano in 4/4, alto in 3/4 or 6/8, tenor in 5/4, bass in 6/4 time. From this result a fascinating play of quite irregular accents and rhythms, and wonderful rhythmical effects that are entirely lost in the eighteenth and nineteenth centuries. The irregularities are being slowly and laboriously rediscovered by some of our ultramodern composers, who usually believe that they are inventing quite novel rhythmical effects and are generally ignorant of the fact that the sixteenth century practiced these free rhythms with a far greater virtuosity. Conductors very frequently spoil these enchanting irregular rhythms because they do not fully understand either their nature or the system of conducting they require, a system very different from the ordinary modern one of beating time.

These polyphonic part songs of the sixteenth century mark a summit in German music, and of their kind they are unsurpassed. Together with the motet-like pieces founded on the new Protestant chorales, they reflect more than any other species of musical composition the German spirit of the time of the Reformation. The style, however, did not have a long duration; in fact, it did not long outlive Martin Luther. Luther died in 1546, and toward 1550 the great time of German music in that century was past. The high tension that animated all Germany, either in favor of Luther or against him, had slowly abated. Protestantism had become an established institution, destined to last for a long time to come; this was manifest to every man of insight. There was no more question of annihilating Protestanism; the Catholic party strove only to limit its further progress, to counteract its deepening influence.

A grave danger for German Protestant church music arose after Luther's death in the second half of the sixteenth century. It came from Italy, and consisted in the sensational success of the new Italian music, the Venetian polychoral style, but still more in the new attainments of seventeenth-century Italian concertizing music: opera, oratorio, cantata, and the new instrumental forms of sonata, concerto, *canzone*, *ricercare*, and so on. The success of this new Italian music everywhere in Europe was fully as complete as the victory of Dutch music had been a century before. The danger for Protestant music consisted in the fact that these new Italian fashions so fascinated musicians of all countries that the serious religious style of the traditional music seemed old-fashioned. Everywhere Protestant church music adopted the new Italian mannerisms, with the result that it was quickly imbued with secular tendencies, that pretty but shallow tunes superseded the noble, genuinely religious older style, and that the church was changed into a concert hall where one heard music that was pleasing, but cheap and thoroughly unecclesiastical in character.

The clever and extremely skillful diplomats of the Catholic Counter Reformation in Rome also availed themselves of the popular success of this Italian music, and their agents in Germany, especially the Jesuits, encouraged the propagation of Italian art and music, i.e., Catholic art, by all means at their disposal. As the Jesuit fathers in many parts of Germany had full control of the schools, and as music was taught very thoroughly in the higher German schools at that time, the Italian and Catholic tendencies could be strengthened by means of the new Italian music which charmed the German people so much. The entire seventeenth century in Germany, from the musical point of view, is a fight for supremacy between the new Italian and the traditional German tendencies. This contest recalls the similar contest between Italian and Dutch music a century earlier, of which mention has been made in the chapter on Renaissance music. It is the merit of the few great and the numerous lesser German masters of the seventeenth century that they turned these dangerous Italian influences in such a direction as to bring more good than harm to German Protestant music. This situation will be discussed in greater detail in the chapter on music in the age of the baroque style.

A glance at the music of Hans Leo Hassler, however, belongs here. Born in Nuremberg, educated in Venice, he became the mediator between German and Italian music. His life extended from 1564 to 1612. Both these dates and his music show that he stands between the sixteenth and seventeenth centuries, between the German and the Italian tendencies. It was his good fortune and it became his glorious title that his music knew how to reconcile the best traits of both German and Italian art. He had insight, flexibility, and skill enough to choose exactly the qualities that could be successfully adapted to each other. Only Mozart equals Hans Leo Hassler in his phenomenal power of assimilating foreign traits, in his faculty of giving the mixture of German and Italian music a sparkling freshness and buoyancy, a fascinating new charm of its own. To these qualities Hassler owes his lasting fame and his popularity, even at the present time, in Germany. Like Mozart he has the secret of eternal youth. His delightful part songs mix the Italian elegance and vivacity of temperament, the grace of Italian dance-rhythms, the beauty and colorful variety of Italian tonal effects with the German emotional depth and sincerity, the German manly vigor, solidity of workmanship, and constructive power. The happy proportions of this mixture have very rarely been equaled. The traditional German stiffness and prolixity and roughness of sound are entirely absent from Hassler's music, and yet it is as thoroughly German as any music ever written. The style and spirit of the Italian madrigal and *ballata* have never been translated into the German musical idiom in an equally felicitous manner by any other composer.

Hassler stands midway between Catholic and Protestant tendencies, and in his music these contrasting, even hostile, elements are reconciled as they were never to be again. Though he was a good Catholic all his life, his music never accentuates that fact in any aggressive manner. What he presents in his music are not the new features that make for division and antagonism but rather the traits common to the German people as a whole, regardless of confession or sectional variation. And these familiar homelike traits that appeal to everybody in Germany are given an added charm of novelty by a peculiarly Italian grace and lightness, a roundness of form, a vivacity and gaiety originally to be found only beyond the Alps, in the warmth and sunshine of Italy. With Hassler begins that interchange between Italy and

Germany, that mutual give and take which is so essential a chapter in the history of music between 1600 and 1800, and, though less intensive and under different aspects, even down to our own time.

In his great achievement of perfect assimilation, however, Hassler was alone in his day. The Protestant movement of the Reformation gave a new and powerful impulse to German music, opened up new vistas, new possibilities that found their final perfection two centuries later in Johann Sebastian Bach, but it also resulted in a lasting division of German music into two branches, distinct from each other and very different in their artistic tendencies. Henceforth Protestant music takes root and flourishes in northern and middle Germany, in Saxony and Thuringia especially, while in southern Germany and Austria, the Catholic countries, music makes its way in another direction. Whether this separation was fortunate or unfortunate is a weighty question on which many arguments pro and con might be advanced. It is well to remember, however, that the Protestant turn in German music led to Bach and Handel, the Catholic to Haydn, Mozart, and Beethoven. Surely we ought to be satisfied, however strange, tortuous, and roundabout the road, when German music brings us at last to such glorious artistic heights as these.

CHAPTER SIX

SEVENTEENTH-CENTURY BAROQUE

➤➤➤➤➤➤➤➤ ❖ ⧩⧩⧩⧩⧩⧩⧩

B Y WAY of introduction it would be useful to define the
term "baroque" as it is used in architecture and painting.
Having once understood the salient characteristics of baroque
expression in these arts we may look for similar traits in music.

The baroque style in architecture follows the style of the Renaissance and dominates the seventeenth century in Italy as well
as in other countries. Its principal characteristic, borrowed from
painting, is the searching for new architectural effects. The
static elements of architecture — the predominance of straight
outlines, vertical as well as horizontal, and clarity of design
and ground plan — lose some of their importance in the baroque
style. Curved outlines instead of straight become fashionable;
effects of light and shade are eagerly sought; picturesqueness,
striking and surprising vistas, vastness of proportion, and splendor of color and ornament are factors of the new style. Baroque
architecture dominates the general aspect of the city of Rome
as we see it at present, as well as the older sections of Vienna, of
Munich, Augsburg, Passau, and many other fine old Bavarian
towns, with their Jesuit cathedrals, their fine public edifices, and
the imposing houses of their noble families. Rome, indeed, possesses architectural monuments of every century since antiquity.
Yet most of the Roman public buildings and palaces and many
churches date back to the seventeenth century. Perhaps the most
brilliant example of the Roman baroque spirit is Bernini's semi-
circle of colonnades which gives so splendid a frame to the im-

mense place before St. Peter's and to the marvelous church itself. Every visitor to Rome will also remember the Piazza d'Espagna, with its magnificently picturesque staircase leading upward to Monte Pincio. The many splendid churches of the Jesuits in Rome are likewise built in the baroque style, especially the ornate church called Il Gesù, with its shining display of gold and its ingenious and surprising effects of brilliant light piercing through darkness.

In painting, the baroque style does away with the plastic out-lines, the sharp contours of Renaissance art. If, for example, one compares Rembrandt's portraits with those of Holbein or even Raphael, the difference of treatment becomes obvious. Outlines are intentionally made dim and unclear; the eye of the spectator is led away from contours to the play of light and shade on the curved level of the face. A new world of picturesque effect is discovered by the baroque masters. The emotional contents are also changed. In both painting and sculpture artists now are eager to represent the titanic, the vehement, the passionate, the terrible, and the elemental. In his later works Michelangelo is a baroque artist, as are the great Venetian masters, Titian, Paolo Veronese, and Tintoretto. If we accept Renaissance art as repre-senting the classical phase, the baroque attitude is an approach to romantic aims: the form of classical art has very aptly been called closed, that of the baroque open. This distinction is also applicable to music. We speak of classical and romantic style in music; we also make a distinction between closed or concentric form, and open or, as it might be called, eccentric form, eccentric here to be understood in its literal sense of spreading away from a central point. But the second sense ordinarily attributed to the word eccentric also fits baroque expression, which often is extravagant and borders on the grotesque. Modesty and unpre-tentiousness become old-fashioned. Artists are no longer inter-ested in economy of means; rather, they are bent on spending lavishly whatever they possess, and elaborate display becomes of prime importance to them.

In the nineteenth century there was a tendency to consider the baroque style, especially in architecture and sculpture, as an art of the second rank, decidedly inferior from an aesthetic point of view to the art of the Renaissance. Jacob Burckhardt, the author of the admirable *Kultur der Renaissance in Italien* and of the hardly less admirable *Cicerone*, gave very strong expression to this opinion, and through his great authority he contributed not a little to the common underrating of baroque art. In the twentieth century, however, a more just estimate of the great artistic value of baroque art has gradually been established through the endeavors of such historians of art and culture as Wölfflin, Cornelius Gurlitt, Lamprecht (in the seventh volume of his German history), Riegl (*Entstehung der Barockkunst in Rom*), M. Dvořák in Vienna, and others.

The causes for the change of taste leading to the new baroque aesthetics are manifold. They must be sought mainly in events of political history, in changing economic and social conditions, in technical inventions and geographical discoveries, and in the natural growth of artistic ideas. Scientific and artistic tendencies, conditions of life, and the mental atmosphere of Europe in general were, of course, profoundly influenced by such occurrences as the discovery of America, the increase of commerce with India and other parts of Asia and Africa, the invention of printing, the Reformation in Germany, Switzerland, and England, and the combat between Catholicism and Protestantism which reached its climax in the Thirty Years' War. One who understands the meaning of such grave events for the cultural life of a period will not have much difficulty in finding their echoes in the music of the late sixteenth and seventeenth centuries.

Let us survey quickly the literature of music of about 1550 to 1750 in order to see how the style and aims of music changed under the influence of the new aesthetic creed. Chronologically the baroque style almost coincides with the rise of the Catholic Counter Reformation and its systematic organization, as we find it displayed at the Council of Trent. In 1550 Vignola built the splendid Villa de' Papa Giulio outside of Rome and described what he called the new "Jesuit style" in his famous book, *Trattato degli ordini* ("Essay on the Various Styles"). At that time the Jesuit order was only ten years old, but it was already very powerful and influential in the cause of the Counter Reformation, directed against the rise of Protestantism as formulated by Luther,

Calvin, and Zwingli. In 1551 the Jesuits founded the Collegio Romano, their Roman headquarters. Two years before, they had made their entrance into Germany in Ingoldstadt in Bavaria, and from there they extended their activities throughout Germany, founding churches and schools. Everywhere the new "Jesuit style," the Roman baroque, followed them, and thus it spread to all parts of Germany, became popular, and was finally accepted even by Protestants. To a certain extent the Jesuit tendencies might almost be identified with baroque tendencies. This order, so shrewd, persistent, and logical in the pursuance of its aims, certainly assigned music a definite part in its policy. Surveying the literature of music from about 1575 through the seventeenth century and a part of the eighteenth, we might say that the greater part of it leans toward the baroque, and a considerable part of it is certainly directly inspired by Jesuit ideals and needs. In other cases the clever Jesuit fathers made skillful use of novel styles of composition that they thought likely to win the ear and the favor of a large public.

The first traces of baroque music become manifest at a time when Renaissance aesthetics seems still to be in full bloom. We can observe them, especially in Italy, from about 1550, at first rarely, later abundantly, until after 1600 they become dominant. Wherever in seventeenth-century Italian music the element of color is accentuated strongly and intentionally, we have the first signs of the baroque attitude. Color effects in Italian music are of two kinds: those of the Venetian polychoral style, with its broad stretches of a certain coloring suddenly changing to another color, and those of the new chromatic harmony of the later Italian madrigals.

Mention has already been made in the chapter on Renaissance music of the Venetian style inaugurated by the great Dutch master, Adrian Willaert, after he had been placed in charge of the music in St. Mark's in Venice. His successors, Andrea and Giovanni Gabrieli, especially the latter, cultivated this style of writing for double chorus — or even three and four choruses — with a mastery and a virtuosity that have left their works unsurpassed of their kind. Pieces like Giovanni Gabrieli's six-part motet, "Beata es, virgo Maria," or his eight-part motet, "O

Domine Jesu Christe," have a splendor, richness, and beauty of
sound effect that had not previously existed in music. The six-
part "Beata es, virgo Maria" gives an enchanting effect of light,
bright colors; at the very first entry of the six voices a wonderful genius for tone coloring becomes manifest. To obtain so
brilliant, sweeping, even dazzling a sound effect with only six
voices is an unparalleled feat. Trained to perfection by the fascinating Venetian painting of Titian, Palma, Veronese, and
Tintoretto, Gabrieli discovered the means of transferring the
effects of baroque painting to music, of translating them into
terms of music. His double chorus, "O Domine Jesu Christe,"
has justly been called one of the most magnificent marvels of
sound-color ever created in music. Imagine a four-part chorus
of low voices — alto, two tenors, bass — starting with a beautiful,
solemn, darkly tinged section. As these dark tones vanish gradually in a slow diminuendo, a second chorus of high voices — two
sopranos, alto, baritone — enters very softly, almost imperceptibly.
When the shadowy deep sounds have almost disappeared and the
brightly shining light colors of the high voices fill space more
and more powerfully with their radiant sound, a moment is
reached in which there is a true and almost unequaled marvel of
sound. It makes the listener feel as if he heard a chorus of angels
singing in heavenly brightness. As it goes on, the music is
no less astounding, with many changes of coloring that give
expression to the sentiment of the words, until finally at the
close something like a broad wave of radiant sounds expands
more and more, with an ecstatic exuberance that produces an
overwhelming impression. Mention has already been made of
the discovery of chiaroscuro by the great painter Correggio. In
pieces like this double chorus it is evident how marvelously
Gabrieli has enriched the powers of music by adding to it the
same quality of light and shade.

This Venetian polychoral style is always suggestive of picturesque effects borrowed from painting. In the seventeenth
century, however, the Roman school that continued the style
gave it a somewhat different aspect, more closely related to the
new baroque architecture, magnificent, brilliant, and pompous
in effect, with its vast proportions, its surprising effects of pers-

pective. The musical equivalent of this ornate baroque style is found in a work like the festival mass written by the Roman master, Orazio Benevoli, for the inauguration of the new cathedral in Salzburg, and performed there on September 24, 1628. This cathedral, well known to visitors at the Salzburg music festivals, is a masterpiece of baroque architecture, and no more congenial music could have been found for the festive occasion.[1] The score is a unique work, one of the greatest curiosities of the entire literature of music. As regards the number of its staves, the Benevoli score of 1628 holds the record of all time with fifty-three on each printed page. Neither Wagner's *Götterdämmerung*, nor Mahler's so-called "Symphony of the Thousand," nor Stravinsky's *Sacre du printemps*, Strauss's *Salome*, Schönberg's *Gurre-Lieder*, nor any other monumental work of the last three centuries can compete in mass array with the fantastic appearance of this score. A short description may be given here of Benevoli's magnificent plan of construction. Two choral bodies, each of eight parts, are accompanied by a mass of instruments. The first eight-part vocal chorus has a six-part body of strings (two violins, four violas) and an eight-part body of wind instruments (two oboes, four flutes, two trumpets), besides another group of two cornetti, three trombones, and the organ. This combination requires twenty-seven staves in the gigantic score. The second eight-part chorus is supported by a similar array of instruments, which again require twenty-seven staves. Here a second organ, eight trumpets, and four kettledrums appear. The whole immense ensemble is kept together by a *basso continuo*, a thorough bass, in which all the bass instruments are combined, violoncellos, double basses, bassoons, bass-lute, two organs, clavicembali, lutes, harps, and so on. Here are manifest the pomp, vastness, and boldness of construction, the brilliant virtuosity, and the elaborate decorative art of the baroque style, translated into music on the grandest possible scale. It is as if Bernini's Spanish staircase and his gigantic colonnades before St. Peter's had been transformed into music.

[1] The score of the Benevoli mass was publish.ed for the first time in a volume of the important series edited by the Austrian government under the title, "Monuments of Austrian Music" (*Denk: mäler der Tonkunst in Österreich*).

The baroque architectural spirit is also manifest occasionally in the great German master, Heinrich Schütz, in his impressive *Concerti ecclesiastici* or his *Geistliche Konzerte*, with their double, triple, quadruple choruses with orchestral accompaniment, their sudden contrasts of fortissimo and pianissimo, of tutti and solo, of voices and instruments. The magnificent organ fantasias of the so-called northern organ school, especially those of Buxtehude in Lübeck, are full of this baroque spirit, and Bach owes to it many of his most impressive creations, like the Chromatic Fantasy, the G minor Fantasy for organ, the magnificent first chorus of the St. Matthew Passion, and the famous Brandenburg concertos with their elaborate structure.

Another very different aspect of the baroque style appears in the madrigals of the great Italian masters, Luca Marenzio, Gesualdo, prince of Venosa, and Claudio Monteverdi. Here the picturesque effects of chiaroscuro and the influences issuing from the finely wrought Italian poetry are rather more manifest than architectural ideas, which are less essential in these smaller lyric forms. Three traits distinguish the new Italian madrigal style from the otherwise quite similar German part song and French and Dutch chanson. The old *cantus firmus* treatment, the folksong arrangement, is abandoned; popular tunes are no longer used as a basis, and composers lay stress on inventing new melodies of their own. There is an increased interest in tone painting. This had been practiced to a certain extent in the older Dutch art of motet and chanson, but now the picturesque qualities of the new Italian poetry employed in the madrigals arouse in composers a desire to vie with the poets and to paint in tone the allusions of the verses.

The third and perhaps most striking baroque feature consists in a new treatment of harmony. The interest in color effects, in light and shade, in striking transitions from one color to another, in a mixture of various colors, leads the great Italian madrigal composers more and more to what we call chromatic harmony, away from the diatonic severity of the medieval church modes that for more than a thousand years had been the unshaken basis of all artistic music. The modern notion of harmonic color, of major and minor tonality, was born in the second half of the sixteenth century, and its surprisingly rapid progress is evident in the publications of the great Italian madrigalists and their successors, a group of extremely artistic monodists of the seventeenth century. The common notion about chromatic harmony nowadays is that, though Bach indeed has some surprising chromatic effects, they are mere foreshadowings of the real discovery of chromatic harmony in the nineteenth century; and the great romantics — Chopin, Schumann, Liszt, and especially Wagner — are credited with the invention of those fascinating and colorful chromatic chords and progressions. In his ninth book of madrigals, however, Luca Marenzio published a wonderful musical setting of Petrarch's famous sonnet, "Solo e pensoso i più deserti campi," in which we find almost exactly, note for note, the sensational "Erda" harmonies from Richard Wagner's *Rheingold* and *Siegfried*, with their amazing chromatic progressions. Certainly Wagner did not copy Marenzio, of whose existence he very probably knew nothing at all; he discovered for a second time something that had been alive centuries before but had been forgotten in the course of time.[2]

Gesualdo, prince of Venosa, in the vicinity of Naples, who lived about 1600, is one of the most romantic figures of the entire history of music. We are not concerned here with his amorous passions, his dueling, his killing of rivals, his luxurious, reckless life, but with his music, which represents one of the great curiosities of our art. His collected madrigals came out in a complete edition in 1614, a precious possession of a few of the largest libraries — precious not only on account of its artistic value, but also because it is perhaps the earliest known publication of a score in the modern sense, all the single voices of the composition being printed together in one book so that they can be read simultaneously.

Gesualdo practices here a kind of chromatic harmony, the

---

[2] This is not a solitary curiosity. A considerable number of such rediscoveries of musical ideas might be cited. Years ago I made this observation the subject of a lecture in Vienna, showing how Wagner is related to Monteverdi and the Italian madrigalists, how Arnold Schönberg takes up, without knowing it, long-forgotten principles of the old Paris school of 1200, how Richard Strauss in certain particulars has a strikingly congenial predecessor in the amazing Italian madrigalist, Gesualdo, prince of Venosa.

like of which we find only two hundred and fifty years later. Chopin, Wagner, Liszt, Strauss, Reger, Debussy exhibit no more striking chromatic effects than this Prince Gesualdo of Venosa. He knows as early as 1600 what might be called the quintessence of the harmony of 1900, namely, that all chromatic tones and even all imaginable chords may be inserted in any major or minor tonality without necessarily destroying the effect of tonality. If in a composition of our time we meet with a C major cadence in which the F sharp major chord suddenly shines out, if Chopin places a luminous A major within an E flat major cadence, we are prone to praise such effects as admirable accomplishments of our own age. But one finds such effects everywhere in Gesualdo's madrigals, and it would not be at all difficult to extract from his works a series of daring modulations and chromatic progressions which one could label 1900 with no fear that the deceit would be easily discovered. Here the baroque attitude in music reaches a climax.

Turning now to the greatest genius of these times, to Claudio Monteverdi, we find baroque tendencies on a still broader basis. The name Monteverdi is generally associated with opera, a form of dramatic music which originated in the city of Florence about 1600. Opera is perhaps the most characteristic musical realization of the baroque. Originally, it was meant to be a revival of ancient Greek drama with music. In its practical realization, however, this idea, thoroughly imbued with the spirit of the Renaissance, was colored by the dominating baroque aesthetics of the time, and it turned out to be a combination of dramatic poetry, acting, music, and — in the stage decorations and costumes — painting and architecture.

Music was now fundamentally changed. No more counterpoint, no more madrigals; instead, a declamatory monodic style with instrumental accompaniment above a thorough bass or *basso continuo*. Giving up its dominating position, music became a servant to poetry. Rational declamation was preferred to beautiful melody. The musical result of the first operas by Caccini and Peri in 1600 was accordingly meager, and opera probably would have died very soon in consequence of its anemic condition and frail physique had not Monteverdi's genius saved it. Monteverdi's *Orfeo*, performed in 1607 at the court of Mantua, follows closely all the newly developed rules of dramatic aesthetics; nevertheless, it is full of magnificent musical ideas and strikingly expressive features; it makes use of a new type of melody, of chromatic harmony, of instrumental accompaniment, and of new forms of vocal music. One of the most sensational elements of this score was an orchestra of many different instruments, capable of a wealth of tone color. It required thirty-six instruments: two cembalos, two contrabassi da viola, ten viole da braccio, a double harp (*arpa doppia*), two little violins, *alla Francese*, two *chitaroni* (big bass guitars), two little organs, three *bassi da gamba*, four trombones, a regal (a small organ with labial registers), two cornetti, a piccolo flute, a high trumpet, and three *trombe sordine*. The opera *Orfeo* had a phenomenal success, and Monteverdi very soon wrote a second, *Arianna*, hardly less striking in effect. Of *Arianna* nothing has so far been discovered except the famous "Lamento d'Arianna," an admirable solo that became a model for the new baroque style of passionate dramatic expression. Through a great many subsequent works, in part lost, Monteverdi became the leading master of baroque music in all its various aspects, and he has hardly been equaled in the wealth and variety of his innovations. Nevertheless, these were the revolutionary beginnings of a new style, and, like all beginnings, they were bound to be superseded by later works of art; like the foundations of an immense structure, they became invisible as the structure grew higher.

In these dramatic works Monteverdi is a pioneer, the discoverer of a new world which it was denied to him to exploit fully. None of his operas, highly interesting as they are to the student of musical history, would obtain lasting success if revived in actual performance. In another species of composition, however, the madrigal, he was active not as a pioneer who showed the way to later generations but as a finished artist who brought to its highest perfection the long development of a certain style. Works that represent the highest perfection in any given form are more likely to achieve what is euphemistically called immortality than even the most striking and interesting pioneer attempts, which are bound to be superseded by a later development.

This explains why Monteverdi's madrigals must be ranked among the greatest masterpieces of their kind, giving an effect of great finish and satisfying even a very fastidious modern critic, whereas his operas, in spite of their undeniable genius, must always be judged as representing the very beginnings of the form, failing, without exception, to meet the demands of listeners who know the later attainments of opera.

We find other baroque traits in that peculiar genre of composition midway between the dramatic and lyric chamber music styles which Monteverdi called *ballo*, a term translated very imperfectly by our "ballet."

What Monteverdi and the first Florentine dramatists, Caccini and Peri, introduced as a new element into music is the "concertizing style" that became eminently typical of the entire seventeenth century and the first half of the eighteenth, and includes the music of Handel and Bach. This concertizing style is one of the most complete and accurate expressions of baroque aesthetics applied to music. It is founded on the new invention of thorough bass, or *basso continuo*, a new manner of instrumental accompaniment in harmonic style. Formerly instruments had never effected a change of style in a polyphonic vocal piece. One could double or replace with instruments one or more vocal parts, but the relation of the single parts to each other remained unchanged, whether these parts were sung, or played, or partly sung, partly played. The new thorough bass, however, brought in a contrasting element: a chord substructure, comparable to a broad layer of bricks, a foundation supporting the vocal parts which was thematically quite independent of the bass. The solo parts now could be reduced in number without loss of harmonic effect. One solo voice, for instance, could be worked out in a virtuoso style that was quite impossible to the older polyphonic manner, or two solo voices could be made to concertize with each other in brilliant dialogue fashion, one competing with the other in virtuosity and effectiveness of treatment. Here the baroque tendency toward brilliant display and rich ornamental work found ample opportunities. The style became popular because it expressed the dominating spirit of the entire epoch. The seventeenth and eighteenth centuries make virtuosity a legitimate and indispensable element of artistic writing and cultivate it with great zeal and enthusiasm, not only in singing but also in purely instrumental music. There were, of course, many degrees of virtuosity, from empty display to a highly accomplished mastery of structural complexities. We must never forget that the greater part of Bach's work is virtuoso music of the purest and highest type, demanding for its writing an extraordinary technical skill in polyphony, harmony, and construction, and for its rendering an equally remarkable skill in singing, conducting, and playing.

After this extended discussion of the musical problems of the baroque style let us return to the broader basis of general culture. Repeated reference has been made to the Counter Reformation, the systematic, cleverly organized defense of the Catholic Church against the powerful and dangerous attacks of the Protestant Reformation. It has also been mentioned that music was used by the Roman Church both in defense and in attack. With profound insight into the propagandistic possibilities of the new concertizing and dramatic style, the Roman Church made a speedy and effective use of the sensational invention of opera about 1600. The opera plots of Monteverdi and the Florentine writers, based on classical mythology and drama, were transformed in Rome into allegorical works with a moralizing Catholic tendency, into a kind of religious drama. This variation of opera was baptized oratorio. In its more primitive form the oratorio goes back a half century earlier to St. Philip Neri of Rome, Palestrina's friend, who about 1552 had founded a sort of organization of priests who met in the oratory (called *oratorio* in Italian) of a convent. At this point the Counter Reformation got hold of the new movement, and in 1575 Pope Gregory XIII sanctioned the constitution of the so-called "Congregazione dell' Oratorio," a carefully organized institute for the education of lay priests, as a means of Catholic propaganda. In 1600 the first opera, *Eurydice*, by Caccini and Peri was performed in Florence. At once Rome felt the importance of the innovation. It was very speedily utilized for the aims of the Church, and in the same year a kind of spiritual allegorical opera, *La Rappresentazione di anima e di corpo*, was performed in Neri's oratory. This was written by Emilio dei Cavalieri, who for years had been in charge of the festive musical performances of the Congregazione dell' Oratorio in the convent of Santa Maria in Valicella, and it is generally called the first oratorio, with a curious misunderstanding of the word *oratorio*. Gradually in the course of the seventeenth century the oratorio was changed from a kind of allegorical religious drama, hardly distinguishable from early opera, to what we now call oratorio. At any rate, the Catholic Church appropriated it and made it a purely Catholic specialty for a long time.

At the beginning of this chapter the term "Jesuit style" was used in connection with architecture. In music the same term might be applied to oratorio. For more than a hundred and twenty-five years oratorio was the Jesuit style in music, and was fostered and propagated by the Roman Catholic Church. In the course of the seventeenth century, oratorio, in Italian as well as in Latin, became a vast receptacle for the new forms and new musical effects that are so important for the rise and growth of modern music. To the older choral forms like the motet, villanella, madrigal, and *canzonetta*, it added new forms of solo, choral, and orchestral music, such as the aria, cantata, concerto, and fugue in many varieties. In the wealth of its subject matter, its novelty, and its entertaining variety it vied successfully with opera. It was in a sense a continuation of the medieval mystery play and treated both Biblical episodes and legends of the saints. Usually it had two parts, with a sermon as intermission. In its outward form it passes through several stages, changing from religious opera to a semidramatic production with a *testo*, or an evangelist, who tells the story, as in Bach's Passion music later. A species of especial artistic interest is the Latin oratorio of the Roman master Carissimi and his school, which used the chorus as the principal means of expression. The style and manner of this form of oratorio have been recently revived in very much modernized form by Stravinsky in his *Oedipus Rex*, which is a combination of opera and oratorio. Oratorio reached its artistic culmination and its greatest popularity, however, only after the great Protestant masters, especially Handel, took hold of it.

In 1600, nearly eighty years after the beginning of the Reformation, the hostility of the Roman Catholic Church toward all liberal developments and its intolerance in religious matters were so great that the great philosopher Giordano Bruno was publicly burnt on the Piazza Navona because he refused to make his philosophy agree with the dogmas of the Church. This religious zealotry animated both parties, Catholic and Protestant, and their long fight for supremacy finally led to the Thirty Years' War (1618–1648) in Germany, an event of the gravest consequences for the country in political, economic, and cultural respects for many years.

This destructive war not only devastated and impoverished nearly all parts of Germany but also destroyed its flourishing culture and prevented the progress of the arts by interrupting tradition and by depriving the younger generation of a proper education. The seventeenth century in Germany is marked by an enormous decline in the arts; music alone was an exception, and this exception was due almost entirely to the activity of several generations of Protestant musicians who turned to religion and religious music as their sole comfort and support in the common misery of everyday life. Between 1600 and 1700 these Protestant cantors and organists, mainly in Saxony and Thuringia, kept the tradition of their art alive, and by their sincere, unpretentious work prepared the ground on which a Johann Sebastian Bach could grow and prosper. This century of Protestant German music is well known to us through a long series of modern publications, the *Denkmäler deutscher Tonkunst*, published by the German government from about 1900 on, with the aid of a number of eminent musical scholars. We are thus in a position to survey conveniently the growth of the church cantata, of organ and piano composition, of instrumental chamber music, of suites, sonatas, and concertos in Germany. In all these various species of composition the Italian baroque tendencies of the epoch are clearly evident, though they are modified very perceptibly by their Protestant admixture. In church cantatas and organ music, especially, Germany very soon became superior to Italy.

Perhaps three-quarters of all the German music of the seventeenth century originated in the narrow district of Saxo-Thuringia, which must be called the real home of German Protestant music well into the nineteenth century. This country, the very heart of Germany geographically, lies about equally distant from Bavaria and Austria in the south and the Baltic Sea in the north, between the rivers Elbe and Weser, both of which flow from south to north. By rail one may pass through the entire region in three or four hours. Yet this little district is full of musical associations, and almost every town is more or less famous in the history of German music. A few of the more prominent names may be mentioned to suggest what it means to say that a country is musical by nature, a statement that might also be made about the Flemish country and northern and central Italy. Let us start our musical trip at Dresden, to this very day a great center of music. Here the venerable Heinrich Schütz, the greatest composer of German church music before Bach, was active for nearly sixty years at the head of the famous Saxon court chapel. He is the senior leader and undisputed chief of German music in the seventeenth century, otherwise so ill-fated. He had brought the principles of baroque music from Venice, where in his younger years he had been a favorite pupil of the great master Giovanni Gabrieli, a younger colleague of Monteverdi. Like Hassler, who was mentioned in the preceding chapter, Schütz had the great gift of assimilating the essential traits of both Italian and German music so perfectly that something new, vital, and powerful arose from the mixture. In Schütz's work we find a continuation of the older German polyphonic choral style, but he also makes use of the new Italian monody, baroque dramatic tendencies, the attempts of Monteverdi at tone color, the polychoral style of Venice and Rome, the new orchestral arts, the concertizing style, and the cantata, always blending the new with the old in a wonderfully skillful way. Schütz's music, accessible in a magnificent, complete modern edition by Philip Spitta, the famous biographer of Bach, is almost entirely unknown in America. To perform it, however, would amply repay the labor spent on it, for much of it is religious art of the first magnitude, with a loftiness of inspiration and a mastery of treatment rarely reached even by the greatest masters.

Progressing on our musical journey we come to Leipzig, the commercial and scientific center of Saxony. Everybody knows of St. Thomas' Church, and Bach's activity there. For nearly two centuries before Bach, however, St. Thomas' Church had been famous in the history of German music, and after Bach, in the nineteenth century, Leipzig became the real center of German music. Richard Wagner was born here; Schumann lived here; Mendelssohn founded the world-famous Leipzig Conservatory; and the Leipzig Gewandhaus concerts became the model for symphonic concerts all over the world. In Zwickau, not far from Dresden, Schumann was born. Handel was born and educated in Halle. A hundred years before Handel's birth, however, Halle had become important in music, chiefly through Samuel Scheidt, one of the great German organists, who was the real founder of the German Protestant organ composition, the choral prelude with variations, in his important and fundamental work, *Tabulatura nova*, of 1624. Near Halle is Wittenberg, the town associated with Luther and the birthplace of Protestant music.

Journeying westward, we reach Weissenfels and its huge castle, a town of musical importance which we connect with Bach as well as Handel. An hour later we find ourselves in Weimar, where Bach spent several years as organist of the court chapel. Later Weimar became famous as the residence of Goethe and Schiller, and still later Liszt made Weimar a center of romantic music. Passing by Erfurt, known because of Luther, a city well worth visiting for its magnificent Gothic architecture, we reach Eisenach, where Bach was born, where Luther wrote his translation of the Bible, and where the castle of Wartburg reminds us of the medieval minnesingers and the great German poetry and music of the twelfth century. Other places of note in this district in the history of music are Rudolstadt, Arnstadt, and Cöthen, which are known in connection with Bach. In the part of Saxony bordering on Bohemia otherwise insignificant places have musical importance — Freiburg, Annaburg, Joachimsthal, and Zittau, in the latter of which lived Andreas Hammerschmidt, the most popular German composer of the seventeenth century, whose motets, religious concertos (*geistliche Konzerte*), and spiritual madrigals and dialogues were sung in all Protestant sections of Germany, even in the smallest towns and remotest villages of the Thuringian forest and the Saxon and Bohemian Erzgebirge.

The great publication of the "Monuments of German Music" (*Denkmäler deutscher Tonkunst*), which thus far comprises some sixty large volumes, forms a museum of German Protestant music of the seventeenth century.[3] It contains the work of masters like Scheidt, Hieronymus Praetorius, Hammerschmidt, Ahle, and the ancestors of Johann Sebastian Bach; Johann Kuhnau, Bach's predecessor in Leipzig; Melchior Franck; Johann Rosenmüller; Adam Krieger, the greatest German song composer of the entire century; Friedrich Wilhelm Zachow, Handel's teacher; Georg Böhm in Lüneburg, and Johann Walther in Weimar, Buxtehude in Lübeck, and Pachelbel in Nuremberg, masters of organ composition who greatly influenced Bach. To these admirable volumes must be added the complete new editions of the works of Heinrich Schütz, who has already been mentioned, and of Hermann Schein, the greatest composer of the seventeenth century in Leipzig. For an adequate idea of the chorale prelude for organ, one of the most valuable achievements of German music — and one of the most thoroughly German — the publications of Karl Straube, the eminent organist and choral conductor of St. Thomas' in our day, should be consulted. His selection of German organ chorale preludes previous to Johann Sebastian Bach serves to show how admirable an art Bach found when he started his life's work. But it also serves as a standard for measuring Bach's achievements and reveals the heights to which his immense and solitary genius was able to soar, high above the very respectable attainments of the generation of German artists preceding him.

Just as each art has its own peculiar ideal of form or color that changes with changing styles, so music has its changing ideal of sound which corresponds to the particular style in vogue. The question has not yet been properly investigated whether a new sound-ideal engenders or is a consequence of a new conception of style. Perhaps these apparently contrary possibilities may be active simultaneously, in mutual collaboration. Certainly

---

[3] It was my privilege to edit for this publication a selection from the immense mass of Hieronymus Praetorius' and Hammerschmidt's works.

there is a sound-ideal that belongs to baroque music, and
this ideal corresponds clearly to the stylistic properties of baroque
architecture, sculpture, and painting. Baroque music has a
predilection for impressive sound, vocal and instrumental, and
the seventeenth century witnessed an extraordinary development
of instrumental music from the point of view of both composition
and technique. Until 1600, instruments had been subservient
to singing voices, and, though much used, they generally merely
replaced one or several vocal parts in a vocal polyphonic ensemble. After 1600, musicians became more attentive to the
individuality of various instruments, their tonal qualities and technical possibilities. Thus a new, purely instrumental style was
evolved for the various wind and string instruments, the organ,
and the harpsichord. The great preponderance of wind instruments in the baroque orchestra gave it a sound quality totally
different from that of the now familiar Viennese classical orchestra for which Haydn, Mozart, and Beethoven wrote, with its
basis of string instruments. Unfortunately most of the baroque
instruments, especially the numerous family of cornetti, have
become obsolete, so that in most cases it is practically impossible
for us to reproduce the orchestral sound of the seventeenth
century. We realize more and more clearly, however, that an intimate connection exists between a musical type and the composer's idea of its tonal realization. We have now become aware
of the fact that the musical work of art is falsified if its sound
quality is fundamentally changed in the reproduction. The consequence is a return to obsolete instruments for certain purposes.
Thus in the twentieth century we have had a revival of the harpsichord and of the viol family of the sixteenth and seventeenth
centuries, and, especially in Germany, a reconstruction of the
baroque type of organ, which has partially preserved the sound
quality of many otherwise obsolete baroque instruments. How
far the instrumental idea (in German baroque, at least) is predominant can be seen even in Bach's cantatas and Passion music,
where the assimilation of vocal and instrumental treatment is
carried to such an extreme that any vocal part is almost identical
in appearance with a part written for flute, or violin, or even
for an instrument like the trumpet.

In a valuable essay, "The Changes in the Sound Ideal of the Organ," [4] Willibald Gurlitt enters into the psychology of what he calls "the immanent sound mysticism of the baroque age." The player of early baroque music does not care to extract from his wind instrument, his recorder, his *Blockflöte*, or his cornetto, an expression of personal sentiment; he avoids soulful expressiveness, shuns that *affetto* which in the eighteenth century is so eagerly sought, and strives to make his playing impersonal. Hence the tendency to reproduce the sound utterances of animals, birds, and even insects — the cuckoo, the cock, the bee. For the German musician of 1650 these impersonal sounds had a symbolical value and were credited with a mysterious power to lift man beyond himself.

French music of the baroque style had a peculiar quality, different from both the Italian and the German. The court of Louis XIV in Versailles represents one of the most dazzling manifestations of the baroque, and from about 1660 French music is a very attentive servant of the court. Lully's opera is typical of the theatrical music of the time, quite equal to the task imposed upon it of ornamenting an entertainment of grand proportions and solemn severity. It reflects the somewhat cold glitter, the majesty, and the vastness of the architecture of the period. It translates into musical declamation the rhetorical splendor and magnificence of Corneille's and Racine's classical tragedy, and it succeeds in molding the brilliant theatrical display and the rigid formality of the traditional French *ballet de cour* into a style of classical purity. We must not look here for lyric effusions, for intimate confessions of the soul. All "expression" in this style remains typical, neglects the personal tinge and accent. The composer is concerned only with certain set molds, certain patterns designed to illustrate musically certain typical situations. In this French opera the theater is never for a moment forgotten; the composer never tries to give us the illusion of real passions and emotions. Yet the very severity of this artificial attitude is productive of a genuinely artistic style. The methodical seriousness of the action and the firm construction

[4] *Die Wandlungen des Klangideals der Orgel im Lichte der Musikgeschichte* (Augsburg, 1926).

of the theatrical sketch finally make convention itself convincing and impressive. It is this intellectual greatness, this power of creating style, that makes Lully so significant a figure in the history of music. This artist in himself sums up everything that the French baroque spirit was able to give him and to demand from him. Alone he completed a task which in Italy and Germany fell to a whole generation of composers, most of whom far surpassed him in purely musicianly capacities. Though only a second-rate musician, he became a first-rate theatrical composer, and the model he set for French opera was valid for seventy-five years after his death, until the last of Rameau's work and the beginnings of Gluck's.

It would be interesting at this point to show the reaction of English music to the baroque spirit. In comparison with Italy, Germany, and France, however, the baroque is not pronounced in England during the seventeenth century; it gains real importance only in the eighteenth century, and then mainly through Handel. Owing to the Puritan Revolution the tradition of English music was interrupted in the middle of the seventeenth century, just at the time when baroque art became deeply rooted in Italy, Germany, and France. In the last quarter of the century the baroque influence begins to be manifest in Purcell's dramatic music, but it is mixed with popular English "tunes," almost untouched by the changes of style in artistic music through the centuries. In his sacred music Purcell writes for chorus and orchestra, with thorough bass, in a manner similar to that of Heinrich Schütz. Here we have something decidedly baroque, as also in Purcell's colorful chromatic harmony and in the architectural structure of the "grounds," the English equivalent of the Italian *passacaglia* or *ciacona*. Everywhere, however, the tuneful melody and the slender elegance of melodic contour and form conteract the pompous fullness and solid breadth of the original high-baroque manner.

Italian opera all through the seventeenth and a part of the eighteenth century is baroque music par excellence in a number of varieties. Cavalli and Cesti, successors of Monteverdi, are full of the theatrical pomp of baroque art in the gorgeous architecture of their scenic decorations and the fantastic splendor of their costumes as well as in their elaborate stage machinery and in the music itself. Cesti's opera *Il Pomo d'oro* (performed in Vienna at the Emperor Leopold's wedding), published in part in two volumes of the "Austrian Monuments of Music," illustrates these baroque traits particularly well both in the music and in the fantastic stage designs of the painter Burnacini, which are preserved in the Vienna library. The same traits appear in Roman opera, in the later Venetian opera, and in the Neapolitan opera of Provenzale and Alessandro Scarlatti and his school. Since, however, these scores are not generally accessible and are known to a few specialists in opera only in part, a brief mention will be sufficient here.

The climax and final achievements of baroque music are to be found in the work of the great masters Bach and Handel in the eighteenth century. The outstanding importance of their art, however, demands that it be given more detailed treatment in a special chapter devoted to it.

CHAPTER SEVEN

BAROQUE AND RATIONALISTIC
TRAITS IN BACH AND HANDEL

I N GENERAL an outstanding importance for music is attributed to the years around 1600, as being the time when the
modern conception of music was born. Historically, it is true,
the period is of great importance. Indeed, the entire seventeenth
century is significant, for it saw the evolution of those new forms
of construction, new means of expression, and new aesthetic
maxims which together have created music in the modern sense.
Yet from the point of view of outstanding artistic achievement
the eighteenth century is still more remarkable. If the seventeenth century may be called the childhood and youth of the
new music, the eighteenth century represents the early manhood, the vigorous, still young, yet maturing activity of the new
spirit. If we add the musical achievements of the nineteenth
century, it may justly be said that between 1700 and 1900 the
art of music reaches its full maturity, the maximum of its power
and possibilities, the undeniable climax of its history of two
thousand years.

Compared with the music of Bach, Handel, Haydn, Mozart,
Beethoven, Schubert, Schumann, Wagner, and Brahms, all former music seems a product of adolescence — and in rather
modest proportions. In spite of great artists like Josquin de Près,
Orlando di Lasso, Palestrina, and Monteverdi, in spite of the perfection of certain limited species like the madrigal and the motet,
one is justified in asserting that the older music reached perfection
only in the smaller forms, that in boldness and magnitude of

conception, in power of construction, in emotional profundity, in wealth of imagination it cannot stand a comparison with the later phases of musical art. The two epochs compare somewhat like a charming, idyllic river and the vast, majestic ocean. Neither of architecture, sculpture, and painting nor of literature, poetry, and philosophy can it justly be maintained that their summit was reached in the last two centuries. No matter what magnificent achievements we may boast of in those fields between 1700 and 1900, the past always beats us easily on our own ground and maintains its spiritual power by achievements of the very first magnitude which it would be next to impossible to surpass.

This will be evident from a glance at a few of the high-water marks of former times, chosen at random, without any attempt at completeness or thorough analysis. In architecture one may point to the Egyptian pyramids, the Greek and Roman temples, palaces, and aqueducts, to the glorious cathedrals of the Romanesque and Gothic styles, to the wonderful achievements of the Renaissance — St. Peter's Church in Rome, the Florentine and Venetian palaces — to the sumptuous baroque. If we compare with these achievements our more recent architecture (including the skyscrapers of New York) with all its undeniable merits, we certainly cannot swell with the pride that animates musicians when they consider the great epoch of musical art between 1700 and 1900. In painting, Italian, Dutch, German, and Spanish art up to the eighteenth century has not been surpassed. In sculpture the preëminence of ancient Egyptian, Greek, and Roman art, of Gothic and Renaissance work, is so firmly founded that even a most superficially instructed observer never seriously questions it. In poetry, literature, and philosophy it is sufficient to point to the Bible, to Homer and the Greek tragedians, to Virgil and Horace, to Dante and Petrarch, to Shakespeare and Milton, to Plato, Aristotle, and Spinoza, to realize that the most brilliant achievements of recent times can hardly advance the center of gravity to 1800 or 1900. In music alone the opposite holds true. The two centuries from 1700 to 1900 have brought music to a towering height far beyond anything formerly achieved. Comparing the exalted rank of music with the moderate height reached by the other arts, one is well justified in asserting that music is without question the most representative art of modern times.

Why it is that only music attained such an incomparable height in the last two centuries is a problem that involves a most complicated analysis of a great many different factors. To solve that problem is beyond the scope of this book. We are not concerned here with the profound causes of the phenomenon but with the phenomenon itself, and for the present purpose it suffices to point out the leading ideas of the period, to see how these ideas affected the art of music, and to illustrate the most important phases of the problem in brief outline.

This late coming has been the fate of music all through its history. Music is the youngest of all the arts; it was still in a primitive, undeveloped state at a time when poetry, architecture, and sculpture were already old, laden with the harvest of a thousand seasons of reaping. The music of Greek antiquity, compared with the power, range, and perfection of poetry, drama, sculpture, and architecture, is decidedly primitive, an art of the second order. Painting, too, in antiquity and in the Middle Ages was an art of secondary importance, a servant to architecture, as music was to poetry. But painting reached the full command of its powers as early as the fifteenth century, whereas music did not attain a corresponding degree of power and perfection until the eighteenth century, three hundred years later. The purpose of this book is to show how the dominating spirit and ideas of a certain age left their mark on music, influenced it more or less profoundly. It would be a grave mistake, however, to believe that the relation of music to the other arts and to the spiritual contents of a certain age has a fixed ratio, that all the arts progress "in parallel motion," to use a musical term. In reality, parallel motion has been a rare exception; as a rule an "oblique" or even "contrary" motion prevails in the progress of music with respect to the other arts.

In order to gain some clearness as to the peculiar musical situation in the eighteenth century it may be useful to make a cross section of three especially significant periods in this century. The years 1730, 1760, and 1790, representing three successive generations of artists, are both convenient and appropriate.

The year 1730 falls in the age of Louis XV. France is the dominant power of Europe. England's main interests are turned overseas to her widespread colonies. Italy, divided into dozens of
little states, has not much political importance for European
affairs but continues to enjoy a leisurely life artistically, con-
suming the interest of her accumulated artistic wealth, the heritage of her great Renaissance and baroque epochs. Prussia is
slowly but steadily rising to political power under the strict,
pedantic rule of her severe king, Frederick William I, but is an
almost negligible factor in the arts and sciences. Austria still
boasts of imperial power, though this power is more apparent
than real. But Vienna continues to be the only rival of Paris in
matters of art and culture. In Europe generally, peace prevails;
no revolutions disturb the normal rhythm of life. In literature no works of the first rank make their appearance in any
country; architecture and painting are mainly influenced by
French models, the late baroque and early rococo spirit dominating taste in almost all European countries.

In this atmosphere of uneventful, though by no means dull,
tranquillity, the only startling events took place in the fields of
philosophy, mathematics, science, and music. In philosophy the
work of Leibnitz in Germany and the English idealism of Berkeley, midway between Locke and Hume, inaugurated a new
epoch of speculation, preparing for one of the greatest achievements of modern philosophy, the Kantian criticism. In physics
and mathematics the discoveries of Isaac Newton and the theory
of differential calculus developed by Leibnitz and Newton were
achievements of the very first order, surpassing in importance
anything done in the arts, with the exception of music. Linnaeus'
comprehensive system of botanical classification, Muratori's vast
collection of the sources of Italian history, and Christian Wolff's
encyclopedic system of philosophy might be added. How this
systematic, encyclopedic spirit influenced music will be shown
later in this chapter; here it may suffice merely to mention works
like Bach's *Well-Tempered Clavichord*, his chorale preludes, his
Art of Fugue, his Passion music, his two hundred cantatas,
his *Klavierübung*, and so on. About 1730, however, one of the
most glorious epochs of musical history had begun. It was the age

of Johann Sebastian Bach and George Frederick Handel. In France masters of the rank of Couperin and Rameau were active. Throughout Europe Italian opera was a great sensation. Compared with these magnificent achievements, what happened in the other arts appears of much less significance. One is well justified in calling the early eighteenth century primarily a musical age.

The question, of course, may be raised in what manner these great discoveries in science and philosophy could have affected music, whether there is really any connection between Newton, Leibnitz, Berkeley, Wolff, and Linnaeus, on the one hand, and Bach and Handel on the other. Nobody for a moment believes that Bach had to study the philosophy of Leibnitz and the maxims of differential calculus, or that Handel ever busied himself with Linnaeus' system of botany and Berkeley's idealistic philosophy. These studies would have been superfluous to the great musicians. What they needed urgently, however, and what helped them immensely in their artistic achievements was the new spirit of large conceptions, of profound philosophical meditation, which led to monumental, encyclopedic systems and to a view of science as something comprehensive and universal. Bach and Handel bring the epoch of baroque music to a towering climax and to a definitive close. If we ask what enabled them to rise so high above their most gifted predecessors in baroque music, the answer is that with keen vision and penetrating instinct they had seized the spirit of their age, and had realized as a result of the achievements of science and philosophy that music, too, was ready to undertake huge tasks, to grapple with monumental problems of form and contents, with systematic and exhaustive applications of new aesthetic ideas. To what they had learned from their predecessors in music they added a new grasp of the larger systematic problems of art, an insight which the seventeenth century had not possessed. Their mastery of the art was equal to the immensity of the tasks they imposed upon themselves. Their boldness was based on self-confidence and adequate strength. In the subsequent paragraphs it will be pointed out in detail how the new scientific and philosophical spirit is reflected in the art of Bach and Handel. Building upon a

broad baroque basis, the two masters raised a superstructure of
an encyclopedic, philosophical, and rational character that extended the range of their vision back into Gothic art and forward
to what was to be the rococo. The formula for Bach would be
something like this:

Gothic

Baroque + Rationalistic

Rococo

In the case of Handel the retrospective Gothic element is less
pronounced.

These two great artists are generally believed to have so
powerfully impressed their own age that in referring to the
period from about 1700 to 1750 we habitually speak of "the age
of Bach and Handel." We mean, of course, that the music of
Bach and Handel towers so high above everything else as to
make it appear of secondary importance, even comparatively
insignificant. This is certainly true with reference to Germany
and England; less so as regards contemporary music in Italy
and France. But like most broad generalizations this one concerning the age of Bach and Handel is a conception that was
built up a hundred years later, in the nineteenth century, and
from a point of view altogether different from the one prevailing
in the eighteenth century.

It is well to remember that during his lifetime, and for one or
two generations later, Bach was only a local celebrity of Leipzig,
that his music was almost totally unknown in Italy, France, England, and even Catholic Vienna. When Bach died, all his published music could have been put into one volume, instead of
the fifty-nine volumes of our still somewhat incomplete edition
of his works. And though Handel's fame spread over England,
Germany, and Italy, he was not recognized in France as a really
great composer either during his lifetime or for a century after
his death. Though three or four of his forty-six operas were
occasionally given in German opera houses, his great oratorios
did not reach Germany until about a quarter of a century after
his death. In the eyes of their contemporaries one would have
been much more justified in speaking in Germany of the age

of Telemann and Hasse, and in Italy of the age of Neapolitan opera, of Scarlatti and his school.

Bach and Handel are generally coupled together for convenience' sake and following the routine of an old tradition. In reality, they are as different in their artistic tendencies and achievements as in their personalities and the events of their lives. Occasionally, however, they do meet on common ground, along with the French masters Couperin and Rameau, and the Italian Scarlatti, Corelli, and Vivaldi. In such circumstances these great artists are like members of an international art club, so to speak, representing not so much their own personal ideas as the general artistic tendencies of their age, common to Italy, Germany, France, and England. To point out these common features is, of course, important for our topic: they show music as a part of general culture; they form the neutral background against which individual traits stand out in sharply drawn contours.

What is this neutral background of eighteenth-century music? What are those significant traits which permit us to place an anonymous piece of music, newly discovered, in the earlier eighteenth century? There are a number of stylistic qualities common to all the music of this epoch. These may be called the topography of the prevailing baroque style. They are: (1) certain melodic types and certain types of accompaniment in the mutual correlation that results from the prevalent practice of what is called *basso continuo*, or thorough bass; (2) certain clearly defined patterns of vocal and instrumental treatment; (3) certain aesthetic maxims governing the expression of the musical work of art; (4) certain musical forms, or types of construction.

These four categories cover fully all music between 1700 and 1740. They form the musical background — even more, the musical soil from which all products grow. In this age individual artists are never concerned with overthrowing any of the generally accepted fundamental maxims, but only with varying their manner, though one artist may be more inclined than another to use contrapuntal or harmonic complication, to enlarge the proportions of his art, the scope of his emotional expression. The age is not revolutionary in tendency. None of the great artists of this epoch, neither Bach nor Handel nor Scarlatti nor Couperin nor Rameau, ever made it a point to overturn the universally accepted basis of music. Their ambition was not to create a new style but to perfect the style of the time, to surpass their rivals on their own ground. In this respect the age is very different from the period about 1600 and from the later eighteenth century, when Gluck, Haydn, and Beethoven created a new style, new aesthetic creeds, a revolution in art. If we ask ourselves why great artists like Bach and Handel felt so little inclined to revolutionize their art, the answer seems to lie in the tranquil mental atmosphere of their age, as pointed out at the beginning of this chapter. This general satisfaction with existing methods in all the arts, in architecture, painting, literature, sculpture, and music, may, of course, lead to tiresome conventional work, to dull routine, but need not prevent a great artistic development. At the close of a long period we find ourselves cultivating a certain definite style, the baroque thorough bass. We are approaching the perfection, the climax of this style. Art rises to prodigious heights, but it does not explore new regions; it only mounts higher, digs deeper than ever before on its own familiar ground. In this respect Bach is like Palestrina, who also realized the ultimate possibilities of a long-practiced, familiar style, and unlike Monteverdi and the Florentine reformers of 1600, who started on an adventurous journey into unknown, distant regions.

Here in art the same eternal cycle of events, a law of nature, can be observed. A certain style, manner of living, view of the world is established, explored, and developed to its final possibilities; where these possibilities end, a need is felt of a new way of living or of a new style, which makes its entrance more or less violently and sensationally. Yet the fundamental changes themselves are not brought about all of a sudden. Before they become visible they grow for some time silently, hidden underground, sometimes sending their roots far back into the preceding epoch, to which they are so violently antagonistic but of which nevertheless they are the offspring. Very much the same thing takes place here as in an old family which for generations has lived according to a certain standard, formed a tradition, accumulated wealth. The time inevitably comes when this steady, sure rhythm of living reaches a climax and a close, either through inner exhaustion or through powerful outer forces, and ultimately one branch of the family breaks away from its tradition and starts life on new lines, bound either to perish, or to become altogether insignificant, or to found a new prosperity.

Viewed in this way one can also find in Bach the seeds of a new art, though he himself probably paid little attention to the incidental traits that were destined to become the germ of a new species. These matters can be perceived only as one looks back into the past. Bach himself could never have known just which aspects of his art would become important for the future; they are apparent only to later observers, who are able to compare the newly grown art with the older style and to trace back to their source certain striking features.

If treated in detail the four stylistic qualities of eighteenth-century music just pointed out would require a special book on the technique of composition in the baroque period. In this rather general review the dominant idea will be illustrated sufficiently if we single out for closer inspection the third, which is concerned with the aesthetic maxims governing the manner of expression in the musical work of art. The other three topics would involve a highly specialized discussion of purely musical technicalities; the question of aesthetic tendency, however, has to do not only with the technique of composition but also with the prevailing cultural state, with taste, and with the demands made on music in a certain age, and it is problems like these that are of especial interest from our present point of view.

In order to be able really to appreciate the art of Bach and Handel it is not sufficient to be a lover of music, a susceptible and attentive listener. It is not even sufficient to be a very excellent musician. It is necessary in addition to understand the aesthetic theories of the early eighteenth century in order to know what the artist's aim was, what problems he set for himself, and how he solved them. Between the aesthetic maxims of Bach and Handel and those of 1930 there are far greater differences than most musicians are aware of. Three items especially call for our attention: (1) a most comprehensive, subtle, and impressive conception of tonality and construction; (2) a profoundly mystical symbolism of expression; (3) a complicated doctrine of emotional expression, going back to certain primitive correlations of rhythm and melodic line with the various emotions, what in German is called the *Affektenlehre* of the eighteenth century. Closer investigation of these three topics reveals the presence of a comprehensive treatment on the part of composers which is genuinely systematic and scientific. It is of minor importance whether this new scientific spirit was introduced into music by Bach and Handel as a part of their individual contribution to advancement of the art, or whether it was a common property of their time, taken over by them from the technique of the great Italian masters. The music of the leading Italians, Scarlatti, Porpora, Bononcini, Vivaldi, Tartini, and others, is too fragmentarily known at present to decide questions of priority. The new spirit — scientific, systematic, psychological, philosophical, whatever one may call it — is undeniably a powerful factor in music about 1720. Whoever introduced it, we associate it with Bach and Handel because these two masters utilized it with a superior artistic instinct and ingenuity. To their works, therefore, we turn for the most convincing and impressive application of the new principles.

As to tonality in Bach and Handel, we have of late gained new insight into a system of surprising extension, the existence of which was not even suspected twenty-five years ago. Handel, the great dramatist, makes a most scrupulous choice of keys for the arias in his operas and oratorios. It matters very much to him whether he writes a piece in F major, or F sharp major, or F flat major, in F minor or F sharp minor. For him every one of these keys has a well-defined color, atmosphere, and meaning, to which he adheres strictly during his entire artistic career of over fifty years. F major, for instance, is the key of the pastoral idyl all through the eighteenth century, and it is certainly not by chance that Beethoven a hundred years later chooses it for his Pastoral Symphony and for his "Spring" Sonata for violin and piano, op. 24. F sharp major for Handel is what one might call a transcendental key; indeed, all keys with signatures of five, six, seven, and even eight and nine sharps are associated by him with the idea of heaven, with ecstatic visions of a world beyond earthly toil and pain, with eternal peace and heavenly consolation. F minor and F sharp minor are both tragic keys, but there is a subtle distinction between them. F minor is generally chosen for the expression of profound sadness, melancholy; it is a dark, pathetic, lamenting key. Certain aesthetic conceptions of the eighteenth century still survive in Beethoven, and again it is not by chance that he wrote his *Egmont* overture in F minor, and that the gloomy prison scene in the second act of his *Fidelio* has the F minor tonality. For Handel F sharp minor is full of tragic intensity, less melancholy and sentimental than F minor. It sometimes has a heroic note, a sound of brave resistance to a cruel fate. G minor in Handel's operatic music is preferably used for the agitation of jealousy; E minor is reserved for the expression of an elegiac mood. It is interesting to remember that one of the most admired masterpieces of elegiac music, Brahms's Fourth Symphony, chooses the same key, E minor; we also remember that Brahms was a close student of Handel and took many a hint from this great master. G major in Handel suggests bright daylight, sunshine, green meadows. C major is used to express manly vigor, military discipline and the elemental power of nature. Beethoven uses it in the same way. It is the key for plain, straightforward action, without psychological complication; it is the *Naturtonart*, as the Germans call it. In this way one might go through all the other keys. Handel's entire harmonic system and style of modulation is based on the underlying meaning of the various keys.[1]

There is another aspect of tonality in Handel's music which had not been perceived until the decade between 1920 and 1930, when as the result of a great Handel renaissance actual performances of Handel's operas were given. The start was made at the University of Göttingen by Dr. Osker Hagen.[2] For years Handel enthusiasts met in summer in the idyllic little university city to hear one or two new Handel operas; from Göttingen this new Handel movement spread all over Germany, and in the course of about eight years approximately one-fifth of the mas-

---

[1] I have treated this subject at greater length in an essay for the *Musical Quarterly* (New York), April 1935, in the memorial number devoted to Bach and Handel.

[2] At present professor of Fine Arts at the University of Wisconsin.

ter's dramatic output of forty-six operas were heard. Naturally a close study of these neglected scores followed, and the musical experts of Germany were unanimous in the opinion that since the revival of Bach's Passion music and cantatas, a century back, nothing of equal importance had been saved from oblivion. One of the most remarkable discoveries, due to Dr. Rudolf Steglich,[3] was Handel's use of tonality as a constructive factor of the widest imaginable proportions. In addition to making use of the emotional and expressive meaning of the various keys, Handel builds entire acts of his operas and oratorios of four hours' length according to an ingeniously devised architectural plan of tonalities, making use of the relationship of the various keys and grouping them in symmetrical order, or, when necessary, destroying this symmetry by a striking contrast. Drawing up a sketch of the various keys as they follow each other in a Handel opera or oratorio, one is strikingly reminded of the constructive plan of an architect. In my comprehensive book on Handel (Berlin, 1924) I have tested Professor Steglich's observation in a number of cases. From this book (p. 643) I quote the analysis of the plan of tonalities for the first act of Handel's opera *Amadigi*:

"The first act of *Amadigi* shows the following order of keys in the arias:
Overture C

g-g-C-B flat-e-B flat-g-F-E flat-A-B flat-B flat-g

G minor is heard at the beginning, in the middle, and at the close. B flat major occurs twice in each half, shortly before G minor in the middle and G minor at the close. C major has the same relation to E minor in the first part as F major has to A major in the second part. C — B flat — e in the first part corresponds to F — E flat — A in the second part, the second complex being a fourth higher than the first one. Moreover, in each part an entirely foreign, distant key jumps in, E minor next to B flat major in the first part, and A major between E flat and B flat major in the second part. These strikingly distant tonalities are carefully chosen for the purpose of giving especial and definite emotional

[3] Now professor at Erlangen University.

expression and coloristic effect according to the demands of the dramatic situation. Melissa sings of her amorous grief in the elegiac key, E minor, Amadigi of his amorous delight in A major. The recitatives between the arias lead over in modulation from one key to the next one, besides living their own harmonic life in themselves."

In the same book, acts from Handel's *Siroe* and *Orlando* are analyzed with regard to tonal architecture. Surprisingly, we find that there is no fixed scheme but that in every dramatic score the master devises an ingenious new ground plan of tonalities. How clever and inventive he is in combining the logical constructive outline of whole acts with the emotional expression of single keys in individual parts can only be hinted at in the present essay. Here, too, we can only raise the question whether this system of tonal architecture and its relation to the emotional, expressive, and color values of the single keys is entirely Handel's own property, or whether part of it was inherited from the Italian opera of about 1700. What prompted Handel in this systematic, subtle, carefully planned use of keys and tonality? It was certainly the *Zeitgeist*, the spirit of the times, the rationalistic trend of thought characteristic of the eighteenth century, the inclination toward systematic, subtly thought-out workmanship. The mathematical and philosophical progress of the earlier eighteenth century, slowly pervading the entire mental atmosphere of the age, at last reaches music, and its influence becomes manifest in various ways: in the impressive, clear, well-proportioned, and strikingly effective construction of Handel's music, in his systematic treatment of keys and tonality, and in his method of psychological synthesis in opera, of which some illustrations will be presented in the latter part of this chapter.

In Bach as well, the mathematical and philosophical tendencies of the age are plainly evident, though in a somewhat different manner. They lie in the convincing logical power of Bach's music, in its delight in complicated problems of construction, in the masterly elegance, the crystal clearness, with which the greatest complication of counterpoint is presented. In a word, Bach's fugues show, as nothing else in music does, the inner relationship of mathematics and music. And Bach's own profoundly meditative personality is reflected in the philosophical aspect of certain of his compositions. In his cantatas, his Passion music, and his chorale preludes for the organ he interprets the meaning of the Holy Scriptures and the Christian creed with a fervor, persuasiveness, penetration, and vast imaginative power never again exhibited by religious music. His religious music has, indeed, much similarity to a profound sermon of a great preacher. At the present time Bach scores like the St. John and the St. Matthew Passion music and the B minor mass are being studied in Germany with a view to finding out whether Bach had a system of tonal architecture similar to Handel's or different from it. In his larger works there is certainly a rhythm of vast proportions that escapes most listeners but is real and effective nevertheless, a series of symmetries and contrasts that suggests the broad rhythm of the seasons of the year. It has not yet been sufficiently observed whether Mozart's operas and Beethoven's *Fidelio* and *Missa solemnis* follow a similar plan, but of late the brilliant Wagner studies of Professor Alfred Lorenz have disclosed the remarkable fact that Wagner also makes use of a certain well-planned succession, correspondence, and contrast of tonalities in his operas.

Another topic in the list of the aesthetic features of the art of Bach and Handel is concerned with the symbolism of expression practiced by these great masters and with their peculiar manner of tone-painting. The eminent French musicologist, André Pirro, and the venerable physician, theologian, and musician, Albert Schweitzer, were the first to point out and to interpret the symbolical meaning of Bach's art. In his scores one finds a considerable number of typical rhythmical motives, whole classes which recur again and again with slight variations. These motives have a symbolical meaning for Bach; they represent formulas on which he bases his emotional expression. They are so flexible that in spite of their fixed rhythms they can be made to express a surprising variety of emotional nuances. Though at first glance the proceeding might appear mechanical, Bach knows how to avoid this danger and is capable of expressing emotionally almost anything he desires, varying the formulas most skillfully and subtly to adapt them to each new case.

In Bach this symbolism is so closely linked with the words of the text that it gets its meaning and its artistic weight from the inseparable association of word and tone. It may certainly be called an art of tone-painting. What distinguishes it, however, from the tone-painting of other music of the eighteenth and nineteenth centuries is the fact that it does not interfere in the least with sound musical construction, with absolute mastery of musical workmanship, with the logical progress of the piece. It does not try to supplant the architectural system of music by a pictorial system. Architectural construction and picturesque expressiveness go side by side, assisting, not impeding each other; the symbolism adds charm to the severity of the constructive art of this music, and the firmly built structure gives an impressive background to tone values. Only the sum total of constructive and picturesque elements makes the work of art complete. One who is incapable of appreciating the symbolical meaning of Bach's picturesque traits still hears a soundly constructed piece of music, interesting in itself.

It is remarkable that Bach, like Handel, makes a great distinction between his vocal and his instrumental music. The vocal music is full of picturesque symbolic touches, while the instrumental music relies almost exclusively on purely musical constructive features. It does not try to describe anything; it has no titles, no poetic programs. *The Well-Tempered Clavichord*, *The Art of Fugue*, the organ preludes and fugues, the suites, the Brandenburg concertos are not program music in any sense of the term, but music as absolute as has ever been conceived. An apparent exception is to be found in some of the organ chorale preludes, which occasionally seem to go beyond the self-sufficiency of absolute music. But it is to be remembered that these chorale preludes are really a musical expression and interpretation of the religious poetry of the German chorale, and that a detailed knowledge of the text is indispensable for the full comprehension of Bach's wonderfully constructive and at the same time wonderfully imaginative and expressive musical sermon.

In Pirro's and Schweitzer's books on Bach one can find long lists of the motives used by Bach for the expression of joy, pain, melancholy, agitation, peace, ecstacy, consolation, fear, and so on. But Bach does not stop with shaping the emotional element into symbolical formulas; the actual happenings described in the text are translated into music with the help of certain motives. In particular, everything connected with motion, with rhythm, has an extremely realistic interpretation. Walking, running, jumping, rising, falling, climbing, resting, flying, swimming are translated into musical terms of admirable ingenuity and distinctness, as the listener realizes when he has once comprehended the meaning of these rhythmical and melodic formulas.

Handel practices a similar art in the arias of his operas and oratorios. Usually he lets the accompanying obligato instruments suggest the scene, while the emotional and rhetorical accents are given to the voice. Hundreds of striking examples might be given from the inexhaustible mass of Handel's works, but we have space for only a few, chosen at random. In the opera *Giulio Cesare* there is an aria expressing greed for revenge that makes use of the metaphorical picture of the furious snake, which once attacked does not rest until it has killed its foe. The snake's winding, darting, and recoiling, its furious hissing, are rendered by the figuration of the orchestra as well as by the coloratura of the solo in a manner that is both fantastic and exciting. After his miraculous escape from death, Caesar regains his courage and compares his strength to the irresistible power of the torrent rushing down from the mountain. In its restless motion the accompaniment suggests strikingly the idea of the torrent. Another aria compares justice with a warrior about to shoot his arrow from the bow. In its sound, and even in the appearance of the notes on paper, the accompaniment suggests the release of the arrow from the bow, and its swift flight toward its aim. A most realistic scene occurs in *Solomon* when the king is about to decide the quarrel of the two women who claim the same infant. Solomon sings, "Justice holds the lifted scale," and in his music Handel succeeds most surprisingly in evoking the idea of the slowly rising and falling scales. *Belsazar*, *Semele*, and *L'Allegro ed il pensieroso* are also full of delightfully picturesque, ingenious, and effective accompaniments of this kind.

No less interesting and varied is the manner in which Handel translates emotions into music, making his men and women

express their feelings and reveal the secrets of their souls characteristically, convincingly, naturally. In Handel's manner of
psychological analysis and characterization the systematic, rationalistic spirit of the age is reflected. A character in a Handel
opera is expressed musically by the sum of the arias given to
him. Each aria reveals a different characteristic. Thus, for instance, in the opera *Alceste* the heroine, Alcestis, expresses in her
arias the various sentiments agitating her in such a manner as
to reveal to the listener her individual character. Sacrificing her
life in order to save her husband, Admetus, she takes leave of
him in her first aria, which has a noble elegiac quality full of
tenderness and love. Her second aria, before her death, has a
note of proud courage and satisfaction, and when Hercules succeeds in bringing her back to life from Hades her singing is full
of exuberant joy and expectation. Finding her beloved husband
in love with another woman, however, she gives vent to her rage
and disappointment in an aria full of passionate outbursts of
jealousy, but her next aria corrects this unrestrained outburst
with new expressions of love for Admetus. Back from Hades in
her palace she sings out her delight in life with enchanting grace
and elegance. And her last aria, after her reconciliation with
Admetus, expresses her heartfelt joy in a plain melody that is all
the more impressive for its plainness. Each of these six arias
presents a different feature of Alcestis' character, and together
they reveal the penetrating nature of Handel's delineation.

We often speak of the psychological analysis of character in
dramas and novels, but the term synthesis is more appropriately
applied to Handel's dramatic art, for he adds one trait to another
until he has built up the entire character. Modern dramatic
technique is almost diametrically opposed to this in tendency.
Its psychological method is not synthetic but analytic. The
modern dramatic poet starts with a complete conception of the
dramatic character, and separates from this initial compound,
this complicated mixture of emotions (*Affekte*), this precon-
ceived sum total, a certain momentary state of mind to be expressed in dramatic terms. Handel leads his public in an opposite
direction, presenting every emotion in isolation, unmixed, pure,
and leaving it to the listener to form an impression of a character

as a whole. Certainly this synthetic manner is more appropriate to melodic expansion than the complex analytical Wagnerian method, which needs the help of word, of gesture, of scenery, of orchestral commentary, to reach its aim. Wagner's music is primarily a music of gestures and declamatory accents, an illustration of dramatic situation, with emotional expression as a resultant factor. Handel's dramatic music is primarily a melodic expression of emotion, and all the other factors — imitative action, the emphasis of declamation, scene — are secondary. The contest of emotions *in abstracto*, rather than the acting characters, is the central point of interest; a drama of emotions is here made visible by those who feel the emotions, the dramatis personae. It is evident how different this dramatic style is from the later dramatic art of the nineteenth century, and how little the modern type of operatic performance would fit the Handel opera. It becomes manifest also that the Handel opera cannot be properly appreciated, cannot produce its full effect, unless the listener knows something of the artistic creed of its author. The same applies to Bach. Every great musical achievement, in fact — the work of Mozart, Beethoven, Wagner, and Brahms, and modern music as well — is based on a certain aesthetic system with which the listener ought to be acquainted. Only from that particular aesthetic point of view can a clear and comprehensive outlook be attained. Even the most revolutionary art has its conventional traits — one may go so far as to define style as a sum of conventional features — for without certain well-established conventions no great art of any kind can exist. When we study art under the aspect of its relation to general culture, these conventional traits become of prime importance. This often misunderstood truth is mentioned here in connection with Handel and Bach in order to show that even the greatest artists cannot escape from the irresistible power of the ideas that dominate their age.

After all these digressions it seems appropriate to return to the basic substance of the art of Bach and Handel, to the baroque attitude of which this art is so brilliant and impressive a result. It represents indeed the summit, the most powerful, perfect, and final expression of the baroque artistic spirit, an achievement so great that it put an end to the successful use of the ideas underlying it. A great period of musical art comes to its close with Bach and Handel. Bach, indeed, goes back to Dutch polyphony and once more revives that magnificent art, but it was by connecting the Gothic traits of polyphony with the conceptions of his own age that he achieved a result beyond the mere technical feat of rivaling the Dutch masters in skill. Compared with the monumental style of Bach's St. Matthew's and St. John's Passion music and his B minor mass, the achievements of all other choral composers except Handel appear insignificant. In these gigantic structures the Gothic art is revived again, but on a greater scale and with an additional wealth of picturesque ornamental design that is derived from baroque taste and style. These ornamental and picturesque traits are manifest mainly in the solo sections for voices and in the concertizing of the instruments. The same, in lesser degree, may be said of the two-hundred-odd Bach cantatas. In their structure, in their well-ordered ensemble of many different formal features they represent a musical architecture of a magnificence never before attempted in music. This combination of sinfonia (or concerto) and fugal chorus, recitative, solo aria, and concertizing duet with elaborate instrumental accompaniment and orderly thorough bass, the whole interspersed with plain chorale tunes — this combination represents in its vast proportions and its wealth of constructive features something closely akin to the elaborate baroque architecture. The epic tendency of baroque art also has its parallel here in the breadth of the musical narrative and the great care given to every descriptive detail.

Handel realized the baroque spirit in his music in another manner. In his operas and oratorios the dramatic element of baroque art is predominant, and their monumental style, their vast proportions, their picturesque treatment of details, and their elaborate constructive plan are the logical outcome of the baroque style. The influence of dress on mental bearing has been described by Carlyle and other observant philosophers; certainly the stately dress we see in Bach's and Handel's portraits — the splendid coats with broad silken and velvet bands, the immense wigs — is not without influence; it is merely another outward aspect of the baroque. Finally, the cosmopolitan, international nature of baroque art is splendidly illustrated by Bach and Handel. Bach's art represents a combination of German, Italian, and French elements, and Handel's power of assimilation, with its use of German, Italian, English, and French traits, is perhaps even greater than Bach's.

After thus considering the common ground of Bach's and Handel's art, we are better prepared for a proper estimate of the essential differences in the music of the two great masters. Our description of the prevailing spirit of the eighteenth century was essentially historical; a treatment of the differences in the music of Bach and Handel touches the really vital points, those features through which these great musicians of the eighteenth century remain great musicians for us children of the twentieth century, unlike them as we are.

In brief, Handel's eminence lies in dramatic choral music; Bach's in religious and instrumental music. Handel is generally ranked among the great masters of religious music, but only once in his long career did he write an oratorio, the *Messiah*, which may justly be called Christian and religious in spirit. Its universal success has led to the identification of Handel with it. The truth is, however, that though he occasionally produced religious music Handel was essentially a composer of dramatic music. He had written no less than forty-six operas before he finally turned to oratorio, forced to it by the collapse of Italian opera in England. And his passion for dramatic music did not leave him in the oratorios, which are merely a continuation of his operas, though on an imaginary stage. The Handel oratorio can be comprehended properly only if one recognizes its dramatic character. In the oratorio Handel gave up not drama but its theatrical aspect. He progressed now to dramatic subjects of a far greater and more sublime style, and through the experience of thirty years of opera writing and producing he perceived that it was possible to write musical drama of the most impressive type free from the limitations of the actual stage and of theatrical conventionalities and traditions. No theater could have produced the powerful dramatic plans that agitated him now; the sublime ethical conceptions of his oratorios could only be realized in a new version of the drama.

Opera had been fashioned to please the taste of the upper classes of society. The wealthy, capricious, dissipated, and somewhat brutal English higher society had twice caused Handel's financial failure. He finally had courage enough to turn his back upon it and to seek a new support in the bourgeois middle class, less frivolous and less spoiled than the aristocratic society of London. It is to these sound and receptive people that Handel speaks in his oratorios. He conveys to them the monumental ethical conceptions of his great soul and powerful intellect by means of musical stories, expressed in terms understood by everyone, based on the most popular and yet profoundest of all books, the Bible. He no longer makes use of the myths of classical antiquity, understood only by educated people who had studied Latin and Greek. The well-known stories of the Bible supply his themes. But the people of Israel are meant to be the English people, the German people, any people. Handel addresses his contemporaries directly, holds before them a mirror in which they may see a reflection of their own actions and ideas. Through the powerful dramatic interest and the concentrated emotional expression of his stories, without ever assuming the tone of a preacher, Handel manages to convey to his public his ideas of morality, his ethical ideals. The universal, eminently human aspect of the Handel oratorio explains its longevity. Its characters are not the products of a particular age, of a particular cultural type and social convention, like those of Italian opera, which tend to appear antiquated and artificial in another age. They are people in whom we see the most elemental aspects of human nature, its nobility and courage, its baseness, cruelty, and weakness: never fashionable but never out of fashion, always essentially the same.

These oratorios are popular and yet at the same time full of masterly art. In the combination of these two apparently irreconcilable traits Handel is unique among composers, though Beethoven occasionally resembles him in this rare faculty. The vastness of Handel's creative power becomes evident only by degrees, when one finally reaches a point of view high enough to survey the magnificent chain of mountain peaks in their totality, and not merely singly. In the series of national dramas, such as

Israel, Athalia, Belsazar, powerful individuals stand out with sculptural clearness, characters like Saul, Samson, Joseph, Joshua, Belshazzar, Judas Maccabeus. Between these monumental dramas smaller, more lyrical works are inserted as intermezzi, works like *Acis and Galatea, L'Allegro ed il pensieroso,* the *Ode to St. Cecilia,* and *Alexander's Feast.* Another smaller group continues the mythical subjects of opera. *Herakles* and *Semele* are the most perfect and admirable music-dramas in the antique spirit, truly a renaissance of the Euripidean art of drama and of the psychological interpretation of tragic characters. In some of these oratorios the whole nation is the hero, as in *Israel in Egypt.* In other oratorios Handel represents the combat of hostile nations; in *Belsazar* three peoples are represented, the Persians, the Babylonians, and the Jews.

For these impressive themes Handel finds an appropriate means of expression, unparalleled either before or since, in his treatment of the chorus. The chorus in the Handel oratorio represents the voice of the people. Accordingly, primitive mass feeling, elemental emotions, plain ideas fill the choral pieces, but the musical means employed to obtain this plain mass effect are sometimes very elaborate. No composer knew more about choral treatment than Handel, and from him one can learn how to write effectively for chorus in the most diverse manners. The fugal style prevails, as in Bach's choral works. But Handel knows many other types besides the strictly constructed music of the fugue: plain choral song, with solo arias in dialogue, choral recitative and arioso, choral suite or cantata, motet and madrigal, passacaglia or chaconne (i.e., variations on a bass theme repeated several times in succession). In his use of the chorus Handel stands easily at the top among all composers. Even Bach cannot compete with him in these respects. A whole book, as yet unwritten, might be devoted to Handel's choral art, and such a book, if adequately written, would be a valuable guide through the vast regions of the choral empire which this composer rules with uncontested power. Compared with his achievements in choral writing, everything of this sort previously attempted seems insignificant; even the highly respectable Roman master Carissimi has the appearance of a slender young boy beside the gigantic figure of Handel. And everything accomplished in oratorio in the two hundred years after Handel is most profoundly indebted to him. Haydn, Mozart, Beethoven, Mendelssohn, Brahms, and Bruckner are his pupils in their choral art, and even these great artists have never surpassed their master.

In solo arias Handel displays most effectively the old Italian *bel canto*, the virtuosity of brilliant coloratura; and the thousands of arias that occur in his forty-six operas, thirty-two oratorios, and nearly a hundred cantatas contain a world of music. In addition, the hundreds of characters in these works represent a vast *comédie humaine* comparable to that of Shakespeare, but, alas, known to only a very few lovers and students of Handel's art. For all these amazingly varied types Handel finds convincing emotional expression. In this respect he is in advance of all composers. Bach, being a composer not of opera but of cantatas and Passion music, cannot be compared with Handel in the variety and wide emotional range of his characters. It is only exceptionally that Bach thinks musically in terms of human character, whereas this is Handel's regular practice. Bach's arias in his two hundred cantatas are sung by any soprano, alto, tenor, or bass voice, not by a well-defined individual with a certain name, of a certain finely expressed mentality, temperament, and character. This trait alone explains the great difference in the artistic intentions of the two artists. Bach almost always sings of his own emotional world, whereas Handel, in true dramatic manner, puts himself into the soul of his character and, like a great actor, discards his own personality and assumes the characteristic accent of speech, manner of expression, and tone of the person he wishes to portray.

Handel's art of suggesting landscape in music also represents an outstanding feature of his art, to which the barest allusion must suffice here. These scenes, scattered throughout his opera and oratorio scores, present pictures in tone — impressions of overwhelming elemental power or of enchanting beauty and loveliness. This highly attractive topic demands special treatment beyond the limitations of this book, but a brief comparison between Bach's and Handel's ideas of scenes from nature in music seems appropriate here. Handel uses them in the desire to illustrate his drama and make it more interesting, charming, or impressive. Bach's landscape painting in his cantatas has not this direct, immediate appeal; he seems rather to use allusions to nature as picturesque symbols to reënforce some dominating sentiment of a quite different type.

On the other hand, Bach is superior to Handel in pure instrumental music, in what we call absolute music. Works like the organ preludes and fugues, the chorale preludes, *The Well-Tempered Clavichord*, *The Art of Fugue*, the Brandenburg concertos, and the Goldberg variations are unequaled in the mass of Handel's instrumental music. Impressive, masterly, and beautiful as the Handel pieces are, they seem plain — sometimes too plain — and light in style compared with Bach's work of similar type, with its wonderful constructive power, its elaborate contrapuntal virtuosity, and the specific weight of its ideas. One really ought not to compare the instrumental music of Bach and Handel at all, for they represent two entirely different conceptions of the problems of construction and expression. It is better to take each as he is. The aesthetic pleasure we might derive from a Handel *concerto grosso*, with its spacious, finely proportioned architecture, its clear, plain melody, will only be marred by our recollection of Bach's more elaborate, ingenious, and emotionally penetrating instrumental art. The art of enjoyment in music as well as in life is based on the faculty of relishing the peculiar excellencies of any object fully, completely, without weakening the impression it makes by reflective activity or by a critical comparison with other objects in different categories.

It is generally recognized that every age has its own spirit, more or less fine and valuable, that the spirit of a period long past cannot be awakened to life again later, and that it is useless to imitate the style of a period of the past, because such an attempt results only in artificiality, lifelessness, and superficiality. Granted the truth of this observation, there are still in all art certain elementary, fundamental traits, permanent and vital in their importance, not subject to changes of taste or of fashion, inherent in all works of true art, no matter what their style may be. One may therefore supplement by the following corollary the aesthetic maxim just expressed. Imitation is bad and useless when it relates to the changing outward aspects of art, but it is good, and indeed indispensable, when it relates to the fundamental basis of an art, to its permanent, unchangeable ideas. No master of music has ever shown these elementary, unchanging laws of musical composition more clearly, convincingly, and impressively than Bach. It is true that Bach is a son of his age and that he pays his tribute to the manner and mannerisms of the earlier eighteenth century. It is also true that those features of his music which reflect the conventional traits of the eighteenth century in Germany are not fit for imitation, charming as they often are. But below this outward, fashionable layer, this coat of eighteenth-century coloring, there is a solid substructure of a granite-like firmness, almost indestructible, potent throughout whole ages, formed of those elementary basic laws of composition which have everlasting validity because they are the rational outcome of the conception of the nature of absolute music.

Bach shows us in the clearest, most exhaustive, and most penetrating manner the meaning of such musical conceptions as form, construction, logic, coherence, proportion, progression, melodic contour, background, dialogue, characteristic emotional expression, symbolical expression, picturesque expression, gravity, weight, lightness, contrast, and so on. These traits in Bach's music are not part of the spirit of the eighteenth century but the constant underlying foundation of the art of musical composition. No artist ever had greater powers of penetration and concentration, or greater ability to distinguish between what is essential and what is merely accidental. For this reason, once its essential nature is recognized, Bach's music can never become antiquated. The fundamental traits must always be present, will always be fashionable, and the lasting value of a piece of music is finally determined by the strength and clearness with which they shine out through the superficial outer color of a particular age. It is for these reasons that musicians see in Bach their greatest teacher, the master who sets the standard in essential matters of composition, the sure guide who shows the right way. If he has some musical instinct by nature, even if he is not particularly well educated in the subtleties of the composer's professional studies, the amateur, the music lover, can nevertheless recognize Bach's unequaled mastery through the impression he gets from Bach's music. He cannot help feeling Bach's superior intelligence, his peculiar elegance and lightness, the elasticity of his part writing, the clearness of his contrapuntal web, the noble beauty of his melody, the total absence of everything cheap and vulgar; and behind all these qualities he feels a mysterious, awe-inspiring emotional power, a faculty of looking into the hidden depths of the soul, of unlocking the inner secrets. He feels a quality quite unique in all music, something that cannot be re-placed by any other music, no matter how much we may love it, something sound and balanced, easy and natural, yet mysterious and exciting, and at the same time calming and consoling. We may safely judge a person's understanding of music by his atti-tude toward Bach, and we may also safely consider that a man who is bored by Bach is completely ignorant of artistic music.

A word remains to be said on the rococo spirit in music. This graceful, charming, and somewhat frivolous daughter of baroque art dominated the middle of the eighteenth century. In music, at least, the rococo appears like a little appendix, a charming coda, an interlude between the vast baroque epoch and the new Viennese style of Haydn, Mozart, and Beethoven which was destined to become so monumental and glorious an achievement. In architecture, painting, and literature the rococo is the baroque in little. It leaves out all the grandiose, passionate, and powerful traits, and accentuates all that is ornamental, adding still more elegance, grace, and refinement, a new touch of fragile beauty, a somewhat artificial but nonetheless charming pastoral attitude. The exquisite Meissen porcelain of the early eighteenth century is rococo par excellence, and a little of that dainty china pretti-ness pervades rococo manifestations in all the arts. It is evident in the charm of color, the fascinating grace and elegance of Wat-teau's painting, in the work of artists like Fragonard, Lancret, and François Boucher, who represent the fairest, most fragrant flower of the rococo spirit. In its fantastic grace, elegance, and wealth of ornament, the Zwinger in Dresden is perhaps the most perfect architectural realization of the rococo spirit. And the literature of France in the eighteenth century, also dominated by the rococo, is full of a sparkling wit, an exquisite culture, a subtle elegance and ease of attitude that had never before been reached. The over-refined, somewhat frivolous French salon of 1750 is the product of this spirit.

In music we find it reëchoed in small pieces of sparkling *esprit*, of tender, delicate sound, but also of an extremely brilliant virtuoso style. Its finest products are to be seen in the clavecin pieces of Couperin and Rameau, the greatest French musicians of the early eighteenth century. But the elegant rococo spirit is not a stranger to Bach and Handel, and in Bach's clavecin suites there are exquisite examples of those pretty little French minuets, gavottes, gigues, musettes, and sarabandes which are the musical counterpart of costly Meissen porcelain. Domenico Scarlatti's piano sonatas, elegant, lively, clever, brilliant in their virtuosity, are rococo music of the finest type.

A languid, weak, somewhat degenerate coda to rococo art makes its appearance in the so-called "gallant style" of Philipp Emanuel Bach and his school. One might liken it to what the Germans call a *Schluss-schnörkel*, an elaborate flourish of the pen in the signature of a letter. The aristocratic French rococo is here taken over by the sober and parsimonious German *bürger*. Even as late as Haydn and Mozart it is still manifest here and there, most charmingly in the humorous, witty, and elegant minuets of their sonatas, quartets, and symphonies. Here it takes its final leave, retiring with that smiling grace, that lack of pathetic gesture and emotional display which is characteristic of it. A great epoch of art has fulfilled its mission. A new world looms up on the horizon, the nineteenth century, an era too troubled and serious after the terrors of the French Revolution to care much for the delicate, fragile, slightly artificial charms of rococo art.

CHAPTER EIGHT

CLASSICAL TENDENCIES OF THE LATER EIGHTEENTH CENTURY

I N THE preceding chapter three periods of significance for the music of the eighteenth century were chosen for closer inspection, and a start was made with 1730. The second period, 1760–1780, is the subject of the present chapter. The date 1760 has been selected because it represents a turning point for the art of music. It takes us to the beginning of the activity of Joseph Haydn and the Mannheim school, to Mozart's first steps in music, to the opera of Gluck. Bach had died ten years before; Handel in 1759. The glorious art of these two giants had come to an end, and it left no possibility of further growth within its domain. Music had either to stagnate in imitation of Bach and Handel, or to relinquish the familiar roads altogether and turn to new regions. Happily for the future, the spirit of reform was strong enough to build up a new style, appropriate to the spiritual demands of a new age. What was this age like? In 1760 Europe was no longer so tranquil as in 1730. The Seven Years' War was still going on, and both Austria and France were involved in the struggle of Frederick the Great to raise Prussia to a position of power in Europe. General attitudes in France, Germany, and Austria had changed considerably. The middle classes had bridged to some extent the vast abyss between the common people and the nobility. The popular rationalistic philosophy of the day, with its enthronement of reason as the most valuable guide in all situations of life, gave adequate expression to the views of these newly enlightened and educated middle classes. Transcendental problems, the profound mysteries of life and death, flights of imagination, exalted passion lost their interest. The mass of the people, especially in France and Germany, had advanced considerably in education and in general culture, but the price of their progress was a lack of great achievement; in both the sciences and the arts mediocrity was dominant.

A certain mental attitude had grown old and exhausted, had become incapable of further great achievements, and though a new attitude had been developing since the middle of the century, it had not yet become strong and mature enough to produce works of great weight. In music, after the glorious achievements of the age of Bach and Handel, a flatland appears, a period of little things. Yet the barrenness of these years from 1750 to 1770 is only apparent. In reality a new style of great moment was already growing — but underground and silently, so that very little of its future greatness was perceptible — and the years 1750 to 1760 mark the start of a revolution in music hardly less memorable and important than the famous artistic revolution of the year 1600.

The childhood of the great classical Viennese school appears insignificant indeed, compared with the work of Bach, Handel, and Rameau. But modest as these beginnings were, they gain significance through the freshness of their ideas, to which tradition contributed little. In this intermediate epoch between the two masters, Bach and Handel, and Gluck, Haydn, Mozart, and Beethoven, music turned away from the immediate past. The style of Bach and Handel seemed too heavy, too much burdened with thought, too elaborate in construction, too full of emotion. Everything was seen and felt now on a smaller scale, in a smaller angle of vision and feeling. One desired less display of skill, greater simplicity, less sophistication of expression, greater naturalness of style. At the same time, however, one wished for a certain refinement and cultivation; one abhorred vulgarity.

We are in the age of what the Germans call the *galanter Stil*, a term coined by its chief exponent, Philipp Emanuel Bach, the second son of the great Sebastian. This "gallant style" is noticeable in poetry and painting as well as music in both France and Germany, particularly the latter. It is part of the decline of the rococo, when it had been taken over by the bourgeoisie. In this phase rococo art lost its fantastic, exuberant aspect, and degenerated into a somewhat sober, artificial grace, fit for everyday life. Everything in it was small, sentimental, weak, fragile, but on a certain respectable level; there was always about it a "genteel atmosphere," as the term *galanter Stil* may perhaps best be translated.

German lyric poetry of this epoch is closely allied with a new type of German song practiced by the composers of the Berlin school. Max Friedländer has described this phase of music in a classical book on German song in the eighteenth century, in which the mutual relations of lyric poetry and German song are treated exhaustively and clearly. The difference between the earlier and later poetry of the eighteenth century is noticeable at once if one compares the texts of the cantatas of Johann Sebastian Bach with the poems used by Philipp Emanuel Bach and his school. In all English and French literature of the past five hundred years hardly anything can be found to equal the poetry of the Bach cantatas in ponderousness, in bad taste, in inartistic exaggeration, and in diction devoid of all poetic grace and beauty. Nothing less than Bach's gigantic genius could have created out of these poor and repulsive verses music of the highest type. Coming from this crude poetry to the graceful verses of Hagedorn, Gleim, Gellert, Haller, Klopstock, and Hölty, it is as if one had gone from a dusty room, overfilled with old-fashioned furniture, into a garden in the first days of spring. As regards the music to which these pretty verses were set, however, it must be said that the poets were decidedly in advance of the musicians. The hundreds of song melodies written at this time in Germany seem almost primitive in their bare harmony, their intentional lack of all artistic complication. Nevertheless, it was out of this artless style that Schubert's incomparable songs grew in the course of time.

The same tendency toward the popular, the plain, and the uncomplicated is manifest in the instrumental music of this age. Bach's *Art of Fugue*, his *Well-Tempered Clavichord*, and his Brandenburg concertos no longer invite young musicians to try their skill at similar complicated problems. A new kind of simple

orchestral music becomes fashionable. We find these forerun-
ners of the later Viennese sonata and symphony in several
regions: there is Philipp Emanuel Bach, whose piano sonatas
Haydn admired as masterpieces of a new style; there is a school
of Viennese composers of popular orchestral music; there is the
Mannheim school, whose leaders were Stamitz, Richter, and
Cannabich, composers of symphonies celebrated throughout
Europe, much played even in Paris; and finally there is Johann
Christian Bach, Sebastian's youngest son, who won fame in Italy
and in England as a composer of opera and symphony and who
influenced the boy Mozart considerably. All these composers
of the second and third rank prepared the ground for Joseph
Haydn. Their symphonic music seems extremely simple and
unpretentious, compared with what was later achieved by Haydn,
Mozart, and Beethoven; nevertheless, in all its simplicity it is
the result of a new attitude toward music, a new and energetic
activity. All stress is now laid on melody as the main factor of
the entire composition; everything else — harmony, construction,
counterpoint — becomes subservient. This new melody was
greatly indebted to the folk songs and dance tunes of the ordinary people; it was indeed of the same type, but a little more
finished, shaped by an artist's hand, fitted for use in a composition of larger dimensions.

Melody of this sort needed an accompaniment different from
that appropriate to the melodic type used by Bach. The time-
honored thorough bass, for a hundred and fifty years the
indispensable basis of all music, is abolished with surprising quick-
ness about 1760. Contrapuntal complexity finds no place in the
new symphonic type, which, in accordance with its plain melodic
material, is perfectly satisfied with a very plain harmony, with
chords that hardly go beyond the range of tonic, dominant, and
subdominant. Melodic contour, bass line, and harmony are well
adapted to each other; each, being justly proportioned, is corre-
lated with the others, and the whole they create is fully alive,
moves vigorously, walks with a firm, light step.

Yet this music is remarkable not only for its simplicity and
for what it omits. It has some positive contributions to its credit,
innovations born of the spirit of its day, perfectly adapted to the

nature of its melodic subject matter. These innovations are concerned mainly with two things — dynamic effects and tone color, or timbre — which in the art of Bach had almost no significance in comparison with what they were destined to acquire later. Dynamic effects — crescendo, diminuendo, sforzato, the various gradations of loudness from fortissimo to pianissimo — have much less importance in Bach's music than in the new instrumental style. The Mannheim orchestra was famous throughout Europe for its effective and exciting crescendo and diminuendo, its precise and powerful accents, its faint pianissimo and thundering fortissimo. This new dynamic scale was introduced because the new melodic type demanded it, and thus a new kind of musical expressiveness was found, perhaps in imitation of rhetorical speech, where accents and gradations of strength are of the utmost effectiveness. Closely connected with this new dynamic scale is the new art of tone color. In Bach's music the different orchestral instruments are chiefly representative of a certain pitch or tone region. For Bach the instruments are mainly of soprano, alto, tenor or bass character. A violin, a trumpet, a flute interest Bach more by their ability to play a soprano part than by the sound, or color, peculiar to them. In the new style the colors of the various instruments are utilized systematically, and new effects are discovered. The suggestions made for the first time in the Mannheim orchestral music, with its individual use of the string and wind instruments, its crescendo and diminuendo, its sforzato, pianissimo, and fortissimo, are perfected in the art of Gluck and Haydn; the Beethoven orchestra is based on that of Gluck and Haydn; and the orchestral technique of Berlioz and Wagner is an elaboration of Beethoven's. In this way and from these unpretentious beginnings the modern orchestra was slowly evolved. Another remarkable feature of the new style which had its importance for the future is its versatility of emotional expression. The thematic material of the Stamitz and Richter symphonies combines a variety of different emotions, far beyond anything ever attempted so far. In this quick leaping from one emotional mood to another, one of the roots of Beethoven's art is laid bare.

In the dramatic music of the later eighteenth century the event of outstanding importance was the reform instituted by Gluck.

Its significance and nature cannot be properly comprehended unless one takes into account the spiritual atmosphere of Paris about 1760. In the hands of writers like Voltaire, Jean Jacques Rousseau, the Encyclopedists — d'Alembert, Diderot, Baron Grimm, Batteux, and others — literature, criticism, and aesthetics had attained a remarkable height. All of these men, except Voltaire, were passionately interested in music and were actively engaged in aesthetic speculation, in musical research and criticism. The leading motive of their aesthetic creed is the return to nature. Technical complications, artificiality, exaggeration of emotional expression were for them faults of style, and for many years they preached its reform. This influential Parisian Areopagus revolutionized the aesthetics of the day. Without its assistance, its brilliant and lucid arguments, its long-continued agitation, Gluck could neither have gained the clearness of conception nor have found the firm footing in Paris that made his final victory possible.

As it happens, the new operatic style was also foreshadowed in a famous Italian essay by Count Algarotti, *Saggio sopra l'opera in musica* ("Treatise on Opera"). This pamphlet, published in 1755, was translated into French two years later and reprinted in the important periodical, *Le Mercure de France*. In it Algarotti expounded his theories with reference to the plot of *Iphigenia in Aulis*, and we are reminded of Gluck not only by this drama but also by the critical contents of the essay as a whole.

But Gluck is obliged to others besides Algarotti and the French Encyclopedists. His pure conception of Greek tragedy would hardly have been possible a generation earlier. Just about 1760 a renaissance of antique art made considerable stir in Germany. Winckelmann, a German scholar, discovered the incommensurable and incomparable beauty of ancient sculpture in Italy, and his writings profoundly influenced German literature, aesthetics, and art. A little later the enthusiasm for Greek and Roman antiquity received new nourishment from Lessing's *Laokoon*, and we can trace its progress through German poetry until the nineteenth century. Goethe's *Iphigenia*, Schiller's *Braut von Messina*, Voss's translation of Homer, and Hölderlin's poems are a few of the highest peaks of this Greek renaissance, and in this series of masterpieces Gluck's later operas find their proper place. It must not be forgotten, however, that Gluck had several strong competitors in his reform of opera, outstanding masters of the later Neapolitan school. Composers like Jomelli, Traetta, and Maio in their best productions come quite close to Gluck; he surpasses them by only a slight margin, but to attain it required his particular genius, his unique capacity for disregarding certain traditional features that until his time were considered basic and of inviolable sanctity.

In Gluck's operas one can observe the change from the baroque to the rococo, and finally to the classical style of the later eighteenth century. In his earlier Italian operas Gluck is a follower of the Neapolitan school, of the baroque manner par excellence, as we find it in the elaborate operatic music of Handel, Bononcini, Porpora, the earlier Hasse, Leonardo Leo, and others. His smaller comic operas, operettas, and ballets, such as *Le Rencontre imprévue*, *Le Cadi dupé*, *Cythère assiégée*, are full of a pure rococo grace, charm, and refinement; in the great works of Gluck's last period, *Alceste*, *Orfeo*, *Iphigenia in Aulis*, *Iphigenia in Tauris*, *Paris and Helen*, the classical ideal dominates. This new classical style is distinguished by great simplicity of form and an absence of mere ornament. The highly ornate "genteel" style, with its abundance of elegant turns and twists, its little phrases, its coquettish feminine grace, its attitude of politeness, had died of exhaustion by this time. Musicians tired of the endless repetition of these mannerisms and found new possibilities in the revival of the classical.

Similar ideas had been uttered a hundred and fifty years before, when opera was invented in Florence and when the monodic manner of Caccini, Peri, and Monteverdi invoked ancient Greek drama and declared war on the time-honored contrapuntal style. At that time monody was shaped artistically, with a scrupulous regard for the right accents of declamation and the grammatical inflection of Italian, in accordance with the metrical art of Greek tragic poetry. In the later renaissance of Greek drama, the ideal of musical expression and impression seems to have been sought not so much in Greek drama as in Greek plastic art, newly rediscovered by Winckelmann and explained so enthusiastically by

Lessing in his *Laocoön: On the Limits of Painting and Poetry.*
No composer equals Gluck in the plastic quality of his melody
and in the purity of his melodic contours; the incomparable
beauty and purity of form in Greek sculpture has never since
found so adequate a translation into musical terms. The picturesque and the poetic, though they are found in Gluck's music,
are of secondary importance. Though in his famous manifestos,
the prefaces to *Alceste* and *Paris and Helen,* Gluck dwells on the
importance of the word in dramatic music, though he asserts
that music is only a servant to the dramatic idea expressed by
word and action, it would be wrong to judge his music solely
by the standards he set. His artistic practice and his theoretical
reasoning do not quite agree, just as later Wagner's music does
not strictly conform to his theoretical maxims. In both cases the
creative artist speaks as a philosopher of art occupied with aesthetic speculation. But in both cases the aesthetic speculation
seems a little amateurish in comparison with the achievements of
the creative genius, who follows the powerful impetus of his innate musical instinct in spite of the self-imposed limitations of his
aesthetic system. In Gluck the plastic character of the music
touches the very soul of his invention. The wonderful purity
of his melodic contour, its touching expressiveness and noble
simplicity impress the listener far more profoundly than his fine
declamatory manner, admirable though it is in itself. In this
declamatory music one can perceive Gluck's reaction to the
rationalistic spirit of his age. The clearness, the luminous treatment of speech, the immediate correspondence of word and
sound, the logical, rhetorical aspect of his musical recitation — all
this reflects the French philosophy of art, the aesthetic attitude
of Voltaire, Diderot, d'Alembert. Yet behind this clear, perspicu-
ous, logical surface something more subtle and evasive is hidden,
something mysterious and touching, in the sound, in the wonderful shape of the melodic line, and this essential aspect of
Gluck's music can hardly be expressed adequately in words.
The comparison with the plastic ideal of antique Greek sculpture
seems to come closest to it.

Yet the plastic quality of Gluck's music, which is essentially
different from the pictorial expressiveness of Bach and Handel,

is only half of what makes his music unique. He possesses in addition the most sensitive ear for sound quality as a factor of artistic expression, quite apart from melody, rhythm, harmony, and form. The sentimental tendency of the later eighteenth century, which will be discussed in more detail later, a trait quite universal in that period in music, poetry, painting, and literature, appears in Gluck in a concentrated and purified form. Gluck's abnormal sensitiveness to sound enabled him to make wonderful new discoveries on the basis of this interest in feeling. What is meant will become clear by a comparison of a Gluck opera with any Bach score for voices and instruments. Bach is somewhat indifferent to the realization of his music in actual sound. Provided the piece is accurately performed, clearly enunciated, uttered with the proper expression, it does not matter very much whether a violin, a flute, or an oboe plays a certain obligato solo. To Gluck it matters immensely whether a violin, a flute, or an oboe is chosen for a particular phrase. He is the first composer who has a really profound feeling for the individual character of each instrument, and he shares with Haydn the distinction of being the real creator of the modern orchestra, though he precedes Haydn by about a decade in the masterly practice of the new orchestral art.

Hector Berlioz, who was endowed by nature with a similar abnormal sensitiveness to sound quality, or timbre, has acknowledged again and again his indebtedness to Gluck; and every student of Berlioz' classical *Traité d'instrumentation* knows how many striking examples he took from Gluck's scores, and how eloquently he comments on their beauty and their captivating expressiveness. In explaining the nature of the oboe, for instance, he writes with reference to an aria from *Iphigenia in Aulis:* "These complaints of an innocent voice, these continued supplications, ever more and more appealing — what instrument could suit them so well as a hautboy? . . . and again, that childlike cry of the orchestra, when Alceste, in the midst of her enthusiasm and heroic self-devotion suddenly interrupts the phrase of the theme . . . to respond to this touching instrumental appeal with a heart-rending exclamation . . . . All this is sublime: not only in dramatic thought, in profound expression, in grandeur and beauty of melody, but also in instrumentation, and the admirable choice of the hautboy from amidst a throng of instruments which are either inadequate or incapable of producing such impressions."

Listen to these words of Berlioz describing the famous flute obligato from Gluck's *Orfeo:* "Only one master seems to have known how to avail himself of this pale coloring, and he is Gluck. . . . Gluck's melody is conceived in such a way that the flute lends itself to all the uneasy writhings of this eternal grief, still imbued with the passions of earthly life. It is at first a scarcely audible voice, which seems to fear being overheard: soon it laments softly, rising into the accent of reproach, then into that of profound woe, the cry of a heart torn by incurable wounds, then falling little by little into complaint, regret, and the sorrowing murmur of a resigned soul. What a poet!"

It may be helpful to make a few more specific remarks on the sentimentality that is so striking a trait of the time between about 1760 and 1780. This characteristic feature of the age found its final, classical expression and representation in Goethe's *Die Leiden des jungen Werthers* and in Rousseau's *La Nouvelle Héloise.* Sterne's famous *Sentimental Journey* is another masterly example of this tendency of the age. An almost feminine sensitiveness, a melancholy shyness, a marked refinement of feeling, speaking, acting, a readiness to indulge in tears and emotional outbursts are some of the characteristic traits of this sentimental attitude, which may perhaps be explained as an imaginative excess that counterbalances the sober, logical, passionless rationalistic intellectuality prevailing in this epoch. In painting and music as well as in literature it became the signature and fashion of the day. The pictures of Greuze, perhaps the best known examples in painting, accentuate the value of virtue with a suspicious didacticism which cannot quite keep a certain frivolous sensuousness from shining through. In music we have an abundance of this sentimental beauty, full of sensuous charm, of sweet, soft melody, but rather more prone to affectation than to true emotional expressiveness. The operas of Pergolesi, Hasse, Traetta, Maio, Piccini, of Johann Christian Bach, the youngest son of the great Sebastian, and others, abound in this type of melody. In oratorio, too, this soft, pale, sweet Italian melody dominated for a half century, at least, between Handel and the last Haydn oratorios, *The Creation* and *The Seasons*, with which an entirely new chapter in the history of oratorio begins. Hasse's famous *Miserere* of 1728, written for the girls' chorus and string band of the Conservatorio degl' Incurabili in Venice, is one of the earliest, yet most enchanting examples of this style. Pergolesi's equally famous *Stabat Mater* is also a model of the type.

Gluck has this sweet melody at his command whenever he is in need of it. The difference between him and the Italian melodists, however, is that the Italians are obedient servants of their melodic mannerism, from which they have neither the wish nor the power to escape, whereas Gluck is not a servant but the commanding master; he has the strength to reject the demands of fashion, habit, and tradition whenever his artistic intentions urge him toward the achievement of new aims.

The other chief event in the second half of the century, the rise of Viennese classical music, demands attention now. How did it happen that Austria and Vienna became the home of this new art of sonata and symphony? Could it not have prospered equally well in Rome or Naples, in Paris or London, in Mannheim and Munich, in Dresden and Berlin? All these places were great centers of music; artists of high rank lived in each; powerful patrons of art — kings, dukes, cardinals — encouraged art and artists and spent great sums for musical purposes. But the peculiar social and cultural conditions of Austria proved an especially fertile soil and made it superior to any other country for the growth of orchestral symphonic music and of instrumental chamber music.

For a long time Italy had made such a specialty of vocal music, especially opera, that orchestral music never attained a comparable importance there; instrumental solo music and concerted chamber music — as in the violin concertos and sonatas and concerti grossi of Vivaldi, Corelli, Tartini — were so much preferred to symphonic orchestral music that not even in the nineteenth century did the symphony find a home in Italy. In Paris, likewise, interest in music centered in opera. This preference for the theater was a characteristic trait of French musical life until late in the nineteenth century. In the later eighteenth century there was an important school of composers of violin sonatas, headed by Leclair and Gaviniés, and there was the famous institution of the *concerts spirituels*, which set a model for public concerts in the European capitals. But for orchestral music the Paris *concerts spirituels* had to rely mainly on the productions of the Mannheim and the Austrian composers. The really remarkable and exciting events happened in opera. Rameau's great operas had no rival in France until about 1760, when charming and witty Italian intermezzi, like Pergolesi's *La Serva Padrona*, paved the way for the new French comic opera, a genre that appealed particularly to the Parisian public. For many years Parisians were kept in a state of excitement by the quarrels between the adherents of French and Italian opera, the *bouffonists* and the anti-*bouffonists*, the Lully party versus the Rameau party, and still later the Gluckists against the admirers of Piccini. This state of affairs explains why Paris excelled in opera but had only a secondary importance for creative work in the symphony.

Germany, especially Prussia, had been impoverished by the Seven Years' War. By nature North Germany was not a country rich in musical talent. The Saxon countries absorbed the best musical powers of Germany, and after Bach's death a decided decline is noticeable even in the Saxo-Thuringian district which for two hundred years had been the home of Protestant church music. Through Frederick the Great, Berlin became a center of music, but the King inclined toward Italian and French music, and valued German music little, in spite of the compliments he once paid Bach when the great master was his guest in Potsdam. The famous Mannheim orchestra could not maintain its supremacy for any length of time. Because its startling innovations were not supported by artistic personalities of the first order, its technical achievements were copied everywhere and became the common property of orchestral music throughout Germany and France; after one generation Mannheim had little of special interest to offer and quickly lost its prominence. Dresden, for centuries an important center of music, still retained its rank. But the Dresden court was interested only in Italian opera, and under these circumstances Dresden had not much part in the formation of the new symphonic style.

Austria was in a different position. Here was a country full of musical talent, with an atmosphere that had been saturated in music for centuries. It was not only that the imperial court in Vienna patronized art and artists in a grand style; the whole country was steeped in music. All the wealthy Austrian magnates and noble families had private orchestras and even private opera houses in their castles. Good orchestral musicians abounded, and every butler and manservant in a princely household was expected to play an orchestral instrument fairly well. In every little town there was a music master who provided orchestral music for all occasions — for parties, dances, weddings, serenades, and funerals. Usually a dozen or more talented young apprentices lived in his house and had to be ready at any hour to play in his service. The Bohemian musicians were famous all over Europe; as late as 1900 one could hear Bohemian bands everywhere, and even American towns were regularly visited by what were called "German bands," though they were generally composed of Bohemian players. Gluck and Haydn started their careers as players in such bands. A long tradition, an abundance of musical talent, enthusiastic love of music among all classes of the population, great wealth and artistic ambition on the part of the dominating caste of nobility — all these combined to establish the understanding and the skill in instrumental music in which the great Viennese art could prosper. Prince Lichtenstein, Prince Schwarzenberg, Count Waldstein, Prince Lichnowsky, and great families like the Esterhazys, rivaled each other in the excellence of their private orchestras. In summer they lived in the country in their magnificent castles, with music as a daily pleasure. In winter they moved to their Vienna palaces, always taking their musicians with them. Thus practically every house in Vienna was inhabited by musical people, professional musicians or enthusiastic amateurs.

Josef Haydn was in the service of Prince Esterhazy nearly thirty years. It was his duty to drill the orchestra and to conduct its almost daily performances at table, in the opera house and the concert hall of the castle, or in the church. All that distinguished Haydn from dozens of his *Kapellmeister* colleagues, active in the castles of the noble Austrian families, was his greater capacity, his outstanding genius. In the epoch preceding the French Revolution these musicians, great and small, were generally ranked with servants; they were commanded by autocratic masters, who were sometimes good-natured patriarchal lords, sometimes of a haughty and tyrannical disposition, like that Salzburg archbishop who made young Mozart's service so thoroughly intolerable.

When in 1909 the Haydn centenary was celebrated in Vienna, in conjunction with a congress of the then flourishing International Society for Music, hundreds of visitors from all parts of the civilized world had a unique opportunity to cast a glance into this fantastic old Austrian world of music. Prince Esterhazy invited about four hundred guests, of whom the writer was one, to visit his castle in Eisenstadt in Hungary, about three hours' ride from Vienna, in a quiet little country town which looked exactly as it had a hundred and fifty years earlier when Haydn lived there. We saw the magnificent castle with its concert halls and theater, the vast park with its old trees, its romantic vistas. We saw Haydn's modest house, the little garden pavilion in which he used to compose in solitude, fleeing from domestic troubles and his quarrelsome wife, and we saw the little church in which his body was entombed. The atmosphere of the green meadows, the long lake, and the wooded hills that surround the village is part of Haydn's music. Having seen Eisenstadt, one feels that no music but Haydn's could adequately have expressed the soul of this quiet, unexciting, but lovely landscape. The illusion of an excursion into the past became perfect when we were seated in the concert hall of the castle. There sat Prince Esterhazy and the princely family with their distinguished guests. The musicians of the orchestra, dressed in the fashion of 1770 with powdered wigs and colorful coats, waited quietly and modestly. Finally maestro Haydn himself came in, greeting the princely family and his musicians, to whom he was like a father. Then he sat down at his cembalo and performed with the orchestra one of his many symphonies, not one of those brilliant, rather pretentious symphonies which he wrote for London twenty years later, when he had become a world celebrity, but a modest little one that was both masterly and perfectly charming, as was fitting for the country town of Eisenstadt.

Such performances as this Haydn had to give several times a week. He had thirty years' time in which to learn his art to perfection, trying out every new idea that struck him, working day by day with his little orchestra, with his singers — for thirty years accumulating quietly, without nervous haste, an immense treasure of artistic experience. Even yet there is no complete collection of his innumerable compositions.

There was nothing to divert him from his artistic work. Each day had its task, which was accomplished with precision and loving care. For a few weeks in winter Prince Esterhazy moved to his luxurious palace in Vienna, generally taking Haydn along, and in these Vienna holidays Haydn came into personal con-tact with the international world of music, with the celebrities of his age, famous composers, singers, virtuosi, and patrons of music. Always, however, notwithstanding his growing Euro-pean fame, Haydn was a servant of his prince, an esteemed and privileged servant, to be sure, but still without freedom to shape his life as he might have wished. Tied to his duty, he was never at leisure to indulge in fanciful extravagances. He was nearly sixty years old when Prince Esterhazy died and he at last gained his independence.

It is merely by chance, of course, that Haydn's triumphs in London, his first independent activities, began in the year in which the French Revolution started, but it is interesting to observe that his entire artistic career had been shaped by the standards of the old régime, which was overthrown in France by the Revolution and later received a severe shock in other countries as well. We find ourselves here, about 1790, at the last of the three cross sections through the eighteenth century — 1730, 1760, 1790 — on which the present discussion has been based. 1790 means the close of the *ancien régime*, the beginning of the French Revolution. The last remnants of the rococo spirit disappear. Kant's epoch-making *Kritik der Urteilskraft* is pub-lished. The "liberal" emperor, Joseph II, who did not adequately reward Mozart's touching devotion, dies.

There seems to have been something fateful in the circumstance that Mozart died in 1791 just as the French Revolution reached the height of its frenzy. Haydn, robust and masculine, could still profit from the tremendous changes that were brought about by the French Revolution. Mozart, more delicate, extremely sensitive, with an almost feminine susceptibility, was so thoroughly a child of the dying rococo age that the rude shocks of the French Revolution were a fatal blow to him and to the world in which he had grown up and which in his short life he had never outgrown. He died on the threshold of the new world that was slowly rising out of the turmoil of the corrupt and perverted rococo spirit. In his music the dying age reaches its most enchanting and delightful expression, in which all its characteristic features are idealized.

Here the chief emotional factor is erotic, to an extent far greater than in the music of any composer before Mozart and, one might say, after him. Nowhere have the mutual relations of the sexes been expressed with such delicacy, refinement, variety, penetration, and clearness of vision. Mozart's music is concerned only secondarily with religious or ethical aspects, with the heroic and the pathetic, with constructive problems, with tone painting, with the purely intellectual. Its constant theme is the emotional aspect of the human soul in love. The key to his wonderful achievements in this line we find in his operas, which are concerned almost exclusively with giving musical expression to the emotions of love in the most varied aspects with an almost unparalleled intensity and vitality. In these operas — *Idomeneo, Entführung aus dem Serail, Figaro, Don Giovanni, Die Zauberflöte, Così fan tutte*, and others somewhat less conspicuous — the ultimate expression is found for all shades of amorous passion, from the purest, most ethereal sentiment to the most brutal and most outspoken sensuality. A whole literature of novels is surpassed by Mozart's operatic arias, which present the most concentrated, persuasive, and telling expression of the erotic emotions ever created by art. Once the essence of Mozart's opera is realized, it is easy to perceive the same groundtone in his instrumental music. The symphonies, quartets, and sonatas are filled to the brim with that peculiarly spiritualized variety of erotic sentiment which gives Mozart's music its incomparable value. If Mozart's music should ever be lost, the world would have lost something irreparable; nowhere else — neither in Haydn, Beethoven, Schubert, Schumann, Wagner, nor in Brahms — can this Mozartian flavor, this lyric expressiveness, this candid and yet modest revelation of the soul, this divine grace, this animated amiability, be found in any comparable degree. The genius of youth is embodied most gloriously in the touching, yet luminous and joyful life and art of Wolfgang Amadeus Mozart.

In his short life of thirty-five years Mozart brought to ultimate perfection at least two styles: Neapolitan opera and the new Haydn type of sonata and symphony. The latest stylistic achievements of Italian opera he took over from composers like Pergolesi, Jomelli, Traetta, Piccini, Paesiello, Gluck, and Galuppi, and in his thematic material he often seems to be a member of this Italian school. Yet he gave opera what all the Italians were unable to give it, the last perfection of form, technique, and expression, lifting it out of the "opera by the dozen" class into the rank of individual, even unique works. These Mozart operas are Italian in type and German in sentiment, but above all they are "Mozartian," works of an unsurpassable finish and finality. Whether one inspects overtures or arias, recitatives or ensembles, dramatic expression, or the structure of the finale or the orchestra itself, everywhere one finds a *non plus ultra*. Later opera had no chance in competition with Mozart; it had to find new aims and new methods.

In his instrumental music Mozart took over the sonata type as it had been remodeled and improved by Haydn, but he gave it new contents, new accents and colors, so that in spite of the identity of form and constructive technique a Mozart sonata will only rarely be mistaken for one by Haydn. Mozart's more highly differentiated and more complex emotional life is echoed in his music by an almost feminine grace and softness, an elegance of motion, an elegiac touch, and a colorful chromatic harmony very different from Haydn's more masculine sound and more cheerful and forceful manner. As a composer of sonatas Mozart supplements Haydn. Together they bring the new sonata form to a perfection that is classical in its vivid sense of harmonious proportion, its perfect equilibrium between form and contents, and its lack of experimentation. Chronologically and artistically, linked to the past as well as to the future, Mozart stands midway between Haydn and Beethoven. Some of his latest work has a decided tinge of the passionate utterance, the noble pathos of the younger Beethoven. It cannot be maintained, however, that Beethoven's art is supplementary to Mozart's as Mozart's was supplementary to Haydn's. The Mozart sonata, concerto, and symphony have the classical perfection that excludes later improvement or adequate continuation. Looming up between the mental horizons of Mozart and Beethoven stands the French Revolution. For a short time the two masters meet on common ground; very soon, however, Beethoven moves more and more decisively away from the eighteenth-century *fin de siècle* attitude of which Mozart's music is the most enchanting and sincere expression. Had Mozart, achieved only this echo of his time he would be interesting and important merely historically, like many of his contemporaries and companions in art. His greater glory is based on his power of superimposing on the temporal the unchangeable truth of utterance that makes an appeal to every age.

The French Revolution pronounced a crushing condemnation on the prevailing attitudes of the eighteenth century. Yet one ought not to confound an ethical standard with an artistic one. Many morally debased epochs have produced great art, not perhaps in consequence but rather in spite of the low moral status that prevailed. That the conditions of the eighteenth century, with all their objectionable features, were not at all unfavorable to music is proved by the glorious names of Handel, Bach, Couperin, Rameau, Scarlatti, Gluck, Haydn, Mozart, and hosts of other artists of high rank. It is too early yet to ask whether the conditions of the enlightened twentieth century will lead in music to artistic results comparable with those of the eighteenth century. But there is little doubt that we shall have to achieve prodigious artistic feats in the remaining sixty-two years of the present century if we are to compete honorably with the undemocratic but artistically fertile and abundant eighteenth century.

CHAPTER NINE

THE FRENCH REVOLUTION AND THE NAPOLEONIC AGE

➼➼➼➼❖❮❮❮❮

THE years 1730 and 1760 were taken as the starting points of our investigations in the preceding chapters, and we have touched on 1790 in connection with Mozart; now we must undertake a somewhat more detailed inspection of the musical situation about 1790.

In 1790 the French Revolution had already begun. The tremendous agitation it caused was not only a political event of the very first magnitude but a social and cultural event that is almost without parallel in its influence on life, social creed, culture, and art. The mass of the people, the thus-far subdued *tiers état*, gained by it new rights and a power they had never possessed before, an influence on government. In short, the democratic principle in its extreme form overturned the autocratic principle that until then had been omnipotent. Such violent upheavals necessarily influenced the manner of thought of great masses of the people, potentially changed the spiritual atmosphere, and consequently profoundly altered the soil from which the arts grew. Even before the French Revolution the influence of these growing democratic ideas became apparent in literature, the theater, music, and the opera. The Revolution was not, of course, a sudden explosion; in France the dissatisfaction leading to it had been slowly growing for fifty years or more, and in other countries the democratic principle had already achieved such weight and authority that it could serve as a model for the French people. England was the home of liberal democracy. The United States of America had been founded on the basis of democratic ideals years before the outbreak of the French Revolution. In Austria at the time of Haydn and Mozart the liberal edicts of Emperor Joseph II ushered in a new era, and the order of the Freemasons began to influence the civilization of Austria and Germany in a humanitarian way. Mozart was a Freemason, and how seriously he was imbued with the spirit of Masonry can be seen in many of his letters, as well as in a number of his most valuable works, especially *The Magic Flute* and the Masonic funeral music.

Beaumarchais, the great French writer, was one of the spiritual leaders of the French Revolution, and his famous play, *The Marriage of Figaro*, satirizing an antiquated but often-practiced prerogative of the nobility, served as a libretto for one of Mozart's most delightful operas. Voltaire and Jean Jacques Rousseau also helped very materially to reform the mental atmosphere in a liberal sense. Yet for a considerable time the tremendous upheaval of the French Revolution impressed art in other countries, especially in Germany and Austria, much more than in France. This may seem strange, but the explanation is simple. The Reign of Terror in France, the immense excitement of the whole nation, the years of warfare in the Napoleonic campaigns caused such unrest and such unsettled conditions in France that the arts, which need peace and prosperity, could not flourish. France did not produce one great composer during the epoch of the Revolution. The great celebrity after the death of Gluck was Luigi Cherubini, an Italian, who lived in Paris for more than sixty years without ever learning to speak French well.

In the period from 1790 to 1800 Cherubini was the only musician of the first rank living in France. Mozart had died in 1791, and the great Haydn was just rising to the heights of success and celebrity in London and Vienna; Beethoven so far was little known. The most successful composer of lighter music in Paris between 1770 and 1800 was Grétry, the composer of the famous opera, *Richard Cœur-de-Lion*, and of countless comic operas and operettas. He, too, was not French but Belgian. The only French composer of note in this period, Etienne Nicolas Méhul, did not attain maturity in his art until much later; his masterpiece, *Joseph in Egypt*, was written in 1807. Even in the beginning of the nineteenth century, until about 1820, French composers had little part in the music of weight and importance produced in Paris; the two most famous composers of the Napoleonic years there were Luigi Cherubini and Gasparo Spontini, both Italian artists.

Let us look a little more closely to see how the new mental atmosphere of the revolutionary age influenced the art of Cherubini, who at that time and until late in the nineteenth century was universally considered a master of the first rank. Even the fastidious Beethoven had great respect for Cherubini's art and was noticeably influenced by it. Now we seldom hear anything at all by Cherubini, not even the masterly overtures that adorned symphonic programs for nearly one hundred years, but without doubt he will some day be rediscovered and will be generally accorded the rank of a great and venerable master. About 1800 he had no equal as a composer of opera. Two of his operas, *Medée* and *Les Deux Journées*, are especially outstanding as achievements of extraordinary dramatic and musical value. Of the former, Johannes Brahms said — and the comment deserves to be remembered — "This *Medée* is what we musicians among ourselves recognize as the highest in dramatic music." Reflecting in music the classical style of French architecture, literature, and painting during the revolutionary years and in the Napoleonic period, *Medée* is a worthy continuation of the heroic opera style introduced fifteen or twenty years before by Gluck. It has none of the weakness of imitation, for Cherubini adapts Gluck's ideas with the freedom of an independent artist and fits them both to his own needs and to the changed taste of a new era. Cherubini's scores are based on Gluck's noble and austere style, but they reveal softer emotional traits and a richer palette of tone values, derived from Mozart's more intimate, more colorful, and more supple style.

Cherubini's second dramatic masterpiece, *Les Deux Journées*, the most successful of all his operas, is a product of the revolutionary spirit in its text as well as its music. It is a popular opera, but in its tendency and style very different from the unpretentious popular operas of the Grétry type or the German *Singspiele* of Johann Adam Hiller, so well liked in their time. The Grétry and Hiller operas are late descendants of the long-vanished rococo age. With their charming but slightly artificial grace and simplicity, their pastoral and rustic atmosphere, they are more theatrically decorative than realistic. Cherubini's scenes dealing with the people are realistic. Now, after the Revolution, the common people have a different value from what they had before, socially as well as in art. They are no longer treated playfully, in a condescending, jovial manner; they are taken seriously, with respect for their characteristic ways, for their manner of thinking, speaking, and acting. The plot of *Les Deux Journées* reflects another trait born in the revolutionary years. The terrible experiences of the people made fear a most conspicuous factor of daily life; in those years of bloody revolution and bloody wars, violent death was a daily experience, and afterwards, consequently, the joy of life, the ecstasy of relief, became a new subject for artistic expression. In music relief from fear caused a strange outburst of joy that had never occurred before in equal strength. The drama of rescue became the literary fashion of the day, and Cherubini's *Les Deux Journées* is perhaps the most conspicuous work of this type. Beethoven's opera, *Fidelio*, belongs to the same type. The outburst of joy in Beethoven's music is one of its most striking traits; the Leonore overtures, the finales of the Fifth and the Seventh symphonies, the "Ode to Joy" in the Ninth Symphony are only a few of many examples.

The close relation of Cherubini's music to the artistic spirit of the time is also revealed in other ways. Its wonderful purity and clearness of line finds an exact parallel in the work of the great painter Ingres, Cherubini's close friend. The only difference is that Ingres is an accepted master of the first rank in his particular style, fully appreciated by all connoisseurs of painting and recognized as achieving the most concentrated expression of the ideas that dominated painting in the Napoleonic era. Cherubini, however, fully as great and finished a master, is not yet appreciated in proportion to the high qualities of his art. In A. W. Thayer's biography of Beethoven one may read that Beethoven considered the texts of Cherubini's *Les Deux Journées* and Spontini's *La Vestale* the best opera librettos in existence, and a comparison between the scores of Cherubini's masterpiece and Beethoven's *Fidelio* shows how much Beethoven is indebted to Cherubini's art.

It has already been mentioned that the years from 1790 to about 1810 are very meager as regards creative musical genius in France. Nevertheless, the entire reshaping of life after the French Revolution had extreme importance for music, inasmuch as it was about 1800 that Paris gained the prominence as a musical metropolis which it has retained for more than a century. Now Paris became a serious and dangerous rival of Italy, thus far the leading country musically. In addition to grand opera, French comic opera was permanently established in Paris with its own theater; the *concerts spirituels* became a leading institute of fine performance; the Conservatoire was founded and quickly became the leading advanced school of music of the world. The mass of the people, until now hardly aware of artistic music, through the efforts of the revolutionary government developed a great interest in it.

The only center of music comparable with Paris about 1800 was Vienna. Here Haydn spent his declining years in leisure, while Beethoven was just beginning his glorious artistic career. But neither Haydn nor Mozart, who had died nearly a decade before, can be taken as representing the ideas of that new era ushered in by the French Revolution. Of this change in spirit and in the manner and aims of life we speak collectively by applying briefly one significant label; we say "nineteenth century." In music the first and greatest representative of the nineteenth century is Ludwig van Beethoven. Spiritually he is a son of the French Revolution. As a young man, when he was Haydn's pupil in Vienna, he was already fully conscious of his artistic capacities; he showed a lack of reverence for the established powers, a proud demeanor, and a self-assertiveness that shocked the modest Haydn, who dubbed young Beethoven "grand mogul" and "Turkish pasha." Soon we find him the pet of the great aristocratic families of Vienna. But, unlike Haydn and Mozart, young Beethoven would not suffer himself to be ranked as a servant to these highborn lords. He considered himself socially fully their equal, and spiritually, by right of his genius, their superior. He was the first musician able to maintain such an attitude of independence, and by holding his own against time-honored custom he raised the social standing of the German musician not only in his own time but also for later generations. He established a new dignity for the art of music, lifted it to a pedestal it had never before occupied. Henceforth musical culture turned in a new direction. In the preceding century music had been patronized almost exclusively by the rich nobility; in the nineteenth century it was no longer mainly an entertainment of courts and princely families, but it was maintained on as high a level as before by the middle classes, which had risen socially and culturally as a consequence of the French Revolution. In Germany the entire romantic movement is an outgrowth of this new culture of *Bürgerlichkeit*. Beethoven was a passionate democrat, a convinced republican, even in his youth; he was, in fact, the first German musician who had strong political interests, ideals, and ambitions. Haydn and Mozart had been indifferent politically; Beethoven enthusiastically accepted the watchwords of the French Revolution, *liberté, egalité, fraternité*, and was such an ardent admirer of Napoleon that one of the severest shocks of his life was the bitter disappointment he felt at Napoleon's betrayal of the democratic ideal. He had written one of his most impressive and startling works, the "Eroica" Symphony, as a tribute to Napoleon. When the news reached Vienna that Napoleon had made himself emperor of France, Beethoven in a terrific outburst of rage tore the dedication from the title page of the "Eroica" score and trampled it underfoot. Yet Beethoven was himself a Napoleon in his art, vested with an incomparable power and majesty. His magnificent symphonic style, the boldness of his artistic conceptions, his vast imagination, his unshaken belief in himself — all these suggest Napoleon so strongly that one is tempted to believe that such a phenomenon of musical creation as Beethoven's music may to a certain extent have been helped into existence by the presence of a living model.

In the three words *liberté, egalité, fraternité* one finds the fundamentals of Beethoven's aesthetics, or, more precisely, the moral ideals underlying his aesthetics. The close linking of moral ideals and aesthetic creed assumed a new aspect in Beethoven. There had been a union of art and religion in artists like Palestrina and Bach, but the introduction of the humanitarian ideal into art could occur only after the ideas of the French Revolution had been accepted in a purified form by the intellectuals of other countries. In music Beethoven is the first great exponent of this new doctrine of art.

Homer and classical antiquity, Plutarch, Shakespeare, Schiller and Goethe were the great lights shining out into the dark for Beethoven, as we know from his own statement, and the ethical basis of his art can be deduced from these sources and from the French Revolution. One of the most striking features of Beethoven's work is its wealth of lofty impulses, which surpasses by far anything found in former music. Palestrina, Handel, and Bach are, indeed, full of ethical impressiveness, but on a pronounced religious basis and in connection with the religious poetry of the Bible, the medieval hymns, and the Protestant chorales. This basis is to be found in Beethoven only very rarely, and yet his sonatas, his quartets, his symphonies exhale in a mysterious way a powerful moral essence. At root this is religious, but it has no typically ecclesiastical or dogmatic character. It was based in part on the pantheistic idealism of Goethe, whose great spirituality and all-embracing humanity, as well as his cosmopolitan ideas, had profoundly touched Beethoven. Schiller's noble philosophy, through which Beethoven had come into closer contact with Kant's austere ethics, had also deeply impressed him. The sublime hymn-like chanting of Beethoven's adagio melodies has often been observed, but the allegros of his sonatas, symphonies, and quartets have the same seriousness of diction, the same deep impressiveness, for which only a morality of the highest type can find the appropriate utterance, the right accent, the convincing tone. It is this quality more than anything else that makes Beethoven's melody distinct from that of all other composers.

The influence of Schiller and Goethe on Beethoven and on later music can hardly be overestimated, Schiller's influence being manifest chiefly in the dramatic tendencies and moral aspects of later German music, Goethe's in its exalted lyricism. Without Schiller, no Beethoven, no Wagner; without Goethe, no Schubert, Schumann, Mendelssohn, or Brahms. The power emanating from these two great minds is felt far beyond German music. It can be seen everywhere in Europe: in France, Italy, Russia, the Scandinavian countries; least, perhaps, in England, probably because English music of the nineteenth century has no drama worth mentioning and little musical lyricism in the German sense. Schiller's drama gave an impetus not only to the French romantic drama of Victor Hugo and his school but also to French and Italian opera. Auber's *La Muette de Portici* belongs in this category; Meyerbeer's and Scribe's historical operas would hardly have become what they are without Schiller's models; and Italian opera became dramatically more ambitious as a consequence of the vigorous dramatic art of Schiller. Rossini's *Guillaume Tell* and a number of Verdi operas, such as *Luise Millerin, Don Carlos, Gioanna d'Arco*, testify to that influence directly, while many more, such as *Aïda*, show it indirectly and with even greater brilliancy. As for Schiller's purifying ethical influence, it is perceived most remarkably in Beethoven's musical aesthetics, in the total attitude of Beethoven's art. It comes out most palpably in the Ninth Symphony, with its exuberant "Hymn to Joy" finale, but it pervades Beethoven's music more or less subtly almost everywhere, and it is no less evident in the Pathetic sonata, the D minor and "Moonlight" sonatas, the Waldstein, Appassionata, and Kreutzer sonatas than in the *Leonore* overtures, the opera *Fidelio*, and the "Eroica," the Fifth, and the Seventh symphonies.

"Ethical," "moral" are not meant to be taken here in the sense of preaching a just behavior, according to a generally accepted code of morals. A didactic aim of this kind properly belongs to the sermon of a preacher, to the work of an educator. It is not in itself the purpose of any art, and art has always been the loser when it has been deliberately coupled with a moral tendency. But Beethoven's music has an ethical character of the highest kind because it is the direct, sincere expression of a great soul whose compassion for misery and suffering, and whose sense of duty, of justice, and of truth emanated from him into his music and gave it an incomparable beauty that glows with a noble idealism, a sublime pathos, and a transcendental devotion to the divine power. All this is pure and convincing, genuinely artistic, just because it is not in the least didactic and moralizing, just because this great soul, enflamed by the highest and noblest human aspirations, pervades Beethoven's whole being. It gives a peculiar accent, color, and impressiveness to his entire artistic activity, which is nothing but the most exhaustive expression in terms of music of his emotional world, his dreams, agitations, passions, doubts, aspirations, exaltations, and disappointments, his conflicts, tragic experiences, and joy in life. For emotions of so vast a compass and so great a variety, music as it was then was not a sufficiently flexible medium, and it was the task of Beethoven's life to recreate it and shape it to his own ends. Searching for a complete and convincing expression of his emotional life, Beethoven discovered a new world and showed the way to all later musicians for a century to come. His music has ever since remained the firm basis of all that attained musical importance later in the nineteenth century. Schubert and the romantic masters, Weber, Schumann, Mendelssohn, and Berlioz, are Beethoven's pupils, as well as Liszt and Wagner, Brahms and Bruckner.

It is interesting to observe that Beethoven was also the discoverer of humor in music, humor in the Shakespearean sense — that is, not merely the farcical and the comic but the higher type of humor that touches the soul, provoking laughter mixed with tenderness. Humor of this kind comes as a result of realizing the futility of most human endeavors and rising above them by laughing at them, not in cynical derision but in compassion. This quality hardly exists in music before Beethoven. Mozart and Gluck have almost no humor of this type, though Mozart is sometimes witty. Bach excels occasionally in very jocose tone-painting of a realistic type, but without Beethoven's transcendental flight of imagination and emotional profundity. Haydn's music is full of jokes, often clever, and of rustic quaintness, naïve or apparently naïve traits that make one smile or laugh. But Beethoven's humor transcends the rather narrow realism of his predecessors. For the first time in music, gaiety, boisterous fun, even burlesque revelry do not stop at imitation but penetrate beyond outward appearance to the emotions that cause them.

In this self-consciousness, this self-discipline, this steady, carefully planned progress from one achievement to another, in this preference for individual rather than typical expression, we see the new spirit of the nineteenth century manifest for the first time on a grand scale. The foundation of Beethoven's art is traditional — the sonata form of Haydn and Mozart; the interpretation of this inherited sonata form, however, is new and original. Through it Beethoven reaches new conclusions, realizes vast aims, opens new possibilities, discovers a new world, such as he alone could divine in the clearly and soberly set frame of the typical Viennese sonata. Melodic inventive power and masterly musical workmanship were not sufficient for him. His was a mind that bent itself to new problems which had never been seriously attacked in music before him. Having solved one problem, he immediately turned to a new one. This restlessness, this concern with ever-changing problems, explains his creative method. The difficulties of his self-imposed task were so great that even his phenomenal musical talent did not suffice to make his work easy and quick, and his sketchbooks, of which there are hundreds, show plainly the passionate effort he expended on each new undertaking. The single aim of all this painstaking labor was to give his ideas their clearest, most convincing, and most exhaustive expression, and he was never content until he had achieved it.

It is beyond the intention of this book to enter into a detailed discussion of Beethoven's musical technique, his method of construction, his numerous discoveries regarding sonata and symphonic style, piano composition, quartet-writing, orchestral treatment, thematic workmanship, rhythm and accent, and so forth. Only the general aspects of his work, its cultural radius, its ethical basis, the new problems stated and solved by him, can be touched upon here. Attention, however, must be called to the universality of his art as regards the world of emotional expression. Beethoven is not a great master merely in a certain range of lyric expresssion, a specialist in a certain limited sphere of emotion, like many other composers of note and rank. His music, like the work of Shakespeare and Goethe, comprises everything in the vast compass of passion: deep emotion and sentiment; mirth and humor as well as pathos and tragedy; the lyric and the dramatic. It ranges from profound meditation to the exuberance of joy, from the meekness of humility to a Promethean energy.

Religious fervor and Dionysian ecstasy both find a place in it. It is both cosmic and transcendental, expressive at times of demoniac impulses and at others of the straightforward warmth of sincerity. All this and much more is contained in Beethoven's immortal work.

The only works comparable with Beethoven's thirty-two piano sonatas are the forty-eight preludes and fugues of Bach's *Well-Tempered Clavichord*, and the proud series of Bach's preludes and fugues for organ. All three are manifestations of the highest creative genius. In inventive power, constructive art, emotional expression, and elevation of mind Bach and Beethoven may safely be judged as equals. The differences, which clearly reveal Beethoven's new point of view and new concerns, lie in Beethoven's greater variety and wealth of formal treatment, of problems of expression, of contents. A rapid survey may help to show the amazing richness of emotional and intellectual appeal in the Beethoven sonatas, which range in expressiveness from a plain, almost childlike start, through adolescence and youth, to maturity and the wisdom of older age. Bach's preludes and fugues, almost exclusively the products of mature manhood, are much more similar to each other in style and contents than the Beethoven sonatas. The unpretentious, simple little sonatinas op. 49 and 79 represent the untroubled start. The sonatas of the first period (op. 2, 7, 10, 13, 14, 22, 26, 27, 28), which are works of youthful character, nevertheless possess a greater variety of style than all the sonatas of Haydn and Mozart. The "appassionato" character dominates op. 2, no. 1; op. 7; op. 10, no. 1; the Pathetic Sonata, op. 13; the "Moonlight" Sonata, op. 27, no. 2; and the Sonata quasi una Fantasia, op. 31, no. 2. Charming works of simple grace and idyllic temperament are op. 2, no. 2; op. 14, nos. 1 and 2; op. 22; the Pastoral Sonata, op. 28; and op. 31, no. 1. Another group, op. 53 (Waldstein) and op. 57 (Appassionata), represents Beethoven's second manner, the brilliant, vigorous, triumphant type, corresponding to the "Eroica" and the Fifth Symphony. These powerful works are offset by idyllic little intermezzi of captivating charm, op. 54 and op. 78. With the "Farewell" Sonata, op. 81a, Beethoven's last style is reached. The seven works comprising this group (op. 81a, 90, 101, 106, 109, 110, 111) have as many different characters, but a lofty spirituality dominates them all. They are all unconventional, experimental, extremely bold and fantastic in their aims, extremely complicated and rich in their ideas; yet Beethoven always succeeds in finding a convincing and exciting solution for his problems. These sonatas range from *inferno* to *paradiso*. Their magnificent cosmic visions (op. 106, 109, 111) have passed beyond the appassionato and the Titanic phases into metaphysical depths, mystic regions of a world beyond. Again intermezzi of incomparable lyric beauty and intimacy of utterance (op. 81a, 90, 101, 110) tinged with melancholy sing of the enchanting loveliness of the terrestrial world. Truly it may be asserted that the thirty-two sonatas are a world of music in themselves; in them the piano utters confessions of a personal intimacy and visions of a powerful grandeur that had never before been possible to it and that have never been attempted by any composer since.

The nine symphonies represent the highest and noblest type in existence of music that appeals to the mass of the people as well as to fastidious connoisseurs. To call them popular music in the ordinary sense of the term would degrade them; they are popular in the sense that they express the dim emotional longings of a vast mass of people agitated by common griefs, joys, aspirations, and ideals. Here is music of a universal validity — not merely German, not merely religious, but intelligible through its fervor, its eloquence, its force, and its beauty, to all humanity, regardless of nation, language, or creed.

The eighteen quartets, taken as a whole, represent still another aspect of Beethoven's art. In these his spirituality and his idealism shine forth. Here in the masterly treatment of complicated problems of form and construction is evidence of the highest intellectual power. Here is the very essence of emotion, transformed into sound. This is music for listeners of high intelligence, of fineness of spirit, of profound artistic understanding. Beethoven not only conquered whole continents for music; he also cultivated them and made them yield wonderful new harvests. A century in advance, he had a clear notion of the essential problems of modern music, even of the ultramodern music of the twentieth century. To this day the last sonatas and quartets are stupendous monuments of the music of the future, modern music of the highest possible type.

Ferruccio Busoni, one of the greatest artists of our age, who is generally very wrongly credited with a certain lack of reverence for Beethoven, has summed up Beethoven's meaning for him in such original and striking words that I can hardly find a more apt conclusion to these fugitive remarks. He writes to his wife from Basle, May 15, 1912, as follows:

"I have a beautiful idea for a Beethoven monument, and would not like to have this idea lost, so I tell it to you.

"The uppermost group shows Beethoven on a thronelike chariot, drawn by four horses. These horses symbolize the Third, Fifth, Seventh, and Ninth symphonies. The first horse (Eroica) is all in armor. The second one (Fifth Symphony) is bare, very vigorous, with uplifted head; the third horse (Seventh Symphony) is slender and passes on with a dancelike gait; the fourth one (Ninth Symphony) is entirely covered with cloth, including the head, though holes are cut in for the eyes.

"The middle group shows the Ideal in the center, connecting art with the Heavenly; at the right side a boy worshipping, at the left side a girl in worship.

"The lower group, high relief full of figures and motion. In the center Florestan and Leonore, or the rescue of the man by the love of his wife; at the right, among other figures, Josef Haydn and Friedrich von Schiller; at the left Napoleon as a young general; all around, workmen, soldiers, revolutionaries.

"The two great front statues: at the right, love of mankind; at the left, independence, freedom.

"At the back façade: beautiful columned architecture. Below in three (corners): music, lyric poetry, drama. Is this not very beautiful?"

So far Busoni.

Near the great solitary Beethoven there lived in Vienna a modest contemporary, very little known during his short life, overshadowed by the gigantic Beethoven, apparently insignificant in comparison with him, and yet destined to be ranked by posterity among the greatest musicians. Incessantly active as a creative artist in close vicinity to Beethoven for at least fifteen years, Schubert never came into personal touch with him until Beethoven, shortly before his death, became interested in some of Schubert's music. Like Beethoven, Schubert reflects and re-echoes in his art the leading ideas of his age, but his reaction to the problems of the day differs considerably from Beethoven's. First of all, Schubert is a generation younger than Beethoven; his artistic nature is very different; and finally his social position places him at an entirely different angle with reference to life and culture in Vienna. For Schubert the ties that connect him with his native city of Vienna are stronger than the influences of the French Revolution. Like Haydn and Mozart, he is one of those musicians of genius who spring from the people, which no country has produced in such abundance as Austria. The Austrian popular musicians represent a peculiar type, very different from the musicians born in the Saxo-Thuringian district, the home of the Bachs, of Handel, and of whole generations of Protestant church composers. The Saxon musicians are Protestant to the core, devoted to the church service, and practicing operatic and instrumental music only secondarily, if at all. The Austrian, and more particularly the Viennese, musicians are devout Catholics, but their main interest is in instrumental music, sonata and symphony, and in secular vocal music, rather than in music written for the church.

Schubert supplements Beethoven by excelling in the types of music to which Beethoven devoted little attention. He is the ultimate personification of the Viennese musical genius, and represents it more truly than any other of the countless talented musicians that sprang from this music-drenched soil. Beethoven, for example, only occasionally manifests those typically Viennese traits which Schubert possesses in abundance. No composer ever excelled Schubert in his gift of inexhaustible melody, which has the tunefulness and natural grace of folk song and a warm-hearted sentiment that is at once plain and noble. The Viennese sensuous charm, naturalness, amiability, and vivacity of temperament — in short, the Viennese soul — finds its most eloquent and delightful expression in Schubert's music. Dance and song are its roots; the *Ländler* and the waltz give it its rhythmical basis; and a veritable stream of lyric melody — somewhat foreign to Beethoven — flows incessantly through it, an idealization of the familiar, popular Viennese melody.

Schubert's song was born in and for the drawing room of the Viennese house; it was designed not for the palace or the theater or the big public concert hall, but for the music-loving, educated *Bürgerliche Gesellschaft*, for hospitable homes full of Viennese cordiality and *Gemütlichkeit*. We possess descriptions by contemporaries, illustrations by Viennese painters, and literary reminiscences of this charming social life of the well-to-do Viennese middle class among whom Schubert moved all his life.

Schubert is a new type of artist, a free artist without a position at a court, theater, or church as *Kapellmeister* or organist, as had been almost invariably the case with composers of the eighteenth century. The careers of the latter were based entirely on fixed positions which imposed duties upon them both as performers and as composers. In the last years of his short life Mozart declined a call to Berlin as *Kapellmeister* at the Royal Opera because he was waiting eagerly, but vainly, to be called as *Kapellmeister* to the imperial court. Beethoven, as we have seen, was the first artist who did not care to fill a position which interfered with his creative work, the first composer who did not compose to order. He wrote only as his genius prompted him and disposed of his works afterwards as well as he could, selling them to publishers or musical societies. Schubert followed Beethoven's example. Whereas, however, Beethoven always managed to have his own household, more or less orderly, Schubert is the typical bohemian, a type very frequent among the artists of the nineteenth century. Most of the time he had no lodgings of his own, however small or modest, but shared quarters with one or another of his friends, changing his abode frequently, according to circumstances. All morning he used to compose; at noon he took his meal at some inn or *café*; on fair days he made excursions to the Wiener Wald, the beautiful surroundings of Vienna, in the company of jolly fellows, poor devils and bohemians like himself; and at night he was frequently the guest of some music-loving family, delighting the ladies with his piano-playing and singing, trying his new compositions as soon as they had been written down. Though he was usually in debt and sold his immortal songs for ridiculously small sums, the equivalent of a dollar or two, he seems not to have been unhappy in such an irregular, undignified life. It did not keep him from creating an incredible mass of music in an incredibly short time. Nine-tenths of his compositions were not published until long after his death, and he heard only a very few of them adequately performed in public.

Though he composed in abundance every conceivable type of music — operas, operettas, masses, symphonies, sonatas, quartets, quintets, choral music, and piano music — and though he wrote great masterpieces in most of these species, what gives him his rank among the greatest masters is his discovery of two unknown continents of music, or perhaps one should say two new islands in the ocean of music. The first is a vast island, green and fragrant, charmingly diversified in landscape, with idyllic green meadows, fresh springs, cultivated fields, and quiet villages; but towering behind these lovely plains there is visible a more austere landscape of bold outlines, rugged mountains, and wide stretches of solitude. This is the outward frame of German song, as it appeared when Schubert departed from the scene, and it marks his greatest achievement. When he began, German song was merely a narrow side-lane in music, in which the great masters of the art disdained to promenade and which was peopled only by smaller musicians of second and third rank. His second island is smaller, but it is hardly less significant. It represents the smaller lyric piano-piece in one movement, and it means much for the instrumental art of the entire nineteenth century, as will be explained more in detail when we will come to discuss romantic traits in music.

Schubert left nearly seven hundred songs, not counting the hundreds of vocal pieces in his operas, masses, and other compositions. This prodigious creative activity, compressed into less than fifteen years, is without parallel in its field. Though he was imbued with lyric genius as no one before him had been, this gift of nature could not have grown to its full possibilities without the proper soil. Schubert appeared just at the moment when the astounding rise of German lyric poetry (1800–1827) called for a musician of his caliber. Goethe's matchless poetry was like Moses' staff in its effect on Schubert; at its touch a lyric stream, thus far hidden and enclosed, gushed forth. As Goethe towers above the host of minor German poets around him, so Schubert stands incomparably higher, looks incomparably further, than his German predecessors in song. Until about 1815 German song at its best had been agreeable, melodious, but unpretentious and somewhat old-fashioned. Schubert was daring enough to set sail toward unexplored regions. The poems of Goethe, with their wide horizon and their free expressiveness, suggested to him not only a more ambitious, a more elevated, and a more varied type of melody, but also an application of Beethoven's new sonata style to song. This combination of rich new melody with an accompaniment modeled after Beethoven constitutes Schubert's distinctive innovation in song.

Realizing his powers in the still unexplored possibilities opened up by this happy combination, Schubert displayed a boldness and youthful energy without parallel. He explored and conquered musically the entire field of classical and pre-classical German lyric poetry. It was not only Goethe and Schiller who inspired him to songs of incomparable beauty and expressiveness; Ossian, Klopstock, Claudius, Wilhelm Müller, Platen, Rückert, Heine, and dozens of minor poets also helped to quench his insatiable thirst. And what a variety of lyric types! There is a continuation of the plain, folk-song-like form used by Johann Abraham Peter Schulz, Zumsteeg, Reichard, and Zelter. There is dithyrambic ode, religious ecstasy, fantastic ballad, dramatic scene; there is pathos, romantic effusion, magnificent landscape painting, vehement passion, idyllic loveliness; there is an endless variety of emotional moods, a wealth of vision combined with a power of form and artistic treatment that has never been equaled in the domain of song. But this magnificent achievement would not have been possible a generation earlier; it was conditioned by the actual state of lyric poetry in the early nineteenth century and was its direct outcome. Here again we see another proof that music is a part of general culture, the expression of the dominating spiritual tendencies of an epoch.

CHAPTER TEN

THE ROMANTIC MOVEMENT

T HE romantic movement in literature and art is the significant characteristic feature of the nineteenth century. In
music it was so powerful, so productive of new and impressive
results, that more recent music cannot be properly comprehended
at all without an acquaintance with the various factors that make
up the romantic work of art. Germany and France, more than
other countries, were the home of these romantic ideas. To
trace them back to their origin will help in making clear their
nature and their meaning as reflected and reëchoed in music.
The term "romantic" is connected with "romance" in its double
sense as tale and language. In a general sense the romantic is
the abundance of fabulous detail that characterizes the romances
of medieval literature, those French, Italian, and Spanish poems
common from about 1200 to 1500 which so greatly influenced
English and German literature. A significant work of this early
romantic type is the *Roman de la rose*, to which Chaucer is indebted; and romantic qualities characterize the poetry of Dante,
Torquato Tasso, and Ariosto, Spenser's *The Faërie Queene*, and
the dramas of Shakespeare.

According to the evidence presented by the history of the arts
and by the analysis of styles, the romantic inclination seems to
be immanent in the human soul, a natural propensity. Like a good
many other inclinations and atavistic instincts, however, the
romantic is dormant and inactive, locked up, until it is awakened to consciousness and to activity by a peculiar constellation

of psychic stimuli; only when these stimuli are preponderant can one speak of a romantic attitude. In a minor degree more or less subconscious romantic influences may color the artistic product in every style of art, and as such admixtures, spices, they can be traced through all the various phases of artistic utterance. Even in classical art, which we regard as the opposite of romantic art, romantic traits are often latent, or even clearly apparent. It is only when they become dominant, however, when they determine the form and contents of a work of art, that a romantic style comes into existence.

It is extremely difficult, perhaps impossible, to define clearly and briefly the nature of the romantic work of art in all its subtlety and complication. But by a number of antitheses and contrasting terms the direction, at least, may be indicated in which one is to look for romantic traits. For instance, the classical form in music, painting, architecture has a tendency toward concentration; it is a closed form; whereas in the romantic style there is an open form, a loose construction, something "eccentric," as opposed to the concentric classical tendency. One may oppose the classical feature of clear-cut contour to the romantic predilection for picturesque, colorful treatment and shadowy contours. Or one may speak of the rationalistic, logical traits of classical style, of its love for harmonious proportions, in contrast to the experimental, fantastic, and irrational features of romantic art. Or one may contrast the objective, orderly, positive, clearly assertive classical manner with the subjective, irregular, hypothetical, and vague romantic statement. The universal tendency of classical art is replaced, at least in the earlier romantic phase, by national traits and by an outspoken glorification of the artist's own race. The changeful character of romanticism, however, is revealed by the fact that later it returns to the cosmopolitan ideal, amalgamating these contrary national and cosmopolitan aims by a number of ingeniously devised methods, as may be perceived in the music of Chopin, Liszt, Berlioz, and Wagner.

How close these contrasting styles come occasionally may be exemplified by certain works of Bach, where fantasy and fugue in the same work of art represent two different manners of artistic expression without losing connection and unity. Such

works are Bach's Chromatic Fantasy and Fugue, the G minor
Fantasy and Fugue for organ, and the Prelude in E flat minor and
its fugue in the first part of *The Well-Tempered Clavichord*. In
all these cases we have a fantasy or prelude of romantic nature
coupled with a fugue of the severest classical structure. Imagine
a work of art that omits these structurally severe fugues and is
made up of pieces like the Bach fantasies and preludes just mentioned, and one will have a fairly adequate idea of what is called
romantic music. Whatever appeals primarily and very strongly
to the imagination and the emotions, and stresses these fantastic
and emotional qualities with all the means that are available, may
justly be called romantic.

The modern romantic movement flows in two different streams
in Germany and in France. German romanticism springs from
a purely ideal source, French romanticism from a revolutionary
and militant spirit. The causes for the rise of the romantic movement in these two countries were similar, but the reaction to the
new romantic ideas was as different as the German and French
character and temperament. The cool, rationalistic attitude of
mind of the eighteenth century and the revival of classicism had
more or less exhausted their vital power toward the end of the
century. Scorning logic, mathematical exactness, and scientific
clearness, the long-repressed power of imagination now demanded
its rights again. The years from about 1780 to 1830 in Germany
and Austria mark the struggle of the rising romantic spirit with
the still powerful classical spirit, a struggle finally decided after
the death of Beethoven and Goethe in favor of romanticism.
But even after the victory of romanticism the struggle goes on,
with reversed signs, so to speak, minus instead of plus; the classical spirit reënters, and a reaction in favor of classicism exists
side by side with romantic exuberance. This unceasing mixture
of classic and romantic traits, recurring always in different proportions, can be clearly observed in the music of Felix Mendelssohn, in the later music of Schumann, and in Brahms.

The early German romanticism of about 1775 makes its first
appearance in literature, whence it is later transferred to music.
The so-called *Sturm und Drang* period, the storm and stress
period of young Goethe, Herder, Schiller, and such lesser writers

as Lenz, Klinger, Bürger, Heinse, and the brothers Stolberg, is the dawn, the early spring of German romanticism. It began with an influx of English ideas — with an admiration for Shakespeare, who in Germany was considered the ideal romantic artist, for the poems of Ossian, and for the old ballads collected by Bishop Percy. The traits that characterize this literary movement a generation later are reflected in music. Among them are an opposition to academic rules and tradition; an outburst of nationalism; a craving for liberty; the consciousness of the value and power of individuality, of original genius; an enthusiasm for the distant past, especially the Middle Ages, for folklore, for the mystical; and a pantheistic religious feeling that is opposed to dogmatic, confessional faith. The fantastic vagueness of the romantic spirit, however, is manifest again in the strange fact that in spite of the early zeal for undogmatic religion, even for art as substitute for religion, Catholicism in the early nineteenth century once more began to attract with an irresistible power enthusiastic young German romanticists; this Catholic romanticism became quite a distinct and powerful aspect of the whole movement, whereas Protestantism with its more rationalistic, sober, less fantastic aspects failed of fertility for romantic art. Furthermore, in spite of the new enthusiasm for the Germanic past of the Middle Ages, German romanticism always preserved a deeply rooted love, or at least esteem, for classical antiquity. There must also be added as romantic traits a certain feminine refinement and a decidedly unpuritan, unascetic erotic freedom.

Though the ideas of the earlier German romantic poetry had no practical importance for music until the nineteenth century, their application to music was prepared for a generation earlier in the aesthetic ideas of the romantic leaders. They all had an intense love for and interest in music, and liked to speculate on its origin and nature, on its aims, and on its connection with poetry. It may appear strange and paradoxical at first sight to call Kant's cool and subtly constructed *Kritik der Urteilskraft* a substructure of romantic aesthetics. Yet almost all later ideas on music, up to Schopenhauer and Wagner, are hidden in this last great metaphysical work of Kant's, though to super-

ficial observers Kant seems to have had little familiarity with the
practice of music and to have been not at all what is generally
called a "musical" person. His opposition to the rationalistic
aesthetics of the eighteenth century is of especial importance.
According to his teaching, the source of art is not in reason or
intellect but in feeling, *Gefühle*. However narrow and objectionable the details of Kant's musical aesthetics may seem to
musicians of the twentieth century, his main idea, that music is
the language of feeling, *Empfindung*, is the cornerstone of all
romantic music. For Kant music is a language without the form
of a language; it speaks without *Begriffe*, logical conceptions or
ideas. Its theme is an aesthetic idea, which is wholly different
from a rational idea, and this aesthetic idea has its root in the
emotions of the human soul. Music is defined by Kant as the
"art of the beautiful play of emotions" ("die Kunst des schönen
Spiels der Empfindungen").

Herder, the great protagonist of folklore and poetry, has also
expressed his ideas on music in a number of his writings, especially
in connection with the subject that interested him most, the intimate relationship of poetry and music, later one of the basic
maxims of romantic music. Wilhelm Heinse, the novelist, is a
very remarkable pioneer of romantic ideas on music. His novel,
Hildegard von Hohenthal, published in 1795, in particular, is full
of the most interesting musical and aesthetic analyses of the Italian
operas of his time, and gives us a very valuable insight into the
aesthetic basis of late Neapolitan music, as well as into the
social and artistic culture of Italy about 1780. Heinse's earlier
novel, *Ardinghello* (1787), is full of similar romantic effusions
with regard to painting, sculpture, and architecture. The romantic ideal of emotional music has almost never been described more
beautifully and convincingly than by Heinse: "Pure music,
quite apart from all other conceptions of the imagination, touches
the nerves and all organs of hearing and thus changes our inner
feelings. . . . The entire being begins to resound. . . . Our
feeling is nothing but an inner music, a constant oscillation
of the vital nerves. Everything that surrounds us, all our new
ideas and sensations increase or diminish, strengthen or weaken
the state of these inner oscillations. Music touches the nerves in

a peculiar manner and results in a singular playfulness, a quite special communication that cannot be described in words. Music represents the inner feeling in the exterior air, and expresses what precedes, accompanies, or follows all verbal utterance." A little later, toward 1800, Wilhelm Heinrich Wackenroder wrote his *Herzensergiessungen eines kunstliebenden Klosterbruders* ("Confessions of an Art-loving Monk"), a valuable little book with the subtitle, "Fantasies on Art." Here we find a most remarkable discussion of the romantic ideal of music, especially with reference to sacred music.

If we analyze romantic traits still further, we finally arrive at a number of concrete facts, criteria of the romantic style. There is, for instance, the expression of national patriotic sentiment instead of the former cosmopolitan tendency of the classical style. As early as the eighteenth century German, French, and Italian music were clearly distinct from each other — think of Bach, Rameau, Scarlatti — yet these distinctions were only the natural consequence of the composer's descent, and we scarcely ever find the desire to glorify one's own national music by belittling the achievements of other countries. On the contrary, in Germany, for example, though they naturally accentuated German traits, the greatest musicians of the eighteenth century were cosmopolitan in the widest sense of the term. Bach was a close observer and student of Italian and French music; what we call the Bach style is a compound of German, Italian, and French traits, and it is by no means certain that the German traits exceed the French and Italian traits taken together. In the case of Handel, it is almost impossible to estimate justly whether German, Italian, or English traits predominate in his music. Mozart, too, had the astonishing faculty of assimilating whatever seemed valuable to him, no matter whether it came from Germany and Austria or from Italy and France. When we approach German romanticists like Weber and Schumann, however, the international aspect almost disappears, and characteristically German features are deliberately brought out; a new charm, a strong flavor is sought in them. The same trait can be observed in Russian music, in the Polish accent in Chopin, the Bohemian in Smetana, the Scandinavian in Grieg.

This national aspect includes the use of folklore and folk song, an outstanding romantic trait. The predilection for folklore in German poetry began with Herder, Goethe's older friend, and came to its climax in the epoch-making collection of German folk songs edited by Arnim and Brentano under the title *Des Knaben Wunderhorn* in 1805. Even the title is romantic to the core: "The Boy's Magic Horn." The horn is the romantic instrument in German music, with its sound full of longing, of *Sehnsucht*, and "magic," of course, is a thoroughly romantic epithet. "Des Knaben" also has a romantic ring; it means not the school boy but the grown youth, filled with youth's vague emotional turmoil, sensibility, and excitability.

It is a very remarkable fact that none of the great masters of classical music paid much attention to folk song. One finds hardly a trace of it in Handel and Mozart. Bach uses a folk-song melody only for humorous effects and in rare cases, as if folk tune were too primitive and commonplace for serious treatment. Beethoven used folk song only in extremely rare cases, as, for example, in the famous Rasoumoffsky quartets, where Russian folk tunes are introduced, not out of artistic conviction or necessity, but in order to please the Russian Count Rasoumoffsky for whom the quartets were written. Like Haydn, Beethoven once arranged a collection of English, Irish, and Welsh melodies with piano, violin, and violoncello accompaniment. Both these collections may be considered a concession to the rising tide of romanticism, but neither Haydn nor Beethoven can be called real romanticists, though romantic ideas sometimes penetrate into the solid, clear structure of their classical form.

In Haydn the Austrian national element is for the first time not only a natural property of the music but a consciously stressed and prominent feature of the entire melodic invention. Though he rarely uses real folk song, his entire thematic invention grows from the fertile soil of Austrian popular tunes, which he elaborates, develops, and treats with a cleverness that is far beyond the possibilities of genuine folk song. This Austrian local color is much stronger in Haydn than in Mozart, whose horizon reaches to a more cosmopolitan world. It is true that there are Austrian traits in Mozart's music, but while, for example, a rustic tone prevails in Haydn's minuets, Mozart's charming minuets remind us of the more highly cultivated classes of society.

But when we come to the romantic composers, Weber, Mendelssohn, Schumann, and Brahms, folk song assumes an importance that it had not had since the sixteenth century, the great classical epoch of German folk song. In Norway, Bohemia, Hungary, Poland, and Russia it becomes essential as the basis of the new national art that is an outcome of the great romantic movement all over Europe. It is only necessary to recall names like Chopin, Glinka, Rimsky-Korsakoff, Moussorgsky, Grieg, and Smetana, to perceive how powerful the influence of folk song became in the nineteenth century.

Chopin's melodic material is Polish. Though Chopin spent nearly twenty years in Paris, the most cosmopolitan city of the world, though he was welcomed in the most exclusive Parisian society, his soul and his art remain Polish, and what little admixture there is of French and Italian traits seems like a slightly foreign flavor, marring a little the otherwise delightful purity of his Polish music. He was profoundly influenced by German music; yet he has a way of making this German current almost disappear for most listeners. His method of melodic invention combines the manners of Haydn and Mozart, but with reference to Polish national music instead of Austrian. Haydn's rustic quaintness and Mozart's elegance both reappear, but translated into Polish and transferred to the romantic idiom that is characteristic of the nineteenth century.

Another characteristic feature of all romantic art is the new meaning which nature, especially landscape, gains for art. This can be perceived in poetry as well as in painting and music. The romantic artist is interested not in the details of a landscape, in an exact, photographic, objective copy of actual experience, but in projecting his own emotional world into his vision of a landscape. The difference between unromantic and romantic landscape painting in music can be illustrated by a comparison of Haydn and Weber. In his oratorios, *The Creation* and especially *The Seasons*, Haydn is a delightful realist. These scores are full of charming, idyllic bits: the lion roars, the cock crows, the birds call and sing, the dogs race, panting in the excitement of the hunt; the beauty of flowers, of the hills, plains, and fields, of sunrise and sunset, of rain and tempest is suggested. Haydn's model was Handel, who is unsurpassed as a landscape painter of the old school, but Haydn's own love of nature and delight in its beauty made him even more inventive of charming descriptive touches. This representation of nature, however, remains merely descriptive and does not go beyond the idyllic stage. Mozart has almost no interest in nature; Beethoven's interest in it is limited to its sublime aspect, with rare exceptions, as in the "Pastoral" Symphony, which indeed has a decidedly romantic atmosphere.

It was left to Weber's genius to discover the soul of nature for music. In this respect his opera *Der Freischütz* is epoch-making. The permanent quality of this opera is not in its plot, which is dramatically weak, but in its power of revealing in sound the soul of a landscape, of evoking the *Stimmung* of the dark forests. It is not only that the elemental aspect of the German forest is translated into sound — the forest with its countless dark trees, with its clouds and winds, its friendliness and its mystery; the way in which it influences the people inhabiting it is also suggested most characteristically. The dark nocturnal powers of hell, projected into the bright sunlight of day, give *Der Freischütz* its weird and fantastic atmosphere, its romantic color; and the power to evoke such landscape impressions by the peculiar color of orchestral sound is one of Weber's greatest achievements. The *Wolfsschlucht* scene in *Der Freischütz* has become an arsenal from which all later romanticists in opera — Marschner, Nicolai, Berlioz, Liszt, Wagner — have drawn their implements for producing fantastic sound effects. Neither Berlioz' *Symphonie fantastique*, in itself a great masterpiece of romantic landscape color, nor Wagner's *Flying Dutchman*, nor *Siegfried*, to mention only the greatest achievements, could have come into existence without the vital and fascinating model set by Weber's *Freischütz*.

Fairyland and the phantoms of the air had been introduced into German literature by Norse myth and English ballads, by Ossian, and by certain Shakespeare plays, and music soon found new attractions in these fantastic visions. Schubert tried his hand here occasionally (as, for instance, in the magnificent setting of

Goethe's "Erlkönig"), though he did not compete with the achievements of Weber and Felix Mendelssohn.

Light, aerial, fairy music is a specialty of Mendelssohn's in which he has never been surpassed. Many of his *scherzos* have a delightfully fantastic play of the most delicate tones, suggestive of a dance of spirits that float in the air like clouds, soaring lightly in most graceful undulations, hardly touching the ground with their nimble feet, wrapped in veils, like clouds or smoke mounting toward the sky. For example, there is the wonderful scherzo of the octet. Though written by a boy of sixteen years, its light and delicate touch reveals the firm, sure hand, the alertness of imagination of a master. And his ever-fresh young music to Shakespeare's *Midsummer Night's Dream*, with its marvelous overture, is the product of a precocious genius of seventeen years. A more sinister aspect of the fantastic world of spirits appears in his splendid music to Goethe's "Walpurgisnacht." Ludwig Tieck, the German romantic poet, expressed this romantic delight in nocturnal visions in some famous verses:

> Mondbeglänzte Zaubernacht,
> Die den sinn gefangen hält,
> Wundervolle Märchenwelt,
> Steig' auf in der alten Pracht.

> Magic night in moonlight shining,
> Captivating eye and mind,
> World of wondrous fairy tales,
> Rise again in splendor, as of yore.

But it was not only the fairy scherzo that was created and cultivated by Mendelssohn. He also sought to give musical impressions of landscapes. In his "Italian" and "Scotch" symphonies he succeeds in evoking in the mind of the listener the impression of characteristic local color that is suggestive of Italian and Scotch scenery, and his *Fingal's Cave* overture has earned for him the praise of so severe an opponent as Richard Wagner, who called Mendelssohn a great landscape painter in music with reference to this particular overture. Certainly it gives a wonderfully vivid impression of the surging sea, of waves resounding in rocky caves, of the harsh cry of the sea gulls, the odor of the salt air, the sharp flavor of sea weed, and the melancholy soul of this northern scene. What a masterpiece of romantic imagination and romantic tone-painting!

In her famous book *De l'Allemagne* the French writer Mme. de Staël one hundred and twenty-five years ago defined romanticism as originating in the medieval spirit of troubadour poetry and song, in the Christian and chivalric spirit of the epoch of the Crusades. She also asserts that romantic art must be "original"; that is, in her words, "modern, national, popular, grown from the soil, from religion and the prevailing social institutions."[1] This includes an opposition to classical tradition, which is an imitation of Greek and Roman antiquity and is not grown on native soil. This definition of Mme. de Staël's fits romantic music well, especially in Germany. Weber's operas, for instance, fulfill all these requirements marvelously. There are the national, popular element and the Christian religious sentiment in his most famous work, *Der Freischütz*. There is the glorification of the medieval chivalric ideal in *Euryanthe*. To this is added in *Oberon* the fantastic fairy-tale element, the delight in the mythical and in Oriental coloring, which is so salient a feature of German romanticism. These traits are also to be found somewhat later in the operas of Richard Wagner.

This tendency to escape from the sober drudgery of ordinary life into the fantastic world of the imagination was strengthened in Germany by political events. The democratic, liberal flare-up of the European powers against Napoleon's tyranny was of short duration. After the battles of Leipzig and La Belle Alliance in 1814, after the capture of Paris and of Napoleon himself, reactionary tendencies in Germany and Austria speedily extinguished the youthful spirit of liberty, and the national enthusiasm accumulated in the so-called War of Liberation in Germany soon found no other outlet for its high-strung ecstasy than romantic poetry and literature. Here, at least, imagination was free to indulge in adventurous flights — the more remote, the better. Too close touch with the actual state of affairs invited trouble with the reactionary governments. These were the days when the struggle

[1] Part II, chap. XI.

of the Greeks for liberty from Turkish bondage made a sensational stir in western Europe, and Lord Byron's active participation is an episode of genuine romantic idealism. The Polish revolutionaries of 1830, in their luckless revolt against Russian oppression, were surrounded with an aureole of romantic glamour, especially in Paris, where Frédéric Chopin and the Polish poet Mickiewicz headed a distinguished colony of homeless Polish fugitives.

The same reactionary spirit was also dominant in France. But the French people, less patient than the Germans and already practiced in revolution, were quicker to revolt, and the short revolution of 1830 marks the first powerful wave of the romantic movement in France. Starting much later than German romanticism, the movement in Paris was more violent and much faster in its rise. It is interesting to note that the outbreak of the revolution in Brussels in 1830 which resulted in Belgium's becoming an independent state followed a performance of Auber's opera, *La Muette de Portici*. Even Wagner points out the revolutionary character of this opera. In fact, the French romantic movement is much more highly inflamed by the revolutionary spirit, is much more violent, radical, and extreme than the unrealistic German romanticism. Making a hasty review of what happened in the romantic ecstasies of the early thirties in Paris, we note in literature the exciting dramas of Victor Hugo, the extravagantly fantastic lyricism of Hugo and Alfred de Musset, the beautiful elegiac poetry of Lamartine. In music, also, exciting events abounded. Paganini was the great sensation. His marvelous feats of virtuosity, the strange and fascinating novelty of his art, the demoniac aspect of his violin-playing and of his personality combined to make him a very potent factor in romantic music. Franz Liszt and Hector Berlioz both received decisive impulses from his extraordinary art. Berlioz' *Symphonie fantastique* is the strongest expression of the bizarre traits in which French romanticism revels. Whereas German romanticism has something of a *paradiso* character, the work of Berlioz centers habitually around the *inferno* aspect. Meyerbeer's operas, *Robert le Diable*, *Les Huguenots*, and *Le Prophète*, also have this diabolic aspect in parts.

While the art of Berlioz will find its proper place in the next chapter in connection with what was called the "Music of the Future," the theatrical aspects of French romanticism will claim our attention here, opera being the real representative of French romantic music.

Meyerbeer, the most brilliant and successful representative of romantic grand opera, shows in his internationally famous scores, *Robert le Diable*, *Les Huguenots*, *Le Prophète*, and *L'Africaine*, a peculiar application, even exploitation, of romantic ideas. He tried to combine the national and the cosmopolitan tendencies of romanticism by evolving a sort of international style, borrowing from Italian, French, and German opera their outstanding characteristics. Italian vocal effectiveness and virtuosity are combined with German orchestral elaboration, and this mixture is added to the brilliance exhibited by the French in matters pertaining to the theater. It has been vigorously disputed whether this combination of three styles produces a real style at all, and the answers to this question have differed widely according to the aesthetic creeds of the critics. After all, Bach and Mozart had successfully achieved a similar mixture of different national styles. But there can be no doubt as to the romantic origin of Meyerbeer's venture. The choice of plot reveals the romantic spirit no less. Meyerbeer aimed at a kind of historical opera in which he not only treated dramatic intrigues connected with well-known characters but created a dramatic action centering around such important events as St. Bartholomew's night in Paris, with the assassination of the Huguenots, or the uprising of the sect of the Anabaptist fanatics in Münster under the leadership of an insane "prophet," or the discoveries of tropical countries overseas by Vasco da Gama (*L'Africaine*). These attempts at dramatic pictures of various states of culture were later overshadowed and surpassed by Wagner's *Die Meistersinger von Nürnberg*; in spite of this, however, the art of Meyerbeer is not only historically interesting but has more intrinsic artistic values than are generally accorded to it at present.

It has been pointed out in an earlier chapter that masters like Gluck, Cherubini, and Spontini, though foreigners, gained their fame in Paris and became leaders of French opera. The French metropolis asserted its strange power of assimilation again in the case of Meyerbeer, the German Jew. Meyerbeer and the French Jew, Halévy, the composer of the admirable opera, *La Juive*, by universal consent of their contemporaries took a position at the head of French opera. In conjunction with Felix Mendelssohn they form a trio of world-famous Jewish musicians. This is not chance, but a conspicuous sign of the times. The liberal, tolerant, cosmopolitan attitude of the romantic spirit is manifest in the quick rise to eminence of a number of Jewish composers, for the first time in history, after the emancipation of the Jews in European countries, which in itself was an outcome of the romantic attitude. Meyerbeer, Mendelssohn, Halévy, Hiller, Offenbach, and later Goldmark, Rubinstein, Joachim, Mahler, and scores of famous violinists, pianists, singers, and conductors, show how cordially the romantic nineteenth century welcomed the musical excellence of the highly gifted Jewish people. But the paradoxical romantic mind could house side by side apparently incompatible and opposite tendencies. Thus we find along with this large, tolerant, cosmopolitan spirit a nationalism that was narrow, intolerant, and extreme. Richard Wagner, who was surrounded by Jews and highly indebted to Jewish artists and Jewish intellectuals, started the anti-Semitic wave which attained its full force only two generations later, in our own day.

Another characteristic romantic trait is the mutual approach and the mixture of the various arts. The musical world up to this time had been a world quite separate from poetry and painting, though sometimes the various arts had met on common ground, each, however, maintaining its own nature. But the romantic ideal consisted in mixing the various arts, in making music poetical and picturesque, and poetry musical. The glorious German song created by Schubert, Schumann, and Brahms could arise only in a romantic period, for the new romantic idea of the marriage of poetry and music was its aesthetic basis. The old pre-Schubertian song keeps poetry and music cleanly apart. To the soberly recited verses a tune is added, and a thin, unpretentious accompaniment joins music and words together, loosely and superficially. Romantic song is very different: poetry, vocal melody, and instrumental accompaniment are no longer put together loosely but are so thoroughly composed, in the literal sense of the word — that is, mixed together — that tune and words cannot be sharply separated. The three factors together create something new, so that the words interpret the meaning of the music just as the music unveils the inner sense of the words, and the rhythms and harmonies of the instrumental accompaniment give characteristic color, light, and shade, accents and climax, and thus paint the scene of the poem.

Just as music and poetry formed an intimate union in the romantic era, so music and painting became affiliated. Color in the proper sense is a new aspect of romantic music. Conceptions of light and shade, of fine gradations between lighter and darker color, had thus far been found in music only accidentally and exceptionally. In the romantic work of art the idea of color becomes an indispensable factor, and its realization was achieved by an admirable refinement of harmony and of orchestration. Romantic harmony is identical with chromatic harmony. The frequent use of chromatic progressions lessens the distinction between major and minor tonalities and increases immensely the possibilities of varying cadences and modulations from one key to another. One may even say that this sensitive new harmony is the principal achievement of the romantic movement in music, inasmuch as it added something that had not existed formerly in such intensity and richness. Schubert's music is full of the new major-minor tonality, partaking at the same time of both major and minor, soaring from somewhere in the air between the two, and thereby achieving that peculiarly indefinite romantic color which is neither bright daylight nor dark night but various shades of twilight. But the real creator of the magnificent romantic harmony in all its varying aspects is Frédéric Chopin.

It is too little known that Wagner's and Liszt's sensational chromatic harmony is a daughter of Chopin's harmony, that Chopin was the discoverer of this new land of luminous shadows, of transitions from brighter to darker levels of sound, of genuine scales of musical color. For Chopin tonality is no longer, as in classical music, a constructive feature but in the main a coloristic value, a *valeur*, as the French impressionistic painters say. Chopin, the real father of impressionistic music, is much more concerned with these picturesque *valeurs* than with any other aspects of tonality. For him modulation gains a new sense. In classical music modulation was a formal constructive feature, devised in terms of space or time; establishing a key, departing from it, and finally returning to it was an indispensable proceeding in the classical scheme. Chopin does not ignore or deny this constructive function of tonality, but his passionate interest and delight belongs to the picturesque veiling or masking of tonality, to giving music those innumerable delicate nuances of color which romantic painting in France also seeks, especially that of Delacroix, Chopin's close friend. Delacroix once criticized his older colleague, the great classical painter Ingres, saying that Ingres knew only about *coloration*, not about *couleur*. These two terms might also be applied to Chopin's harmony as compared with the harmony of the classical masters. In Gluck, Haydn, Mozart, and Beethoven, melodic design and contour line were of prime importance; harmony gave color to the design in the sense of *coloration*. With Chopin, however, the conception of *couleur*, of color as an independent primary factor in music, gained ground, so far as music permits color to predominate without losing all coherence and melodic sense. More precisely, one might say that the essential and characteristic trait of Chopin's romantic music is melody conceived in terms of color, of constantly changing color, of color in motion, in flow.

In such an art the distinction between light and shade, warm and cool color, necessarily becomes of prime significance, and consequently all available means, including rhythm and dynamics, are employed toward that end. Chopin's tempo rubato, his abundance of dynamic and agogic signs, *sforzati*, sudden irregular dramatic accents, syncopations, his exciting crescendos and his languishing diminuendos and pianissimos, his voluptuous, exhausted *fermati*, his accellerandos, *ritenutos*, sudden changes of tempo are means to express the romantic visions of light and dark color with all their inexhaustible transitions. Romantic painting in France, particularly that of Delacroix, also knows these dynamic accents. Chopin's genius, however, was not concerned with taking over these modern sensational traits into music merely for the sake of giving his art the appearance of being up-to-date.

These means were needed to express the exaltations, the longings, despairs, the passionate outbursts and fantastic visions of
his romantic soul, his unique personality; and this complete agree-
ment of a powerful individuality with the artistic expression of
its emotional world gives Chopin's music its lasting value,
beyond the unavoidable change of artistic tendencies and creed.
As musician Chopin is closely akin to the romantic poets of the
first order, like Byron and Shelley, the greatest English exponents
of the romantic movement, which in England was concerned
much more with poetry than with music.

Nor is it by chance that the rise of romantic music is more
closely allied to the piano than to any other instrument. Neither
the organ nor strings nor wind instruments are so admirably
fitted for this new passionate music as the pianoforte. The older
forms of the piano, the clavecin, cembalo, spinet, and clavichord, were ideal instruments for the piano music of the eighteenth century, for Couperin, Rameau, Bach, Handel, Scarlatti,
and Mozart. But these delicate thin-toned instruments had no
possibilities for the new romantic music, and by the invention of
new technical devices which changed its character completely
the spinet was adapted to the demands made upon it. Hammer
action gave the piano a more brilliant, metallic, and powerful
tone, but even more important is the pedal, which permits the
prolongation of sound, a device unknown in the old short-toned
cembalo. It is true that the organ, even more than the piano,
also has the power of prolonging tone at will. But there is a great
difference between the sustained tone of the organ and that of
the piano, and this very difference gives the piano its power of
producing the romantic spell, of revealing color, atmosphere.
The prolonged organ sound is rigid; it seems to increase in volume, to gain in loudness and penetration, whereas the pedal tone
of the piano is not rigid but shades off most delicately, growing
softer and softer and finally fading away. This colorful resounding tone, this blending of chords into each other, this
Rauschen, as the Germans say, using a term not known in any
other language, this fascinating and fantastic play of sounds in
the air, derived from the Aeolian harp, is the romantic ideal of
sound, and this is the chief reason why romantic music is in

the main piano music. The pedal has been called the soul of the piano, and indeed with its help the great romantic masters, Chopin, Schumann, and Liszt — to a certain extent Beethoven and Schubert — discovered a new world of fantastic, immaterial sound. These pedal sounds cannot be realized by any other means. Neither the organ nor the orchestra can replace the modern piano. Pedal resonance is to sound what the air, the sunlight penetrating layers of clouds, is to color in painting. It makes possible an amazing variety of color effects, and Chopin, Schumann, and Liszt with admirable inventive genius achieved a practical realization of these captivating possibilities, these fleeting shadow effects.

In Robert Schumann we see the incarnation of the romantic spirit. For the most part his romantic qualities are derived from and nourished by literary sources. Jean Paul Friedrich Richter, E. T. A. Hoffmann, Rückert, Eichendorff, Heine are the poets congenial to him. No composer before Schuman had ever devoted his art to making his music "poetic" to a comparable degree. For Schumann "poetic" is a synonym for "musical," and for him the essence of music, its artistic flower, must needs be poetic. The poetic quality he seeks to achieve is that ideal aspect, that elevation above the commonplace, that escape into a world of fantasy which is the desire and final aim of the romantic soul. It is true that much of the music of Bach, Mozart, and Beethoven has a quality of idealism, but romantic idealism is very different from classical idealism. Schumann's romanticism is of an extremely individual type, quite different from that of Weber, Mendelssohn, Chopin, Liszt, and Marschner. What interests Schumann most is not nature and landscape painting, fantastic visions of fairyland, as in Weber and Mendelssohn; it is not the picturesque sound-fantasy of a Chopin, but rather the poetic exaltation, youthful exuberance, and soulful lyricism of romantic art. In short, he is concerned not so much with the frame, the outer aspects, of the romantic feeling as with its inner aspects. This tendency places him in close contact with the romantic novelists, Jean Paul and E. T. A. Hoffmann, whose writings deal not only with humorous, grotesque, and strange — even abnormal — types of people but also with beautiful and enchanting ones.

Schumann's dance fantasies, *Papillons, Faschingsschwank aus Wien, Davidsbündler*, and especially the immortal *Carneval*, show us this aspect of his art most delightfully. What a difference between this fantastic German dance music and Chopin's hardly less fantastic valses, polonaises, mazurkas, which are so genuinely Slavic in character!

Though Schumann is rarely beyond criticism technically, though his weaknesses in construction, in form, in polyphony, and in orchestral treatment are evident, yet the emotional power of his music is so great that in the works of his best and earliest period he reaches his aim in spite of his handicaps. In many of the Schumann melodies there are a poignant expression, a cry of the heart, a touching accent, a purity and sincerity of feeling so irresistible in their effect that even after a century his strange expressive power has not perceptibly lost its strength. What ties musical souls to Schumann is not his intellectual achievement, which is very slight in comparison with that of other great masters, but the emotional aspect of his music. In this field his achievements are indeed almost incomparable, and the strange, magical charm that emanates from his music has been one of the strongest factors in shaping later music in Germany, France, and Russia. The Schumannesque melodic type is noticeable fifty years later. Gounod and Saint-Saëns, Bizet, César Franck, and Massenet are full of it; Liszt, Rubinstein, Brahms, Tschaikovsky, Borodine, and Rimsky-Korsakoff revel in it. Schumann the composer of songs takes us into a fascinating magic land. Here is lyric vocal music fully suited to the romantic exaltations, the fantastic poetry of such writers as Heine, Eichendorff, Rückert, and Platen. There is hardly anything in the immense compass of music that equals certain Schumann melodies in the power of evoking strong emotion, of making tears rush to the eyes, of arousing outbursts of delight — and all this is accomplished with a touching purity and sincerity, a chasteness of feeling very different from Chopin's sensuous refinement, from Wagner's burning passion and voluptuous impetuosity.

The predilection of the romantic masters for short pieces in one movement is a very striking and characteristic feature. They are not interested in complicated design but in inspiration, poetic ecstasy, a mysterious, fantastic background. The fact that the quick flame of fervent inspiration is likely to consume itself as quickly and thus lose its power of incantation seems to be the psychological reason for the somewhat fragmentary aspect of romantic music. The intellectual power necessary for the magnificent architectural structures of a Bach, Handel, or Beethoven is absent from romantic music. The interest is centered on creating not a cyclical work of powerful construction but a short piece, or a loose bundle of short pieces, flaring up in inspiration for as long or as short a time as the flame may burn. Music of pointedly characteristic mood, *Stimmungsmusik*, is the signature of romantic art, of pieces like Chopin's nocturnes, preludes, *études*, valses, mazurkas, polonaises, ballades, and scherzos, Mendelssohn's *Songs without Words*, Schumann's suite-like dance fantasies — his *Carneval, Kreisleriana, Faschingsschwank aus Wien*, and *Davidsbündler*.

Another characteristic feature of music in the nineteenth century is the rise of national schools. In 1800 there were three great countries that had been rivals in music for centuries — Italy, France, Germany. In 1900, however, a number of newcomers claim attention. There is the Polish music of Chopin, the Russian music of Glinka, Moussorgsky, Borodine, Tschaikovsky, and Rimsky-Korsakoff; there is the Norwegian music of Grieg and Sinding, the Danish music of Niels Gade, the Finnish music of Sibelius; Hungary has its Franz Liszt, Bohemia its Smetana and Dvořák. It is true that music had been practiced in all these countries long before 1800, but it gained international validity only in the course of the nineteenth century. Formerly, it had been a provincial dialect, a folklore idiom of characteristic traits but narrow scope; in the romantic epoch this nationally limited folklore expanded into a well-developed language and assumed a style, form, and content that made it interesting to the musical world at large.

During the nineteenth century the position of music was fundamentally changed as a result of the great changes in political and economic conditions and the revolutions of the technical age. Music now became a democratic affair, supported chiefly by the middle classes and maintained by their thriving commercial prosperity. It was no longer exclusive, aristocratic, as in the eighteenth century; neither was it proletarian, as it tends to be in the twentieth century; it kept a middle course. Publicity became an essential condition for its successful existence. Public concerts, symphony orchestras, quartet societies, piano and song recitals, oratorio choruses, music festivals, public opera houses were attainments of the nineteenth century toward which only faint starts had been made up to 1800. Increased ease of travel, the rise of daily newspapers, with musical criticism as an essential feature, increased speed of international communication through the telegraph, the press, and improved mail facilities all helped music in many ways. A prodigious increase in the printing of books and music created new and extensive fields of activity; education of the masses of the people led millions of people toward art and literature; in fact, an enormous new public grew up, eager to experience what art and artists had to offer. Yet this immense widening of artistic activities had its dangers and drawbacks. Art was too often commercialized and was exploited financially to an unprecedented degree. As a consequence it descended to a very low level: late nineteenth-century popular music, for example, is tainted with a vulgarity that is quite new in the history of music. The striving for sensational effect and catering to a vulgar taste prostituted the noble art of music and adulterated its former purity.

One of the more positive attainments of the nineteenth century, however, is the art of reproductive music, which scored triumphs such as had never before been achieved. Wonderfully gifted and accomplished artists interpreted the works of the great masters with an impressiveness and a suggestive power unknown to former ages: pianists like Chopin, Mendelssohn, Liszt. Rubinstein, Bülow, Taussig, d'Albert, Paderewski, Busoni; violinists like Spohr, Paganini, David, Joachim, Wilhelmi, Vieuxtemps, Wieniawski, Sarasate, Ysaye; conductors like Weber, Wagner, Berlioz, Bülow, Richter, Nikisch, Mottl, Mahler; world-famous string quartets, like the Joachim, Rosé, and Bohemian quartets; scores of admirable *Lieder* singers and opera singers.

An acquaintance with the inexhaustible treasures of music, accumulated for centuries, was thus spread far beyond a little circle of fastidious connoisseurs. Toward this discovery and interpretation of lost and forgotten works of art, great and important contributions were also made by the science of musical research, musicology, as it is now called. A quite important achievement of the romantic spirit (chiefly German) not only in music but in all fields of art and science is historical investigation based on love and respect for the great deeds of the past. Thus Mendelssohn's discovery and first performance in Berlin, 1829, of Bach's St. Matthew's Passion is an outcome of this romantic attitude toward historical research. This memorable performance marks the beginning of the great Bach movement in Germany, which a century later had not yet come to a rest. German musicological research, so fertile for the better knowledge of our great art, with all its brilliant achievements, is a child of the romantic movement. The earlier masterpieces of this weighty German musicological literature are Karl von Winterfeld's important works on Giovanni Gabrieli and German Protestant church music, Thibaut's rediscovery of Palestrina, Kiesewetter's and Fétis' discovery of old Dutch music, Otto Jahn's famous biography of Mozart, Chrysander's equally famous biography of Handel, and a little later Philippe Spitta's monumental biography of Bach, a model of German thoroughness, insight, and industry. Ambros' unsurpassed, though fragmentary, history of music must also be mentioned here. France and England also took up these studies of musical history and archaeology. All these achievements summed up mean an immense gain of insight and organized knowledge, comparable to what has been achieved in the history of literature and in the other arts in the collections of the great museums of Europe.

Musicians of high rank once more became ambitious to excel as writers. This ambition was foreign to Handel, Bach, Haydn, Mozart, Beethoven, and Schubert, though it had been common in the two preceding centuries, as is shown by the important writings of Zarlino, Caccini, Galileo, Michael Praetorius, Mersenne, Athanasius Kircher, Rameau, Philipp Emanuel Bach, Quantz, and many others. But the logical, scientific method of those earlier musician-writers is very different from that of the romantic writers, for whom essay writing was not a professional pursuit but a means of getting relief from their artistic nervous hypertension. In this class we find E. T. A. Hoffmann, Weber, Robert Schumann, A. B. Marx, Berlioz, Liszt, Wagner, Bülow, and others. Professional musical journalism and criticism also had an increasing importance in the nineteenth century. The modern critic through his regular, often daily, columns in the newspaper has become a power the like of which had never existed before in the world of music.

Extracts from the writings of the German romanticists revealing their ideas on music would make a most fascinating volume. Musicians, poets, philosophers, critics, and scientists have contributed a vast amount of thought and observation on music, which to the romantic mind is evidently one of the most attractive of speculative problems. Such a volume, not yet in existence, would draw its materials from the letters of Beethoven, the letters and various writings of Weber, Mendelssohn, Schumann, Chopin, Berlioz, Liszt, Wagner, Brahms, Bülow, and other musicians; from poets and authors like Goethe, Schiller, Herder, Heinse, Wackenroder, E. T. A. Hoffmann, Arnim, Brentano, the brothers Schlegel, Tieck, Jean Paul, Novalis, Heine, Rahel Varnhagen, Bettina von Arnim; from philosophers like Kant, Fichte, Hegel, Schelling, Schleiermacher, Schopenhauer, Feuerbach, E. von Hartmann, and Nietzsche; scientists like Helmholtz, and historians like von Winterfeld, Jahn, Chrysander, Spitta, and Ambros. Through such a volume the preponderant weight of German thought on romantic music would be convincingly manifested if one were to compare it with the little that France, England, and Italy have to offer on the subject before 1860 or thereabout.

The romantic philosophy of Fichte, Hegel, Schelling, and Schopenhauer centered around the idea of evolution (*Entwicklung*). This concept, which also dominated the science and literature of the nineteenth century, is carried over into music, and to it we owe the form of the sonata as Beethoven conceived and shaped it. Romantic music is not static, like Bach's music; it is no longer the exhaustive statement of a single idea, a single mood. Its very essence is dynamic. In it are constant flux, progression, change from one idea or mood to another. The terms "tension," "climax," "dynamic accent," "contrast" gain a new meaning. The Beethoven sonata and symphony, models for all later romantic music in large form, are a dialectic process, a dramatic conflict, a reflection of the composer's experiences and impressions of life and nature, a veritable microcosm, often deeply philosophical in character.

Music now began to attach great importance to contents, meaning, expression. The unpretentious play of sounds of the later eighteenth century seemed shallow to romantic musicians. The Dionysian romantic art demanded not a severe ethos but rather an exciting pathos. An ecstasy of creative impulse, the sexual impulse in a sublimated form, dominates the music of Schumann, Chopin, Liszt, and especially Wagner. Magic charms, a revival of the ancient Orphic mysteries, and an orgiastic passion flame up in the arch-romantic *Tristan und Isolde* music. In less pretentious, less powerful romantic music nervous sensibility is the most characteristic trait. The language of the heart means more to the romantic artist than the cold clarity of logic. For romantic music inspiration in its literal meaning — something breathed into the soul, something of heavenly origin, given by the grace of God — is the divine spark which ignites the fire of artistic creation. The role of fantasy becomes of prime importance. Strictly formal problems are of secondary importance, though of course even romantic music could not afford to neglect them. They were refashioned for their new task, which was less architectural, less constructive and mathematical than previously, and associated more closely with poetry, drama, and painting. Sound and color were primary factors, and rhythm, associated with bodily activity, with gesture and elementary vitality, received a new glorification.

Even ancient and medieval mystic speculations on mathematical principles, on numerals and proportions, were revived to a certain extent by some extreme romantic mysticists, like Wackenroder, Novalis, and E. T. A. Hoffmann. Novalis, for instance, observes that "all method means rhythm. If one has perceived the rhythm of the world, one has also comprehended the world. Every human being has his own individual rhythm. . . . Genuine mathematics is the real element of the magician. In music mathematics appears as a revelation, as creative idealism. Here it is authorized as a heavenly ambassador to mankind. All enjoyment is musical, and accordingly also mathematical." Most remarkable are the following words of E. T. A. Hoffmann on Bach: "There are moments — especially when I have read much in the scores of the great Sebastian — when the musical proportions of numbers, nay, even the mystic rules of counterpoint evoke an interior horror. Music! — with a mysterious awe, even fear I call you! Thou in sound expressed Sanskritta of nature!" Ideas like these explain the interest of the romantic period in Bach, and reveal what those fantastic minds perceived in Bach's music. During the past century the "romantic" Bach has been replaced by the "symbolist" Bach and the "absolute" Bach. Almost every generation makes the incommensurable Bach the image of its own dominating conception of music.

Two famous stanzas of German poetry may terminate this rudimentary essay on the meaning of music for the romantics. Schumann takes as a motto for his *Fantasy*, op. 17, the following verses by Friedrich Schlegel:

> Durch all Töne tönet
> Im bunten Erdentraum
> Ein leiser Ton gezogen
> Für den der heimlich lauschet.

> Through all the sounds resounding
> In life's fantastic dream,
> There sounds a faint tone floating
> For him who closely watches.

The intimacy, the penetrating power of this listening, this searching for the hidden meaning of life, is expressed here in terms of sound. Here Schumann's credo becomes manifest, and adding four famous verses by Tieck, we get a most fitting supplement in our analysis of this peculiarly German romantic spirit:

> Liebe denkt in süssen Tönen
> Denn Gedanken stehn zu fern;
> Nur in Tönen mag sie gern
> Alles was sie will verschönen.

Love thinks only in sweet sound
For ideas are too far;
All that love cares to reveal
Only music may surround.

And if we extract the essence of these two little poems, we get the elements of the romantic world, its moving powers — dream and love. With dream and love, fantasy and passion, romantic music is concerned in endless variation.

CHAPTER ELEVEN

THE "MUSIC OF THE FUTURE"

I N THE preceding chapter the nature of the romantic work of art was discussed with particular reference to German music. The present chapter will be devoted to the subject of romantic music in the second half of the nineteenth century with special reference to the French attitude toward romanticism, because it exerted a considerable influence on Richard Wagner, the central romantic figure of the entire century.

The difference between German and French romanticism has already been explained: German romanticism springs from a purely ideal source, whereas French romanticism has a revolutionary tendency, a militant spirit. The chief exponent of this agitated French romanticism is Hector Berlioz, who together with Franz Liszt and Richard Wagner makes up the triad of great names that represent the "new" music of the nineteenth century, the "Music of the Future."

Berlioz' contribution to this sensational new art consists in the exploration of what is called program music. The aim of program music is to extend the possibilities of musical expression by interpreting musically a poem, a story, or a scene. The idea was not at all new, but the manner was. All through the history of music tone-painting had been more or less exploited, particularly in vocal music, where the text gave a clue to the meaning. But even in instrumental music attempts had not infrequently been made to tell a story without words. The most notable earlier examples are perhaps the "Biblical sonatas" of Johann Kuhnau,

Bach's predecessor as cantor at St. Thomas' Church in Leipzig. Kuhnau here attempts to treat music as a sort of language, telling well-known stories from the Bible in a number of curious piano sonatas. Everyone knows Beethoven's Pastoral Symphony, a piece of decided program music, with a title attached to each movement, the entire symphony aiming at presenting various scenes of rustic life and impressions of nature and landscape in terms of music. Beethoven, however, adds the cautious notice: "Mehr Ausdruck der Empfindung als Malerei" (more expression of sentiment than painting). This is Berlioz' point of departure. But he is not satisfied with a few titles that indicate in a general way the dominating emotional moods of each piece. In his *Symphonie fantastique*, the arch-romantic masterpiece of program music, listeners must read a whole little novel before they can properly understand the meaning of the music. Here we meet again the romantic intermarriage of poetry and music. If one had not read Berlioz' fantastic program and did not know the titles of the single movements, there would still remain a kind of symphony after Beethoven's pattern, each movement sufficiently coherent in itself to be comprehended as a piece of music. But one would not comprehend the inner connection of one movement with another; one would be struck by many bizarre and capricious details which could hardly be accounted for merely from the symphonic point of view. To relish all these details, highly seasoned and spiced as they are, it is indispensable to know the program. We may be unimpressed by the literary program, by the story of the impassioned young poet who in a fit of melancholy tries to take his life by poison but, failing, falls into a sort of opium dream with terrible visions. Yet however repulsive these may be in themselves — visions of a ball, of a melancholy country landscape, of the hero's own execution after having killed his sweetheart in jealous rage, of a witches' Sabbath with the dear girl as queen, leading the infernal orgy — this *Symphonie fantastique* is one of the most fascinating, powerful, and impressive manifestations of the romantic spirit in existence.

Attention has already been called to the picturesque power of romantic harmony as discovered by Chopin. Here we must add newly discovered orchestral colors, with Weber as protagonist and Berlioz as inventive genius of the first order. Berlioz' art of orchestral coloring is an achievement comparable to Chopin's chromatic harmony, a fundamental achievement on which the art of Wagner, Liszt, Richard Strauss, and Debussy is based. Here Berlioz' music manifests its romantic kinship with painting. In the power of evoking suggestive associations through sound color, Berlioz has never been surpassed. In pieces like the admirable "Scène aux Champs" in the *Symphonie fantastique*, he suggests the odor of the moist fields and meadows, the solitude of the country, the melancholy of the vast plains, the oppressive atmosphere of a thunderstorm in the distance. But he is equally skillful at depicting all sorts of fantastic scenes, and through his art he increased the expressive powers of music considerably. To understand his music thoroughly, one should read his memoirs, one of the most fascinating of books, for these romanticists cannot be fully comprehended through their music alone; some literary assistance is necessary.

Franz Liszt, the incomparable pianist, the highly distinguished composer, is the very embodiment of the romantic spirit in his fantastic life as well as in his art. His biography reads like highly colored fiction, for his triumphal success as a virtuoso made him perhaps the most universally admired and celebrated man of his time. We are concerned here only with the manner in which he fashioned the romantic ideas of his age to his particular individual needs. His manifold achievements were of the greatest importance for the cause of progress in music, sending stimulating impulses in many directions. Dispute is possible as to the lasting artistic value and the ultimate perfection of his music, but not as to his inventiveness in finding new technical means of expression or as to his wonderful sense of sound and of color. From Berlioz he took over the ideas of orchestral tone color and program music, developing them in a very individual manner. From Chopin he inherited the sensitive new chromatic harmony, which he enriched in many ways, handing over to Wagner an admirably perfected tool to be used in *Tristan und Isolde*. In the matter of musical form he applied for the first time the principle of "cyclic" construction, evolving all the various themes of a symphonic or sonata-like work in several movements from a few fundamental motives, which through rhythmical or melodic transformations could be made to assume numerous changes of expression. César Franck, Vincent d'Indy, and the modern French and Russian school later adopted this *principe cyclique* of Liszt's. Here we see a particularly striking musical application of the dominant romantic idea of evolution. In his various "symphonic poems," his "Faust" and "Dante" symphonies, and his concertos, Liszt has brilliantly demonstrated the possibilities of this principle of organic structure. The cyclic method had been widely employed in the *ricercare*, *canzone*, fantasia, and suite of the seventeenth century, but had been forgotten in the eighteenth century. Probably, however, Liszt knew nothing at all of these two-hundred-year-old ancestors of his method. It is probable that he elaborated it from his studies of the last Beethoven sonatas and quartets, where a very ingenious and complex use is made of a similar transformation of motives. In his B flat minor sonata Chopin also shows an approach to this method, though it received its practically useful, simplified stamp in the work of Liszt.

In conjunction with Chopin, Liszt discovered new possibilities for conveying impressions of landscape. His *Années de pélérinage*, particularly, which translates his impressions of travel in Switzerland and Italy into highly suggestive and picturesque piano music, sounds as fresh and fascinating as ever if played by a master; Ferruccio Busoni produced a stupendous impression with this work, which in spite of Debussy has not yet been surpassed. Toward the end of his life Liszt turned to ecclesiastical music and became the leading exponent of the peculiarly Catholic romanticism, with its mystic, seraphic sound, to which attention has been called in the preceding chapter. His masses, psalms, and oratorios, especially *St. Elizabeth* and *Christus*, anticipated many a Parsifal *Stimmung*.

Liszt's conception of program music is of particular interest because it shows an advanced stage of evolution as compared with Berlioz' more spectacular, theatrical music. Inspecting the series of "symphonic poems," as Liszt called these works, one finds that he draws his titles and his subject matter mainly from poetry (Victor Hugo, Lamartine, Goethe, Shakespeare, Dante), occasionally from painting, but that he always takes scrupulous care to make his choice of subject matter significant and spiritually elevated.

As this type of program music set a model for several generations of distinguished modern composers, a closer investigation of its psychological basis, its *raison d'être*, seems appropriate in this place. Program music has often been belittled of late by believers in "absolute music" as the only true creed. In the eyes of these judges program music is a hybrid art without genuine artistic substance, without artistic purity. This severe verdict may be just in the case of the modern "school" of program music, the pupils and imitators of the initiators, but it certainly cannot be maintained justly against the best works of Berlioz, Liszt, the modern Russians, Saint-Saëns, d'Indy, Richard Strauss, Debussy, and Ravel. The term "program music" is not a skillfully chosen label, for it induces in the less expert public the belief that the composer's aim was to "tell a story without words" in music, the words being supplied by the title or the sketch to be read by the listener before or during the performance. This crude explanation of the nature of program music does not, however, correspond to the actual situation, as found by an exhaustive analysis of the works of Berlioz and Liszt, with whom we are here concerned. In their scores there are titles and in many cases also an elaborate "program," but the musical result is much more than a descriptive illustration — which would indeed be musically incoherent, even senseless. As a matter of fact, we have here a truly romantic compound of simultaneous auditory and visual appeals.

There is Mendelssohn's song without words, the simplest application of this principle, together with Schumann's *Noveletten*, Chopin's *Nocturnes* and *Ballades*.

There is oratorio — opera without theater, but with words.

There is Berlioz' program symphony — opera without words, but with action and scenery imagined.

There is Liszt's symphonic poem — a lyric or dramatic scene, or cantata, or an operatic intermezzo without words, but with imaginary scenery or imaginary action.

There is Wagner's music-drama — a symphony with words, plus oratorio, and with actual scenery and action.

According to such a classification, Berlioz's *Symphonie fantastique* and *Harald en Italie* would have to be called operas without words.

A very just and illuminative commentary on program music has been made in an essay by H. Frömbgen: "Hegel und die musikalische Romantik," published in the German periodical, *Die Musik*, in 1929. Speaking of *Tristan und Isolde* as the final fulfillment of the romantic principle, the author continues:

"Here the last barriers between *Individuum* and *Kosmos* (the individual and the world) have been pulled down. The tension of this romantic dualism could not be intensified any further. What follows is mere decadence. The content of music in the later nineteenth century becomes more and more complicated and more and more highly differentiated. Music is no longer content with being a reflection of the human being; high romanticism has made music a language that can express everything, including the artist's views on matters of the world and of life. This language was addressed to a public enabled to love it and understand it by an incomparable musical and spiritual tradition. Here was the mission of program music, which is nothing but a consequence of romantic thought. Romanticism is always the art of the indirect. Program music has been misunderstood for a long time. It is not musical photography, but musical reflection, meditation. The romantic artists were not in the least prepared or predestined for a mere imitation of nature. If one overlooks this fact one cannot recognize the true basis and conditions of program music. One forms an estimate of it without the least appreciation of the extraordinary spirituality that underlies it."

After these discussions of the central problems of romantic music, we are better prepared to comprehend both Richard Wagner's starting point and his phenomenal progress. Like all great masters of art, Wagner did not hesitate to appropriate anything he considered useful for the achievement of his artistic aims. He took over from Berlioz an orchestra resplendent in color of all shades, full of striking and suggestive new sound effects. Berlioz' program music, however, he continued only in a limited sense. As a dramatist, he had little use for descriptive operatic symphonies *à la* Berlioz. Yet he has often enough incorporated in his dramas smaller stretches of such descriptive music, as, for instance, the "Feuerzauber" in *Die Walküre*, Siegfried's Rhine-journey in *Götterdämmerung*, and the *Rhinegold* prelude, depicting the quiet flow of the Rhine, and in all such scenes it is quite evident how much he learned from Berlioz. From Liszt, Wagner learned the sensitive new harmony which Liszt in his turn had adopted from Chopin. Not that Wagner was merely an imitator. Though Berlioz mastered the brilliant new orchestra earlier than Wagner, though Liszt was a decade in advance in his consummate mastery of the new chromatic harmony, Wagner enriched these accomplishments, transformed them so that they became thoroughly his own, and made them effective tools of a style superior to that of both Berlioz and Liszt.

In these novel traits we see some of the components of the "Music of the Future" which about 1850 began to excite the musical world. The term is derived from three of Richard Wagner's aesthetic writings, namely: *Das Kunstwerk der Zukunft* ("The Work of Art of the Future"); *Dichtkunst and Tonkunst im Drama der Zukunft* ("Poetry and Music in the Drama of the Future"); *Zukunftsmusik* ("Music of the Future"). From the frequency with which this term occurs in Wagner's discussions of art, one can judge its importance for him. It presents, indeed, a key to the Wagnerian domain of art, and therefore it deserves to be given some attention here.

Hardly if ever before in the entire history of music had such deliberate stress been laid on the future. Artists generally had been sufficiently occupied with the present to be indifferent to speculations on the future. There is no exception, even among the greatest musicians. Palestrina, Orlando di Lasso, Monteverdi, Schütz, Bach, Handel, Mozart, Beethoven — whether they were conservative or progressive or even revolutionary in their tendencies, they were all concerned mainly with the creation of art for the needs of the present. We have no evidence to show whether the idea of future fame and immortality ever seriously entered the mind of Bach. That his great art might be awakened to real life only a century after his death probably never struck him, not even in fancy — if this busy man ever had leisure to indulge in playful fancies apart from his art.

The importance of aesthetic speculation in Wagner and the consciousness and full intention of building something for the future may be explained somewhat like this: Wagner's unique twofold gift as theatrical genius and musician was implanted in a strange new soil. Romanticism and the revolutionary spirit, the chief chemical components of this soil, were productive of a strong fermentation. In Wagner the romantic wandering through space and time, the fantastic speculation peculiar to the romantic mind, and the romantic combination of the various arts had been greatly intensified. The Wagnerian *Gesamtkunstwerk*, the great monumental musical drama, had recourse to all the arts, which were to be harmoniously directed toward one central aim, the drama. But besides having this purely artistic comprehensive tendency, Wagner the musician, poet, and actor was also deeply interested in romantic philosophy. He was a close student of Fichte, Hegel, Schelling, Schopenhauer, and Feuerbach. It was his earnest endeavor to clarify the aesthetic basis of the artistic form he had developed and at the same time to fortify his newly conquered territory by philosophical explanation and proof.

In addition to being a romanticist *pur sang* as an artist, Wagner was also a revolutionary politically, in distinction from other German romantic composers. He was a true son of revolution. The two revolutionary movements of 1830 and 1848 embrace his younger years, the very years in which the mind is most impressionable. At the time of the revolution of 1830, which was more vehement in France than in Germany, Wagner was seventeen years of age and just beginning to think of music as his vocation. Nine years later, when he was twenty-six years old, he went to Paris, full of the fantastic aspirations of youth, expecting to conquer Paris and to win universal fame as a composer of opera, like Meyerbeer. He was bitterly disappointed in these expectations, but the disappointments themselves drew him nearer to the spirit of revolution — in life as well as in art — which was gathering strength in those years, particularly in Paris, for the great outburst of 1848. In the meantime a great stroke of good luck had lifted him into a prosperous artistic career — the success of his opera *Rienzi* had gained for him an appointment as *Hofkapellmeister* at the Royal Opera in Dresden. But in spite of the prospect he had of gaining a lifelong position, the revolutionary impulses in Wagner were so strong that he participated actively in the revolution of 1848, a crime which not only cost him his high position but also forced him to leave Germany and to live in Switzerland as a fugitive for fifteen years, without any income worth mentioning, always dependent on the liberal help of friends like Franz Liszt, the Wesendonck family in Zurich, and certain others.

During these years of exile his artistic powers reached their maturity. His greatest works, the *Ring des Nibelungen* and *Tristan und Isolde*, were conceived and to a great extent finished in the years 1850–1860. There seemed to be no possibility, however, of having these gigantic works performed: Germany was closed to the music of the revolutionary Wagner, sought by the police of Dresden; Paris was incapable at that time of seeing in Wagner's drama anything but the thoroughly impractical dreams of a crazy genius. Since the present was powerless to help his art, what else could Wagner do but hope for the future, and persuade himself and as many other people as possible that what he had to offer could only be realized and appreciated by later and more enlightened generations? In order not to lose all faith in himself, in order not to despair of life and art, he turned to this speculation about what was to come. With all the great resources of his powerful mind he built up his belief in the future as an artistic gospel, strengthened with all the arguments of philosophy and aesthetics. Furthermore, he was a revolutionist, and the revolutionary mind always takes the future into consideration.

Analyzing further the components of Wagner's art, we perceive that he made use of Beethoven's symphony as regards constructive principles, of Weber's feeling for the moods of nature, of Meyerbeer's theatrical virtuosity. When one considers the poetry of his drama, one notes its dependence on the romantic ideas of the age, as outlined in the preceding chapter. The great romantic wave of medieval national poetry, of Germanic mythology and archaeology, the great new achievements of literary and historical research had awakened Wagner's enthusiastic interest. Jacob Grimm's studies in the comparative grammar of the Germanic languages, the philological researches on the medieval epics, the Eddas and the Nibelungenlied, and Karl Lachmann's editions of Middle High German poetry, of Wolfram von Eschenbach, Walther von der Vogelweide, Gottfried von Strassburg, and other poets of the chivalric age — all these opened Wagner's eyes and gave him a clear insight into the old Germanic mythology and poetry.

This enumeration of the various sources of Wagner's art is fairly exhaustive if we add one other trait which at first sight looks rather unromantic: his enthusiasm for ancient Greek drama. This one unromantic trait, however, became the final aim, the real object of his manifold mental activities. The vitality of the Wagnerian work of art is the result of the happy union of romantic and classical ideas. Wagner used a romantic style and romantic means for the realization of a classical ideal. Gluck had reformed opera, a century before Wagner, by a renaissance of the antique ideal, but while Gluck sought refuge in Greek mythology Wagner based his dramatic stories on Germanic, sometimes Celtic, mythology, applying the idea of ancient tragedy in form and dramatic technique. The tetralogies of Aeschylus are the distant models of Wagner's Nibelungen tetralogy. In *Tristan und Isolde* and *Parsifal* a certain Euripidean spirit becomes manifest, and in the *Meistersinger von Nürnberg* reminiscences of the comedy of Aristophanes are undeniable. Wagner's genius is revealed perhaps more clearly than anywhere else in this amazingly productive union of severity, ancient sculptural simplicity, and architectural grandeur with the rich detail, the fantastic exuberance of the romantic world. The natural tendency of the romantic toward formal vagueness is wonderfully counterbalanced by the firm constructive art of ancient tragedy. Thus the cool marble beauty of antique form is infused with the warm blood of the romantic imagination, and the lax imagery of the romantic is given shape by the architectural form derived from Greek tragedy.

What is assigned to the chorus in ancient tragedy is confided to the orchestra in Wagner's drama. Just as in Greek drama the chorus comments on the action, approving or disapproving of the dramatic events, so in Wagner the orchestra makes a running commentary on the drama, explaining the inner meaning of the action even where the words for certain reasons fail to accomplish this task. To fit his orchestra for this elaborate, constantly watchful, and varied activity, Wagner used all the descriptive, pictorial, and illustrative means of modern romantic music, its tone-painting, its sensitive and colorful chromatic harmony, its rich orchestral palette. These traits serve to produce the proper emotional mood, the proper *Stimmung*; they also help to illustrate many a scenic effect, making it more impressive by an appeal to the eye and the ear at the same time. The music of the orchestra also reflects in its rhythmical patterns the characteristic gesticulation of the actors. In this subtle explanatory commentary of the Wagnerian orchestra Beethoven's symphonic technique is transferred to the theater. Just as in the "Eroica" and the Ninth Symphony, for example, an elaborate symphonic complication of the various motives in the "working out" sections gives an effect of logical coherence, of dramatic tension, of arresting and exciting development, so in Wagner's symphonic art a number of characteristic motives, the so-called leading motives, are used throughout an entire work, entering into different contrapuntal combinations and changing their aspect through manifold variations of harmonic coloring and dynamic accents. An especially significant feature is Wagner's power of logical, convincing transition from one complex of emotion to another, from one color, rhythm, or melodic design to another. This Wagnerian art of transition is directly derived from Beethoven's symphonic technique, and is most ingeniously adapted to the particular needs of the Wagnerian tone-language.

If we ask ourselves to what extent the "Music of the Future," that is, our present music, has realized Wagner's expectations, the answer must be that it does so only in part. If Wagner meant that his own music would have full validity even after a century, his prophecy, as it seems, will be amply fulfilled. But if he meant that he would be the founder of a great school, that later dramatic music would move along the lines he mapped out, there cannot be any doubt that he was mistaken. It has been proved by actual experience in the last fifty years that Wagner's principles were fit for him alone, that they were born of his own unique personality and are not transferable to other personalities. There has, of course, been no lack of imitation. But for a half cen-

tury not a single opera belonging to the strict Wagnerian school
has been accepted by universal consent as permanent property of
the operatic stage. Even musicians of the rank of Richard
Strauss, Max von Schillings, and Hans Pfitzner failed in their
early Wagnerian attempts. On the other hand, whatever has been
really successful on the operatic stage since about 1885 hails not
from the Wagnerian camp but from that of the opposition.
The only really successful product of the Wagnerian school is
Humperdinck's charming opera, *Hänsel und Gretel*, and its
success is due to a great extent to the composer's clever modifica-
tion of Wagnerian principles. But if we take such successful
works as Verdi's *Falstaff*, Massenet's *Manon* and *Werther*,
Gounod's *Faust* and *Romeo and Juliet*, Mascagni's *Cavalleria
rusticana*, Leoncavallo's *I Pagliacci*, Saint-Saën's *Samson et Dalile*,
Bizet's *Carmen*, and Puccini's operas, it becomes manifest that
these operas owe their success not to Wagnerian methods but
rather to their deviation from them. It is very strange that hardly
a single German opera, besides those of Wagner, won lasting
fame on the operatic stage between 1850 and 1900. There can
be no doubt that Wagner is the sole representative of German
dramatic art in his age. But in France and Italy his influence was
not so powerful as to crush all other attempts at dramatic style.
Giuseppe Verdi, especially, holds his own valiantly against the
aggressive German artist, and in France Bizet, although on a
much smaller scale, successfully upholds French character and
his own personality, and achieves artistic independence of Wagner, a feat that commands our highest respect, all the more because
young Bizet was a glowing admirer of Wagner.

There were three countercurrents to the "Music of the Future"
— one in opera, two in symphonic music — partly opposed to
Wagnerian tendencies, partly influenced by them. One might
well say that the contest of these opposing powers gives the music
of the later nineteenth century its character, and that these countercurrents complement the essential contents and achievements
of the art of music in the years 1850 to 1900. These three opposing forces are: (1) Italian opera, dominated by Giuseppe Verdi;
(2) the music of Johannes Brahms; (3) the symphonic art of
Anton Bruckner.

Verdi's mission was to bring the old Italian operatic art to a climax. He is without doubt the greatest dramatic genius ever produced by Italy, and he stands at the head of Italian theatrical music as Wagner stands at the head of German. Though he was noticeably influenced by Wagner in his later works, this influence extends mainly to form, to greater harmonic refinement, to more subtle symphonic workmanship and orchestral treatment. The substance of Verdi's music, his glowing melody, his unerring theatrical instinct, his passionate soul, remain as Italian as possible from the somewhat crude beginnings in 1839 to the enchanting vivacity, grace, and humor of his *Falstaff* in 1893. His immense dramatic output — no less than thirty operas — makes it very difficult to arrive at a just estimate, a complete appreciation of his work as an artist. Whereas many people have heard, and some have studied exhaustively, all Wagner's operas, no one has actually heard all the thirty Verdi operas. In all countries except Italy and Germany Verdi is known chiefly as the composer of *Il Trovatore, Rigoletto, La Traviata,* and *Aïda.* A few people also know *La Forza del destino, Otello,* and *Falstaff,* but twenty-three other Verdi operas have no practical existence for the world of music lovers.[1] The essential difference between Wagner and Verdi is the difference between the German and the Italian temperament, language, and expression. Wagner's style is based on the German orchestral symphony; Verdi invariably makes the vocal part the essence of his music. This difference in the center of gravity in the art of Wagner and Verdi explains all the differences in style, which are the logical outcome of this fundamental attitude. Though Wagner occasionally knew how to produce magnificent vocal effects, and significant and finely wrought symphonic workmanship had hardly any secrets for Verdi when he found reason for employing it, on the whole the orchestral basis in Wagner and the vocal preponderance in Verdi remain the true sources of invention and style.

Verdi's vocal style, however, is very individual and very differ-

[1] From my own experience I may say that between 1920 and 1930 a veritable Verdi renaissance took place in Germany, so extensive that I acquired an acquaintance with fifteen Verdi operas by actual performance, and I may add that every one of these operas was a veritable feast in spite of certain occasional trivialities and vulgarities in the older operas.

ent from the older *bel canto* style, as used in the operas of Rossini, Bellini, and Donizetti. He is not, like his predecessors, primarily intent on melodic beauty and sweetness, on brilliant vocal virtuosity, but on sharply characteristic, even realistic vocal treatment and invention. No composer equals him in the power of inventing characteristic vocal melody of the most diversified types; its dramatic intensity and emotional strength are so powerful and irresistible that these qualities alone guarantee his perpetual popularity. He is the tragedian par excellence. Only twice in his career of nearly sixty years did he write a comic opera; all the more marvelous that his *Falstaff*, the last of his thirty operas, written at the age of eighty years, should have been a supreme masterpiece of comedy. At the close of his magnificent artistic career, with the wisdom of age Verdi came to the conclusion that the best way to look at this funny world is to take it with good grace as a huge joke, a vast comedy, in which at the end everybody is fooled. We have to make the best of it and to acknowledge with a manly humor the futility of life. It is a pessimistic philosophy, with a tragic ground tone, but uttered with a hilarity, dash, and *brio* that are quite unique. The last scene of *Falstaff*, in which Verdi takes leave of the operatic scene, translates this philosophy into musical terms in that magnificent fugue for ten soloists and chorus on the text "Tutto nel mondo è burla ("Everything in this world is a mockery"— and as counter theme, "we are all fooled"). With this *risata final*, this final laughter, Verdi finished his message to dramatic music.

As a dramatic work of art Verdi's *Falstaff* is hardly less masterly than Wagner's *Meistersinger*, though very different in style and mental attitude. After all, Verdi was the only rival of Wagner worthy of his opponent. The two artists, born in the same year, 1813, never met each other, though they were contemporaries for seventy years. As far as we can tell, Wagner did not take Verdi's art seriously, whereas Verdi was at the same time instinctively repelled by Wagner and magically attracted by him, and held him in a sort of awe mixed with admiration. Verdi, the plain peasant, Italian to the core, with his overpowering, sometimes brutal strength, his straightforward directness, and Wagner, with his mental complexity, his Protean versatility, his German intellectualism of the highest type, his demoniac magic art — these two were too far apart to meet on common ground. In Franz Werfel's fascinating novel, *Verdi*, the psychological basis of their mutual relations, at least spiritually, is laid bare with penetrating insight.

We turn now to the second of the countercurrents that opposed themselves to the elementary strength of Wagner. In the field of concert music, symphony, chamber music, and song, Johannes Brahms is the only great artistic power of his age able to resist the Wagnerian invasion and to build up a great art in opposition to it.

As we have said, Wagner represents the revolutionary German type; Brahms, no less thoroughly German, is the spokesman of the more conservative German attitude, the champion of evolution rather than revolution. Combined, the two give us a complete survey of the widely divergent, yet complementary Germanic spiritual traits that dominated the nineteenth century in music. Brahms, too, is romantic; the nearer it is to 1850, when he started his artistic career, the more romantic his music is. Robert Schumann, the great romantic visionary, recognized a cognate romantic soul in young Brahms at their first meeting; and certainly no composer of twenty could boast of so emphatic and inspired a welcome by a leading master of his art as Brahms received when Schumann wrote that famous Brahms article, his last article in his *Neue Zeitschrift für Musik*. Schumann received his young friend as his equal in genius, as a worthy companion in the elect circle of the great romanticists. Later Brahms bridled his romantic impetuosity and fantastic exuberance by an ever-growing reverence for the art of the great classical masters. It was this apparently reactionary tendency in particular that estranged him from the "Music of the Future," in the close proximity of which he had started his career.

Brahms's artistic genealogy is as follows: Bach is his great-grandfather. Mozart and Beethoven are his two grandfathers. Schubert is his uncle. Mendelssohn is his elder cousin, and Robert Schumann is his father.

Liszt as well as Schumann recognized the extraordinary abilities of young Brahms. Joseph Joachim, the great violinist,

Brahms's devoted friend for about forty-five years, at that time concert-master in Weimar and in close personal relation to Liszt, recommended Brahms so strongly that Liszt invited young Brahms to be his guest in Weimar. Here is the turning point in Brahms's artistic career. It would have been easy for him to cast his lot with the revolutionary Berlioz-Liszt-Wagner party and to become a privileged member of it, but even as a youth of twenty Brahms felt that his artistic ideals led in another direction. This marks the beginning of the rupture which came to so sensational an end in 1860 when the *Leipziger Neue Zeitschrift für Musik* printed the famous manifesto against the "Music of the Future," or the *Neudeutsche Schule*, as it was called. This sharp declaration of war, signed by Brahms, Joachim, Johann Otto Grimm, and Bernhard Scholz, divided German music into two hostile camps for about thirty years. As a creative genius of a fame that later became universal, Brahms, was, of course, the leading spirit in this new movement, which in the literal sense of the term may be called a countercurrent to the "Music of the Future." Brahms had recognized his mission. The disintegrating tendencies of extremely romantic music had to be counteracted. The history of German music in the second half of the nineteenth century may be summed up under two headings: Wagner and Brahms.[2]

For decades the militant Wagnerian party fought a fierce fight, not only for their master's glory but for their master's sole glory; the real Wagnerians were avowed enemies of Brahms. On the

---

[2] How severe the rupture was can be illustrated by a few personal reminiscences. When I was a pupil at the Berlin Royal High School of music under the direction of Joseph Joachim, Liszt's piano music was not officially admitted in the piano classes, and as late as 1898, fifteen years after Wagner's death, Joachim made quite a stir in the academic circles of Berlin, hostile to Wagner, when he conducted the *Meistersinger* prelude in a concert of the Hochschule orchestra for the first time. Professor Bargiel (stepbrother of Clara Schumann), my teacher in composition, and Professor Rudorff, head of the piano classes, used to go into fits of rage when in our youthful enthusiasm we pupils spoke of Wagner in admiring terms. My teacher in counterpoint, Professor Carl Leopold Wolf, occasionally discussed Wagner with us, warning us against the dangerous temptations of Wagnerian music. He condescendingly admitted that in the *Meistersinger* score there were contained some *hübsch empfunden* (prettily conceived) episodes, but *Tristan* he called an *eklen Brei* (a disgusting porridge). On the other hand, when Brahms died in 1897 Frau Cosima Wagner confessed that she had never heard any of his compositions, and probably she never came into closer contact with Brahms's music in her later life.

other hand, there was also a long, though less clamorous fight for Brahms. But finally, toward 1900, the excitement abated more and more, and music lovers at last discovered the truth, that it is not necessary for a Wagner enthusiast to be hostile to Brahms, and vice versa. Both Wagner's and Brahms's music are great achievements, complementing rather than excluding each other.

The reconciliation was brought about by artists of rank and influence who stood between the hostile parties, especially by Hans von Bülow. An ardent Wagnerian, conductor of the first performance of *Tristan und Isolde*, the great pianist retired from the Wagnerian cause after his wife Cosima, daughter of Franz Liszt, had left him to devote her life to Wagner. And in the eighties von Bülow found his way into the hostile camp. The man whose active enthusiasm for Wagner had known no bounds now became the champion of Brahms, and the popularity of Brahms in Germany dates from the years in which von Bülow, conductor of the Meiningen orchestra, went on concert tours all over Germany with his famous orchestra, performing the Brahms symphonies, overtures, variations, serenades, and concertos, and interpreting them so convincingly that he established Brahms as the leading master of his age in concert music. The other great champion of Brahms was Joseph Joachim, Brahms's close friend from about 1850 to 1897, when Brahms died.[3]

[3] About him I trust I may be pardoned a digression into personal reminiscence, for I treasure his playing and teaching among my most precious memories. From Joachim, who was an incomparably great artist, a personality of the highest type, I learned what Bach, Mozart, Beethoven, and Schumann really mean. His quartet rehearsals, his playing of the Bach Chaconne and sonatas, of the Mozart and Beethoven concertos and sonatas, his teaching at the royal Hochschule for music in Berlin, were revelations to me, and the invigorating, purifying, and illuminating power that emanated from him has not lost its vitality for me after more than thirty-five years. Though at that time he was already old and had lost a part of his magnificent virtuosity, his spiritual powers were sublime; never since have I met such a combination of manly vigor, culture of taste, purity of style, and demoniac power of expression as he revealed. Almost every year Brahms paid us a visit at the Berlin Hochschule, and Joachim, of course, never failed at those festive occasions to perform an ample program of Brahms's chamber, orchestral, and choral music. My impressions of Brahms were first-hand, as Brahms was, so to speak, the patron saint of the Berlin Hochschule. We were fed on Brahms, but had to abstain from Wagner, at least at the school. We reveled all the more, however, in the Wagner performances of the Royal Opera House, where a number of the famous old guard of original Bayreuth singers were still active. Albert Niemann, the greatest Wagnerian hero on record, had just stopped

We have hastily surveyed the Wagnerian "Music of the
Future" and the forces, centered in Brahms, that opposed it.
There is one more aspect of note, worthy of close attention, an
art partaking of both tendencies which serves as a connecting
link between these extremes. This is the music of Anton Bruckner. His place is between the "Music of the Future" and its
countercurrents, that is between Wagner and Brahms. Bruckner
is exclusively a composer of symphonies and masses; he has no
dramatic interests at all. Beethoven, Schubert, and Wagner are
his direct ancestors; the Catholic Church is his mother, the convent his school, the organ his friend and companion. Though
Brahms and Bruckner lived in the city of Vienna for thirty
years, they had no personal intercourse and were on rather hostile
terms. While Brahms's fame by and by spread over the entire
musical world, Bruckner's fame came only thirty years after his
death (1894), and the Bruckner movement in Germany assumed
larger proportions only after the World War. It was not until
between 1920 and 1930 that it became clear to musicians that
this modest, shy, old-fashioned, simple-minded composer of symphonies and masses was in reality a great musical genius. Now
in our time his art is being recognized and duly appreciated.
Bruckner himself would have been amazed if he could have seen
the literature devoted to him, the bulky tomes of a thousand
pages or more dedicated to the profound study of his art, if he
could have known that Bruckner societies would spring up not
only in Austria and Germany but in the distant United States of
America (where, however, to tell the truth, he is still a stranger,
in spite of the American Bruckner Society, which was founded
four or five years ago).

Wagner was for Bruckner the one great event of his life, his
fervent love. The son of an Austrian village schoolmaster, a real
peasant, young Bruckner grew up in the shelter of a Catholic
convent, became organist in a church near Linz on the Danube,
and began an uneventful career — in fact, no career at all. This
rustic, provincial organist and composer of Catholic church

singing at that time, but Franz Betz (the first Hans Sachs), Lilli Lehmann, Rosa
Sucher (an unsurpassed Isolde), Julius Lieban, Götze, van Roy, and other
great singers were still active.

music would probably never have left his tranquil church service if it had not been for Wagner's music, which with the elemental power of an electric spark set his dormant imagination aflame and stirred in him vast powers of music. His third symphony is dedicated to Wagner, who was the only contemporary of high rank to take any interest — and that of a rather detached sort — in his music. When Bruckner died in 1894 at the age of seventy his nine symphonies and three masses were played only occasionally, at rare intervals, but he had inspired a number of young artists of rank, mostly young pupils of the Vienna conservatory, with enthusiasm for his work, and these musicians, later famous, gradually obtained a standing for his art. Such famous men as Hugo Wolf, Gustav Mahler, Franz Schalk, Dr. Carl Muck, Dr. Ferdinand Löwe, and Arthur Nikisch were his early champions.

Bruckner's symphonic art is an outgrowth of the romantic movement, mixed with the baroque traditions of the Catholic Church. Its intermediate position is conditioned by its purely symphonic nature, which affiliates it with Brahms, and by its adoption of the Wagnerian ideal of sound. There are, however, profound differences between Bruckner and Brahms. Bruckner's symphonies are monumental, unlyric, saturated with mystical religious feeling, cosmic and grand in conception, full of ecclesiastical pomp, thoroughly Austrian, with rustic elements mixed in, whereas Brahms's symphonies are lyric, Protestant, of North-German austerity, intimate in expression, reticent in display of sound, neither cosmic nor profoundly religious and mystic. Brahms's symphonic style is a magnified chamber-music style; Bruckner has no inclination at all toward chamber music, the small frame. His is not the bourgeois ideal of intimate, lyric music; his vast imagination is at home in the infinity of cosmic space, in transcendental religious ecstasy, in visions of heavenly glory and brightness, in adoration, fervent prayer for salvation, and the despondencies of guilt and sin.

These monumental blocks of ecstatic music are regularly and happily set off in the Bruckner symphony by at least one element that has terrestrial reality, the scherzos. Here Bruckner, the Austrian peasant, records rustic life with a vitality, an almost brutal strength, a realistic power that can hardly be paralleled. In this boisterous merriment, this captivating dance-rhythm, this grand sweep of popular tune, this mixture of grace and vigor, tenderness and almost savage wildness, the spirit of the Austrian Alps, of upper Austria, comes alive with an amazing vitality, just as in Haydn the spirit of the Austrian lowlands is kept alive in music.

To sum up briefly the result of this investigation:

Bruckner is the *Gottsucher* (God-seeker), a humble man, illiterate, a crank, a queer old fellow of childlike simplicity, but full of the holy spirit, inspired by religious ecstasies of a profundity unknown in music since the days of Palestrina and Bach. He is, moreover, a great melodic inventor, a great master of counterpoint, and a builder of vast achitectural structures.

Brahms's real domain is chamber music, with its intimate, refined expressiveness, its clean and interesting workmanship, its lyric melody, its logical and convincing treatment of form. The last, most concentrated essence of Brahms's music is in its noble elegiac quality, its tone of resignation, often austere, always touching in its sincerity and depth of manly sentiment, but always subject to a strict self-control, bridled and restrained in its outbursts of passion.

Unbridled and unrestrained passion seems to be the most characteristic feature of Richard Wagner, but this flaming up of sensuality is in reality controlled by a powerful will, an energetic hand. Schopenhauer's title, *Die Welt als Wille und Vorstellung* ("The World as Will and Idea"), might justly be applied to the Wagnerian work of art. Gigantic will power and boundless imaginative force together have produced in it something incomparably great.

Wagner, Brahms, Bruckner, and Verdi have given the second half of the nineteenth century a special significance, marking this epoch as a high peak in the chain of mountains that make up the art of music. These masters are still comparatively near our age, speak to us in a familiar idiom. What they have to give us is so much that even a most minute study of their art will not exhaust their message to the world. A famous quotation from Goethe's *Faust*, "Du gleichst dem Geist, den Du begreifst," ought to be deeply impressed on the minds of all serious young artists, ambitious students: "You resemble the spirit whom you comprehend." To really comprehend Wagner, Brahms, and Bruckner means not that we make ourselves a part of them but that we make these great and venerable masters a part of ourselves. We are vastly more than before as musicians after our smaller spiritual powers have assimilated the spirit of their great art. In the last analysis one can comprehend something new and great only in proportion to the extension of one's spiritual horizon. What the great masters do for us is to lift us higher, so that our horizons grow wider. In this and not in weak imitation is the significance of penetrating studies in art.

CHAPTER TWELVE

THE TWENTIETH CENTURY

THE intention of this book has been to point out that since antiquity, more than two thousand years ago, all the achievements of music, all significant changes of style, have been subject to the cultural conditions of various epochs and have been shaped by the dominant aesthetic ideas of each. Consequently, we should expect modern music to partake of the nature of the soil from which it grows, to reflect the ideas of our time, the intellectual, moral, social, economical conditions of our world.

We live in an age full of unrest, uncertainty, and dissatisfaction, striving, as we believe, after something new and better. The disagreeable conclusion must be added, however, that we are groping in the dark in our effort to find the way out of our troubles. This is exactly the situation in modern music: much agitation, much speculation and clever experiment, a passionate striving after a new basis, but no clearness about the really efficient measures to be taken, no real style, no well-defined course. This situation gives to ultramodern music, viewed as a whole, a veritably tragic aspect. On the one hand, great energies, strong talents, much courage, sincerity, and passion consumed in a fierce struggle for something new, valuable, representative of our age; on the other, only meager artistic results in comparison both with the effort expended and with the achievements of former epochs, even the now much-derided romantic period.

The twentieth century down to 1938 is made up of two distinct epochs that are divided by the World War. These four years of war destroyed the old order of things everywhere, and the rise from this deep fall has been slow, full of hesitations, doubts, and uncertainties. Thus we have from 1900 to 1914 the last late flower of romantic art, decadent but still full of brilliant intellectual achievement. The period after 1920 is characterized by a tossing overboard of the romantic ideal and by a passionate search for a new ideal that will express convincingly the aspirations of a thoroughly disillusioned generation, full of bitter determination and relentless agitation, but lacking and despising the gentler longings of a refined and sensitive soul. It is the age of grotesque, parodistic, distorted music. The "Music of the Future" of the nineteenth century is now parodied in the "futuristic" music of the twentieth century. Experiments are highly prized, and too often misunderstood as products of a settled, fully mastered art.

Let us at first cast a searching glance at the state of things from 1900 to 1914, when the years of war forcibly ended an epoch, interrupted tradition, and prevented a natural, orderly evolution. Europe had reached the peak of a prosperity beyond compare. Toward 1900 Berlin became the great center of music, and in Germany interest in music grew to a towering climax until the outbreak of the war put an end to those years that were so incomparably brilliant musically. Germany, a country smaller than the state of Texas, at that time maintained at least a hundred and twenty opera houses, which played most of the year, with the exception of the summer months, and then a great many summer music festivals provided excellent music in abundance. Good symphony orchestras, together with an opera house, a theater, and a chorus, were maintained even by towns of twenty-five thousand inhabitants.

This prosperity of the arts had, of course, a very substantial support in the orderly, well-managed state of affairs in Central Europe. Four decades of uninterrupted peace, sound economic conditions, and constantly growing wealth had produced an atmosphere favorable to the growth and culture of the arts. The refinements of modern culture, the great achievements of the new technical age, the great international society of European countries in friendly rivalry and constant intercourse had given the art of music extraordinary opportunities. Romantic music was appropriate to this new society of 1870–1900 and later, for the rise of the middle classes was closely connected with the rise of the romantic movement. Romanticism was, in fact, a child of the bourgeois spirit, its appropriate expression, and the prosperity of one was helpful and even, it may be said, necessary to the prosperity of the other.

The situation in Germany about 1900 had changed somewhat from that of a generation earlier. Imperialism had become the watchword of German politics, and German imperialism left its mark on art as well, particularly music. Its first triumphant expression is to be seen in Richard Wagner, and its continuation in "Richard the Second," as the Germans often jokingly refer to Richard Strauss. This second great master is indeed the representative exponent of what may be called imperialistic music. Yet his music has nothing to do with German nationalism, and it is in no sense, certainly much less than Wagner's, a glorification of German national ideals. The only contributions made by Strauss to German nationalism are a few rather poor military marches, written by special order of the Emperor. Nevertheless, Strauss's music may be called imperialistic because it applies to music the spirit of commanding power, brilliant achievement, dazzling outward splendor, amazing technical finish, the desire to overtop everything that has preceded, and mass display, stress being laid on quantity as much as on quality. These features were an outcome of the materialistic prosperity of an age of luxury, of many refinements, of immense technical advance. Other characteristic features of this culture are a taste for splendid display and high-sounding oratory, both, however, a little empty and lacking in real meaning.

All this we find in Strauss, but, happily, a little more besides, and this inclination of the balance toward the side of genuine art marks Strauss's claim to a permanent position in music. He is not only a child of his age, a mouthpiece of its dominant ideas; he is also a great artist following the voice within him, the command of his musical genius. The real Strauss is a person of fascinating vitality, full of brilliant humor, amiable, witty, and highly cultivated, decidedly a man of the world, capable of representing musically almost anything that pertains to the varied interests of actual life. In a word, he is a great realist.

Strauss is the master of the symphonic poem, which he took over from Liszt, elaborating Liszt's idea of allying music to poetry and painting with the aim of expressing in musical terms an idea originally extra-musical. Strauss's programmatic conceptions are almost exclusively of the literary type. A glance at the titles of his symphonic poems is sufficient to show his predilection for literary tasks. There are *Macbeth, Tod und Verklärung, Don Juan* (inspired by Lenau's poem), *Till Eulenspiegel,* which describes the pranks of the jester Till of German popular tales of the sixteenth century; there is *Don Quixote,* which follows Cervantes' famous novel; there are *Ein Heldenleben* and *Sinfonia domestica,* both musical autobiographies. In his aims, therefore, Strauss is the successor of Berlioz and Liszt; in his technical methods he is in advance of both, since he started as a full-fledged Wagnerian and has adapted Wagnerian methods to his own particular needs in a masterly way. Just as Wagner transferred Beethoven's symphonic principles to dramatic music, so Strauss carried over Wagner's dramatic methods into the new symphonic style. Thus Strauss descends on the one side from Berlioz and Liszt, on the other side from Wagner. It took genius indeed to extract something artistically sound and impressive from a combination of forces that tend to diverge more and more, like the art of Berlioz and Wagner, and to reconcile, so to speak, these dissidents after their deaths.

Strauss has no metaphysical background, no mysticism, no religious fervor, no torments of the soul, nothing tragic and elegiac about him. He is at his best when his magnificent vitality, his delight in the fantastic sensuous experiences of his rich life are shaped by his masterly hand into a series of true masterpieces. His cheerful temperament, his brilliant career, his happy life have left their imprint on his art, a thoroughly optimistic art which is a glorification of bright daylight, sunshine, full of exuberance, wit, and humor. He has a certain relationship to Felix Mendelssohn in his excellences as well as in his occasional weaknesses — the marring of the otherwise noble beauty of his art by sentimental melody of a too-popular cut. Occasionally, as in his operas *Salome* and *Elektra*, he is interested in sexual abnormalities and perversities and Freudian complexes, in accordance with certain literary tendencies of the age that are exemplied by such writers as Oscar Wilde, Wedekind, and Hugo von Hofmannsthal. His extraordinary intellectual gifts, his admirable powers of imagination, and his gigantic mastery of his art, together with a decided anticipation of ultramodern traits, make even the controversial scenes of these operas highly impressive. But under a more penetrating and searching criticism it is evident that these scenes have not the true and convincing ring of the immediate utterances of his genius as we find them in his masterpiece, *Till Eulenspiegel*, in his enchanting opera, *Der Rosenkavalier*, in the exquisite refinement of *Ariadne auf Naxos*.

At first glance there seem to be many similarities between the music of Richard Strauss and that of his contemporary and rival, Gustav Mahler. Both are brilliant masters of the highly complicated modern orchestral art; both take their start from Wagner; both have a gift of plain, impressive melody, and in their high-strung intellectuality, their nervous sensibility, their modernism, their imperialistic attitude, and even their controversial traits, they seem like brothers in art. Closer acquaintance with their music, however, reveals the fact that their differences are greater than their similarities. Their artistic genealogy helps to distinguish them. Strauss is a compound of Berlioz and Wagner; Mahler's music is derived mainly from Wagner and Bruckner. Mahler's excellences are Strauss's weak points, and vice versa; the two supplement each other, and if one could combine them, an overpowering genius would be the result. It is difficult to write on Mahler for American readers because the art of this great musician, like the symphonic art of Bruckner, is not adequately known in this country; the little that has been performed in America has been misunderstood and underrated, for in essence it is too far from the current American spirit. An atmosphere favorable to Bruckner and Mahler still has to be created here. In distinction from Strauss, Mahler is not a realist, but a symbolist; not an optimist, but a pessimist; not a sensualist, but an idealist. His kingdom is not of this world as Strauss's is; his music is transcendental, metaphysical, mystical, imbued with deeply religious yearnings of a pantheistic type. Here we see his connection with Bruckner's mystic religious ecstasies. But the Catholic color, the pomp and solemnity of Bruckner have a different tone and accent in Mahler, particularly in the later works, where a Jewish pathos, a melancholy, elegiac tone that sometimes goes into ecstasies of despair, is characteristic. The earlier works have as their melodic basis a predilection for simple folk song and for march rhythm. Almost always, however, there is a background of the supernatural, sometimes a grotesque humor of a demoniac type, sometimes a pantheistic religious feeling of overwhelming intensity. Mahler is a composer about whom many disputes have arisen, and it is very easy to find fault with him. But in spite of everything that may be said against him as an artist, his nine symphonies remain a monumental effort, a passionate striving after the highest ideals of art, and with all their weak points they reveal such masterly workmanship from many points of view, such an abundance of ideas, so strong and unique a personality, that they will always have to be ranked with the highest achievements of the entire twentieth century. The most highly refined essence of Mahler's art is to be found in his *Lied von der Erde* ("Song of the Earth"), which is imbued with a poignant sadness, and yet is full of an exquisite beauty and delicacy, a fascinating mixture of Occidental and Oriental, German and Chinese feeling and atmosphere. Here indeed is a musical realization of Goethe's "Chinesisch-Deutsche Jahres- und Tageszeiten."

Strauss and Mahler are the leading representatives of German symphonic music in the first decade of the new century. Let us quickly survey the general situation. German and Austrian musical activity in general proceeds at first on the roads laid out by Wagner and Brahms. Gradually a more independent attitude gains ground. The further development has several phases: a great effort to get away from the dangerous influence of Wagner, followed by the preparation of a new basis for modern music. The war years mean a vast abyss for music, and it is only after the war, from about 1920 to 1930, that what we call modern music is built up. France, Italy, Russia, England, and other countries have their share in this transformation of style.

In Germany the schools of Wagner and Brahms had produced a vast mass of imitations in the camp of the so-called *Neudeutschen*, the new Germans, as well as in the academic Brahms circle. The two most prominent disciples of Wagner have already been described — Strauss and Mahler. Of the Brahms school Max Reger is by far the strongest and most remarkable personality. The ten years from 1904 to 1914 were a veritable triumph for Reger, who after a beginning full of hardships and disappointments had finally been generally recognized as a leading master. All over Germany and in the neighboring countries, Austria, Switzerland, Holland, Scandinavia, Reger performed his own works with the help of famous soloists, he himself playing the piano in a unique and very characteristic style, perfectly adapted to his music. His average per season was about a hundred concerts; to these must be added countless performances of his works by other artists. No composer of the present time can boast of even a slight approach to Reger's triumphal presentation of his own works during those luxurious prewar years.

Reger was from the start and remained to the end of his life a Bavarian peasant, with all the vehemence of temperament, the joy in robust jokes and coarse pranks, and the delight in eating, drinking, reveling, quarreling, and fighting which are so characteristic of the Bavarian peasantry. Yet this gigantic man, illiterate as he was, extremely materialistic as he appeared at first glance, could at times be as sensitive and shy, as delicate and modest as a blushing young girl of the old type. His music manifests this strange mixture. A robust, almost brutal force, a pounding with the fist — the manner in which he actually liked to settle many of his controversies — and a boisterous hilarity are mixed with a surprisingly refined tenderness of sentiment, to which must be added a visionary ecstasy, a fantastic religious mysticism, and passionate outbursts of a tragic aspect. It is hard to understand Reger, with his apparent contradictions. This fanatic writer of fugues and crank in counterpoint reveled at the same time in the most extravagant chromatic harmony; devoutly Catholic, he exasperated the Catholic clergy by his constant glorification of the Protestant chorales, to which in his admirable organ music he gave a luxurious, hyperbolic effusiveness of expression of a decidedly Catholic, baroque stamp. In his melodic invention, especially in his very valuable chamber music, he is a son and successor of Brahms, but in spite of this he makes very liberal use of Wagnerian chromaticism, intensifying it even, so as to bring it into close proximity to the extravagant harmony of modernistic music.

His power and facility in the production of music of the greatest complexity were truly startling. For instance, for a Reger concert in Berlin a new violin sonata was announced, of which the finale was still lacking two days before the concert. This did not incommode Reger very much. For him two days were more than enough in which to write an elaborate and difficult finale, rehearse it, and play it in public. In his short life of forty-three years he published no less than a hundred and forty-one extensive works. Much of this voluminous output is only mediocre, according to Reger's own standard, owing to a rather too abundant repetition of his own mannerisms. But about one-third of his music does honor to the twentieth century, is a worthy continuation of Brahms's art, and will probably retain its value for posterity. Works like his organ fantasias, fugues, and chorale preludes, his variations on themes by Bach, Beethoven, Mozart, Telemann, and Johann Hiller for one or two pianos or orchestra, his five string quartets, his violin sonatas, and his Hundredth Psalm are masterpieces of lasting value.

Outside of Germany new tendencies in France have considerably influenced music in all countries since 1900. French impressionistic music is identified with Claude Debussy. This movement, the last offspring of nineteenth-century romanticism, is characterized by a remarkable sensitiveness to color, light, and shade. The romantic courtship of music and painting now becomes a passionate love affair, a mutual fascination, to the exclusion of almost everything else. In order to produce effects of *clair-obscur*, of luminous shades, of reflections of light in water, of clouds tinged by the setting sun, of the play of waves, winds, clouds, and sun, of rain falling on the trees in the garden — in order to produce effects like these, Debussy does not hesitate to sacrifice polyphony, counterpoint, traditional form, lyric melody. The concentrated intensity he desires he can attain only by throwing overboard many other valuable possessions of music. His art thus marks a gain at one point, and a loss at many others. The peculiar intellectual atmosphere needed for this one-sided super-refinement comes from a unique mixture of musical impressions with the ideas dominating French impressionist plein-air painting, that of Manet, Monet, Pissarro, Cézanne, and Renoir. Certain influences from the poetry of the Symbolist school also helped to determine the style of Debussy's art. The poetry of Baudelaire, Verlaine, and Mallarmé is not intent on expressing "ideas"; it aims at word music, at evoking images through the very sound of the words rather than through their meaning. Words serve as symbols for a highly refined sensualism or, at the other end of the emotional scale, for outbursts of a sadistic nature. In his musical interpretation of this poetic symbolism Debussy was less inclined toward these unrestrained and dissolute traits, toward *Les Fleurs du mal*, than toward the luminous, idyllic, lyric aspect of *L'Après-midi d'un faune*. In this score, as everywhere in Debussy's music, there is no passion, no deep feeling, no real emotional art, but rather the cult of suggestive, enchanting sound, observed and rendered with an almost unrivaled refinement. His is an altogether sensuous art. without any marked moral quality, without religious feeling or metaphysical overtones. A combination of the visible with the primitively audible is its germ; the sounds of nature, the rippling of rivers, the various noises of the air and the wind, the rhythm of distant march or dance, the sounding of signals constitute its realistic acoustic base. His formula is the commuting of visual impressions, or even impressions of smell, into musical tones, with the assistance of primitive rhythms and sounds of nature.

It cannot be denied that Debussy has successfully carried out this program and has brought into the domain of music many fascinating new sound combinations. More than that, he has formed a new style. However, the impressionistic aspect of his art is his sole property. It has been much imitated, of course, but to no avail, for the impressionistic principle is not broad enough to admit of manifold variations. Whatever is done along these lines inevitably sounds like a diluted copy of Debussy. What has been more fertile for modern art than the impressionistic principle itself is the technical aspect of Debussy's music, primarily his new harmonic art, on which, in fact, the greater part of all modernistic music is based. While he did not by any means advocate atonality, Debussy dissolved the organism of fixed tonality by lessening or even ignoring the principle of tension and resolution, of tonal function, as we see it embodied in concentrated form in the cadence. In Debussy's music cadence is not entirely absent, but it is so weakened, intentionally, that only very expert, highly trained ears can perceive its faint traces. Instead of the system of key-relationship of major-minor tonality Debussy introduces a system of parallel chord progressions, in a certain sense a revival of the medieval organum and faux-bourdon technique, without regard for key. These chord patterns, moving along uniformly in all parts, have become the signature of modernistic music. We find them in Stravinsky as in Bartok, in Hindemith as in Milhaud, and in all cases they are derived from Debussy. Such uniform patterns exclude poly-phony; melody and accompaniment coincide, are identical, save in pitch; all voices, if one may still speak of part-writing here, run parallel to each other in different planes. The principle of contrary motion, the very essence of counterpoint, becomes in-significant in this style. But strange and fascinating color effects result from this kind of writing, a new harmony, to which also Debussy's predilection for the whole-tone scale with its aug-mented triads contributed considerably. In his piano music may be seen the most remarkable and important addition to the litera-ture of the instrument in recent times. Debussy's predecessor in impressionistic piano music is Chopin, who in his twenty-four preludes anticipated a good many of Debussy's specialities sixty years before the younger master started. Schumann and Liszt must also be counted among Debussy's musical ancestors. In his orchestral music Debussy takes up again certain ideas of Ber-lioz; he is also deeply indebted to Wagner's *Tristan* and *Parsi-fal*. This connection is evident in spite of his deliberate efforts to free himself of Wagner's influence, in spite of his hostile later attitude toward Wagner. In *Pelléas et Mélisande*, his only opera, one may observe both his close approach to the orchestral sound of Wagner and his new style, derived from the use of pure, less mixed colors, quite similar to the palette of the French impressionist painters, to which his delightfully luminous, delicate orchestral sound owes much.

Next to the originator of musical impressionism, Maurice Ravel was certainly the most gifted and the most effective representative of that movement. In certain of his smaller piano and orchestral pieces Ravel is, for a superficial observer, hardly distinguishable from Debussy. Closer inspection, however, reveals individual traits. There may be more intensity, more novelty and real originality in Debussy's music, but there is certainly also more monotony in it, a narrower compass of melodic content and of technical treatment. In his best productions Ravel achieves greater differentiation in the character of the melody; he avoids the vagueness, the misty haziness of Debussy's melodic contour and is not afraid of a real tune occasionally, with a preference for old French folk song. In some of his piano and chamber music he delights in a modern revival of the exquisite clavecin style of Couperin and Rameau. This retrospective, historical spirit is almost entirely foreign to Debussy, who, as regards older music, is content with an occasional hint at church modes, a sort of primitive organum effect of parallel fifths; but even here the symbolic, suggestive, far-away romantic effect of these chains of open fifths seems to be the sole reason for Debussy's interest. In spite of or perhaps rather on account of the narrow compass of his aims and his highly concentrated means, Debussy himself exhausted the limited possibilities of impressionism as he understood it. Ravel prevented a further decadence of this already somewhat decadent impressionism, and even succeeded in rejuvenating the movement by bringing back to it the support of solid formal construction and a certain amount of contrapuntal workmanship, the very features Debussy had deliberately banned. The excessive cult of color in Debussy's music, with its somewhat effeminate delicacy and languor, is halted by Ravel, and is counteracted to a certain degree by linear tendencies, clear-cut melodic contours, a stronger rhythmical backbone, and more elaborate thematic workmanship. In short, Ravel's music represents a more realistic, more varied, forceful, and masculine type.

Impressionistic music could not have attained so prosperous a growth anywhere in the world except the Paris of about 1900. The spiritual and artistic atmosphere of that incomparable city had created the conditions that were indispensable for the growth of impressionistic music. Nowhere else in the world could painters, poets, and musicians have come into a companionship so close as to enable them to exchange the essential features of their various arts, and to give and take so liberally and successfully. It is very significant that impressionism outside of France lost its artistic refinement immediately. Even such talented composers as Ottorino Respighi and Casella in Italy and a number of composers in Germany, Russia, Poland, Austria, England, and America could attain to impressionistic music only at second hand, with the visible label of imitation. The only exception seems to be Frederick Delius, who is called an English composer but who spent the greater part of his artistic career in the vicinity of Paris and was thoroughly imbued with the Parisian spirit.

The next steps in the reaction against Wagner and the creation of the new art of the twentieth century were taken in Berlin, Vienna, and St. Petersburg. In Berlin, Ferruccio Busoni was for twenty years the advocate of all ideas that aimed seriously at creating something vitally new. As an incomparable master of the piano, as a composer, conductor, teacher, essayist, and philosopher of art, Busoni was an outstanding personality of the highest artistic and intellectual type. In Busoni all the various tendencies of the modern movement met; all were familiar to him, and all were searchingly investigated and approved or rejected. Debussy and Ravel, Mahler and Strauss, Delius and Sibelius, Stravinsky and Schönberg, Casella, Malipiero, Pizzetti, Bartok — they were all known to him minutely. Almost every night there was a gathering of young artists from many countries at his hospitable residence, Victoria Luise Platz 11 in Berlin. There were heated controversies on the artistic problems of the day in which everyone spoke freely and which were given great distinction by Busoni's own *esprit* and wit, superior understanding, mature judgment, and illuminating criticism. It is probable that in our confused, nationalistic, impoverished age such social intercourse no longer exists at all. Indeed, those gatherings were a sort of modern parallel to the Socratic symposiums of which Plato gives us so vivid a picture.

Busoni's amazing versatility appears in his compositions — almost unknown in America, except for a few Bach transcriptions. He tried out all the various new tendencies, reducing them to an extract which gave a strange flavor to the fundamental substance of his natural and individual manner of expression without seriously affecting it. By this long process of distillation he finally arrived at a highly concentrated essence of the really valuable constituents. This constant refining, this spirituality and concentration, this absence of everything unessential and commonplace, this simple presentation of extremely difficult and complicated problems gives his style a certain severity and exclusiveness. Popular traits are almost entirely absent, save in the occasional allusion to some gay Italian tune. This accounts for the strange fact that the extremely valuable music of so great an artist should be so little known. The fact is that he addresses an esoteric circle of highly cultivated, fastidious connoisseurs. His artistic testament he deposited in his opera, *Dr. Faust*, to which he had written his own libretto, a drama of extraordinary poetic qualities. *Dr. Faust* is one of the most masterly products of our age, but because of its austerity and the loftiness of its ideas it will probably never be accessible to the mass of the theatrical public. It has been repeatedly produced on festive occasions in Germany, always making a profound impression on those able to follow its high flight. By birth and education half Italian, half German, Busoni combined in his personality and in his art the characteristic traits of both nationalities. The Italian vivacity and gaiety, simplicity, perspicuity, grace and beauty of form, and the Germanic Faustian intellectuality, idealism, weight of contents, and emotional fervor are blended in his art into a unique compound that has almost no parallel. His ultimate ideal was a neoclassicism founded on Bach and Mozart, the masters he most ardently revered, in which there should be combined Bach's constructive art, the logic of his polyphony, Mozart's clearness, grace, and elegance, and all the achievements of modern harmonic and orchestral art.

Busoni's neoclassicism has had considerable influence in Germany as well as in Italy. One can perceive this tendency in the music of Hindemith and Ernst Toch, and of the Italian artists Casella, Malipiero, and Pizzetti. Paul Hindemith, the most successful of this group, shows the anti-romantic tendency, the strict construction, the linear polyphony of Busoni, to which he adds other traits still more modernistic and productive of controversy — the atonality of Schönberg, the dynamic quality of Stravinsky, with its machine-like rhythm, and the quality of the grotesque that is also Stravinsky's. In his best works he succeeds in combining all these various foreign traits so happily that the total impression is one of real individuality.

Each of the great capitals of the musical world — Vienna, Paris, Berlin, Milan, St. Petersburg, and lately London, New York, and Moscow — has its own artistic atmosphere. The atmosphere of Paris and Berlin has already been briefly analyzed. If we turn to the Vienna of the twentieth century we find ourselves in a city of the highest artistic and literary culture, on a soil from which the most precious music of modern times has grown abundantly. Haydn, Mozart, Beethoven, and Schubert are the patron saints of the Viennese music spirit; later Brahms came under its fascinating influence, with the happiest results, and Johann Strauss in the more popular Viennese waltz finds, so to speak, a common factor for all the manifold musical utterances of Vienna, from the symphony to the ballroom. This animated, graceful, enticingly sensuous Viennese spirit continues into the twentieth century, and Mahler is powerfully affected by it. After 1900, however, it begins slowly to disintegrate. The *feuilleton* of the Viennese newspapers, an unexcelled Viennese specialty, much imitated in Germany, shows the popularization of the refinement and culture that is characteristic of Vienna, its change into smaller coin, so to speak. But in the contrary direction an ever-growing intellectual subtlety, a craving for the ultimate in refinement, and a spirit of dialectical sophistry animate the younger Viennese intelligentsia. Here is the home of radical musical modernism, the offspring of the fine old Viennese musical instinct combined with Jewish acuteness, wit, pathos, and energy of will.

This radical modernism began with Mahler and was expanded into a complicated scholastic system by Arnold Schönberg, the central figure of modernistic music. This Viennese musician is the boldest artist of our century. Not satisfied with adding certain new characteristics to the music of his time, he resolved to create a new basis for music, to overthrow the existing state of music, and to build up by himself a new art. He began about 1900 as a Wagnerian, with a sextet, *Verklärte Nacht*, which even as late as 1937 was the only one of his works at all well known in America. One would suppose that so famous a man as Schönberg, who has made his home in America for nearly four years, would find occasions for acquainting the public with his sensational art, the harvest of forty years' work, and that the American public would be curious to hear what the music of the real leader of revolutionary modernism is like. But all that is asked for is his earliest notable work, which echoes *Tristan und Isolde* and appeals to the average taste by its romantic sound, its emotional atmosphere, and its singable melody of the Wagnerian type. Strangest of all, Schönberg himself, as conductor, almost invariably chooses this work of his youth, which, valuable and well-sounding as it is, gives no idea at all of his mature work. Is he himself perhaps afraid of offending the public by his later scores? Or has the great revolutionary, the undaunted fighter, become tired and spiritless? How paradoxical!

But Schönberg's career is full of paradoxes. Of all modern composers he is the one who has exerted the greatest influence on young artists in all musical countries, the one about whom more has been written than any other musician of our day. The entire musical world acknowledges him as the real father of the modernistic movement. Yet his works are little played, even in Europe, and in America nine-tenths of his music is almost entirely unknown. In the last ten years Schönberg's new works have been played once or twice and then laid aside. There are plausible reasons for these failures, to be found partly in the compositions, partly in the attitude of the public, but the curious fact remains that one of the most famous composers of our time is known only to a small number of people in close personal contact with him, and that his fame rests on an exceedingly small number of compositions. His great celebrity is not founded on his music, which is actually unknown to the musical world at large, but on the extensive propaganda of a little party intensely interested in the cause of modernistic music: a little coterie of enthusiastic pupils, radical young composers, a few conductors, his publishers, who specialize in modernistic music (the Vienna Universal Edition), and a few progressive critics in various countries, intent on discussing sensational matters. The musical public, however, has nothing at all to do with Schönberg's fame. This statement is not made in a derogatory sense, but only in order to point out the unique and abnormal peculiarity of Schönberg's position in contemporary music.

Two labels have been attached to Schönberg's music: atonality and the twelve-tone technique. These terms seem to become more mysterious the more one ponders over them. Atonality, according to the Schönberg experts, means the abolishing of major and minor tonality, or any other type of tonality, by overthrowing the harmonic functions of the tonic, dominant, and subdominant, and of the cadence. We are told that the old conceptions of tonality and tonal functions are exhausted and old-fashioned, and that a truly modern composer cannot have anything to do with those antiquated ideas without providing for himself a *testimonium paupertatis*. And as to the twelve-tone technique, we are informed by officially accredited experts that it is one of the greatest discoveries of modern music, providing the long-sought new basis for modern music. The twelve-tone technique has been evolved by Schönberg on an atonal and mathematical basis to replace the antiquated ideas of tonality, cadence, and modulation. It uses the twelve half-tones of the tempered scale, the old-fashioned chromatic scale, in an entirely new manner. Every piece is built solely on one formula of several tones, chosen by the composer from the twelve chromatic tones. For mysterious reasons a strict twelve-tone composition does not allow of the repetition of a tone in the basic formula. One might call such a formula simply a motive, but while the old-fashioned motive had to be invented by the action of the inner ear the twelve-tone formula can be found by mere arithmetic. A piece may be built, for example, on the formula 2, 4, 8, 7, 9, 12, meaning in the twelve-tone series, C to C an octave higher, the chromatic tones corresponding to the numerals. In such a piece, wherever one looks, one sees 2, 4, 8, 7, 9, 12, in a vertical and in a horizontal direction, in melody and in harmony, in inversion, in Schönberg's favorite crab inversion, in diminution and augmentation, in stretta, and so forth. In our case the formula would be as follows:

$$C\sharp - D\sharp - G - F\sharp - G\sharp - B$$
$$2 \quad 4 \quad 8 \quad 7 \quad 9 \quad 12$$

But if one asks what the value of this atonality and the twelve-tone technique is, there is great embarrassment among the commentators. We cannot, of course, attempt here to solve the intricate problems of the Schönbergian theories in a few sentences, but the results of years of observing, analyzing, and testing these theories may be briefly listed.

Atonality is a mystic conception, half hidden by a cloud of vagueness. A real definition of the term, consistent with the actual facts in radically modern composition, is impossible. Schönberg himself has lately considered it advisable to restrain the enthusiasm of his overzealous prophets, and has repeatedly declared that the term "atonal" is not happily chosen. It has no really definite meaning and has been applied to the curious, though often highly interesting harmony of Schönberg in default of a more adequate and correct theoretical explanation. No real atonality exists, or is conceivable, so long as music remains what all the world, including the Schönberg party, calls music. As no architect can do without the idea of the center of gravity, of perpendicular or horizontal line, so no composer can dispense with tonality; if he did his musical structure must instantly collapse.

As a matter of fact, since even the supposedly positive term "tonality" is generally misunderstood, all discussions of atonality are quite aimless. Far from having exhausted tonality, the music of 1930 has not even approached hundreds of possible tonalities. Major and minor scales are only a small fraction of them. There are, for example, the church modes, the various pentatonic systems, the various Oriental and exotic tonalities, the hundred and twelve tonalities discovered by Busoni when he experimented to find out in how many different ways it was possible to fill out the octave C–C above, on the piano. Though we do not yet possess an adequate theory of tonality, we get excited about a nebulous atonality. Moreover, the Schönberg atonality has lately met a rival in a second type of Viennese atonality evolved by Matthias Hauer. What is generally called atonality is only a disguised tonality which may be discovered by sufficiently acute observation.

As to the twelve-tone technique, it is made for the eye, not for the ear. To look at the score of a recent Schönberg opus is a rare treat for one who understands what logical organic construction means, but the most cultivated ear does not recognize even a fraction of all this admirable organic construction, and hears only a mass of rather unpleasant tones, without recognizing their melodic, harmonic, or rhythmical coherence. Twelve-tone composition in its strict form is possible only if the composer is quite indifferent as to the sound effects of his tone-calculations and accepts any combination of sounds as they happen to present themselves in consequence of the ingenious engineering job he has done. Everything would be in perfect order if one were largehearted and unprejudiced enough to call *any* sound effect produced by logical action good and correct. Unfortunately, only a little band of fanatic new-sounders assume this ascetic attitude. Ninety-nine out of a hundred musicians and music lovers are not yet willing to force the ear into utter submission to the calculating intellect. Any regard for quality, color, expressiveness, even — if one may mention it — beauty of sound, would immediately overthrow the entire twelve-tone structure. Form is perfected at the expense of sound; one vital factor maintains itself only by the sacrifice of another vital factor. Here the principle of dictatorship is manifest in music. Here we are witnessing a musically perverse state of affairs: the substitution of the eye for the ear.

Does all this criticism mean that Schönberg's discoveries are senseless? Not at all. His ideas have given a strong impetus to modern music and have led to the discovery of possibilities for striking harmonic and melodic effects and new constructive features. But others seem to have profited more by his discoveries than he has. Alban Berg, Stravinsky, Hindemith, Krenek, and others have interpreted the speculations of Schönberg in a more musicianly manner than the inventor himself. It is probable that he is a greater theorist than creative artist. Like Moses, he has led musicians to the frontiers of the new land, but it has been reserved to others to exploit the new fields profitably. That immature youthful enthusiasts may be led thoroughly astray by Schönberg's difficult speculations needs no proof. Atonality had a certain vogue for about ten years, but of late it has been abandoned by even the most up-to-date composers, and in Stravinsky and Hindemith one can see a return to clearer tonality.

The twelve-tone technique, in itself a highly ingenious, though very one-sided system, may perhaps prove useful when treated less fanatically and less intolerantly, with a greater willingness to give up its tyrannical dictatorship and to amalgamate it with other systems less perilous to sound effect. The premature death of Alban Berg, Schönberg's most gifted pupil, was a severe blow to the cause of twelve-tone composition. As to sound effect, I am inclined to believe that a really well-sounding piece of twelve-tone technique is so, not on account of the application of the principle, but *in spite* of it, owing to the strong musical instinct of the composer, who more or less consciously makes a compromise with the much-abused musical ear and stretches his principles to meet the demands of the ear halfway.

The situation in Russian music needs a brief discussion. Late in the nineteenth century Russian music began to acquire international validity, mainly through Tschaikovsky, who represents the Russian version of hyper-romanticism. This is a subjectivism of the most pronounced type, which revels in extremes, from darkest melancholy to a boisterous animal *joie de vivre* of an almost brutal force. These extremes are joined by music of a very pleasant social type, Russian songs and dance tunes that appeal to everybody, and are treated with real art of sound. It is good to remember that it was Tschaikovsky's international success which paved the way for the other exponents of national Russian music. Until thirty years after his death in 1884 Moussorgsky was almost unknown outside of Russia, and his celebrity even now rests on only two of his works, the opera, *Boris Godunoff*, and the cycle of piano pieces, *Pictures at an*

Exposition, a fascinating work that has called forth about half a dozen orchestral versions by Ravel and other composers of note. Borodine also reached western Europe and America only in the twentieth century. Rimsky-Korsakoff alone had a success at all comparable to that of Tschaikovsky. Two other highly remarkable Russian masters, Glazunoff and Taneiev, have not enjoyed an international success comparable to the esteem and respect accorded to them in Russia. Much more attention has been paid by the musical world to four composers who represent different phases of more recent Russian music. They are Scriabine and Rachmaninoff in the romantic camp, Stravinsky and Prokofieff in the modernistic, anti-romantic camp.

In Alexander Scriabine an exaggerated romanticism reduces itself almost *ad absurdum*. His musical genealogy consists of Chopin, Wagner, Tschaikovsky (though hated by Scriabine), plus the powerful extra-musical figure of Dostoevski. Passionate lyricism in a veritable frenzy, orgiastic turbulence combined with a strange mysticism and fatalism, and a pantheistic religious ecstasy are the characteristic traits of Scriabine's music. Though his music contains hardly anything of Russian folklore – so profusely used by all the other Russians – both his pessimism and his exaltation are very Russian, as is also the mixture of the two. The combination of Nirvana and an ecstatic affirmation of the joy of living is enigmatic to the Western mind, but it is thoroughly Russian. At the present time Scriabine's large orchestral works (*Prometheus*, *Poème de l'extase*, *Le Divin Poème*) with their mystical, orphic traits, their Oriental Satanism, seem to be losing favor. His later piano sonatas, however, are constantly gaining in interest as most remarkable documents of ultramodern ideas of harmony, form, construction, and expression which point to the future.

Sergei Rachmaninoff as a composer is a romanticist who raises no problems. His international celebrity rests on his piano concertos and smaller piano pieces, and on his magnificent achievements as a pianist. Radically modernistic aims are foreign to his art, which is a recapitulation, a last enthusiastic glance backward toward the beautiful regions of nineteenth-century romanticism, rather than labor on barren new soil.

Sergei Prokofieff, a generation younger than Rachmaninoff, is also an admirable pianist and a composer of brilliant and effective piano music. But his mind is of a totally different order. A dazzling play of sounds interests him more than emotion. An entirely unsentimental jester, mocker, caricaturist, he delights in musical antics and buffoonery, taken over into music from the dance virtuosos of the Russian ballet. In this narrowly limited genre he is a master second to none save Stravinsky, who is the originator of this musical type.

Igor Stravinsky is the most successful master of modernistic music. In the list of his works for the last twenty-five years we see more plainly than anywhere else the unrest, instability, and experimentalism of the modernistic movement. There is not one Stravinsky style; there are ten styles. Almost every two years Stravinsky surprises the world with a sensational new variation — sometimes even transformation — of his art. He is the father of the grotesque, mechanical, static, and objective music that was later adopted by Hindemith under the name of *neue Sachlichkeit*. He was in partnership with Schönberg in the matter of atonality, but the two did not agree, and each now likes to call the other a nuisance. What contradictory styles! On one occasion he writes music on a colossal scale, with an orgy of color and excitement, as in the *Sacre du printemps*; on another, as in the *Histoire du soldat*, he is content with the bare skeleton of an orchestra. At one time he is infatuated by rhythm let loose, like an uncontrolled motor car in a mad race. At another, as in *Oedipus Rex*, static music, of a statue-like rigidity, is the creed of the season. Now he outdoes Schönberg in contempt of tonality; now, as in *Apollon Musagète*, he finds a new delight in using C major and plain triads in tonic and dominant of a primitive type, *à la* Lully. For a time the word "futuristic" was his watchword. Of late he has become historically retrospective and has attempted a renaissance of the music of the seventeenth, eighteenth, and nineteenth centuries — Lully, Handel, Scarlatti, Tschaikovsky, Weber. Who can tell what surprises he has still in store?

Yet with all this apparently whimsical versatility, this mimicry, these contradictions in style, Stravinsky is nevertheless a great master of art. His universal success is explained by the fact that, unlike Schönberg, he never forgets the natural demands of the ear; he is never indifferent to acoustic effect. Moreover, the real basis of his music is the elementary power of rhythm, and his masterly use of rhythmical means assures even his otherwise abstruse pieces of an immediate effect, so that they impress even old-fashioned listeners. Personally I am inclined to consider his earlier ballet music, especially *Petrouchka*, his real masterpieces, and am more interested in the Russian aspect of his art than in the slightly snobbish Parisian metamorphosis. But however cold some of his later music may seem, he always succeeds in shaping something that has an extraordinary formal interest, even though the contents may not have an immediate appeal for most listeners. From a style that was hyper-romantic, almost overheated, Stravinsky has moved on to a very sober, cool, classical manner. His personality is so strong that his utterances always command respect and admiration for their musicianly excellence, even if the artistic substance of his later music seems foreign to the artistic conceptions of most of his contemporaries.

The craving of the more mature and serious minds of our time for something of intrinsic worth, something durable and substantially sound in contemporary music has been too often disappointed. If one surveys recent music with the aim of discovering not merely interesting experiments and fashionable isms but an accomplished art of monumental aspect, weighty contents, and ethical values, with a philosophy of life as background, if one looks for something comparable to the achievements of Wagner or Brahms, a "great" art that satisfies many demands and appeals alike to the adherents of nineteenth-century traditions and to the young radicals of our day, one finds it not in the work of Schönberg, Stravinsky, Ravel, or Hindemith, but perhaps in Jean Sibelius, whose symphonic output within the last fifteen years has shown its creator capable of a unique spiritual elevation.

Recognition of Sibelius is not yet universal. Germany has been somewhat reluctant to acknowledge his greatness; in France and Italy he is not adequately known. But the "northern" countries, Finland, Scandinavia, England, and North America, have loudly proclaimed his glory and have given him the rank of a classic master. As yet it is too early to know whether Sibelius' art represents merely a transitory phase or an achievement of lasting value. His great celebrity to some extent has been given him "on credit," and he will have to meet his obligations in the future in order not to lose his truly enviable reputation. But so much at least can safely be said: Here is an art of intrinsic worth and substance, instead of virtuoso showmanship, brilliant technical exhibitionism, and revolutionary experimentalism. Here is music thoroughly modern in spirit, grown not in a hothouse but from its native soil, and fixed in the soil of Finland with far-reaching, firm, and densely knotted roots.

Sibelius' art has three phases: the national, the European, the cosmic. In the first phase Sibelius speaks and sings to the people of his country with the tunes, dance rhythms, and accents of Finland. This northern phase, to which almost all of his symphonic poems belong, is later expanded from a provincial dialect to a musical language of international validity. And in some of his later symphonies Sibelius passes beyond this European phase toward a still vaster horizon, beyond Scandinavia and Europe to a spiritual world where the elect spirits of humanity meet on common ground, freely discoursing on the great themes around which all higher aspirations of mind and soul revolve eternally.

Sibelius has been highly favored by fortune. For forty years he has been maintained by his government, which grants him a liberal pension without imposing on him any duties except to create as his genius moves him, the only composer in the world to be so treated. He has lived a quiet life, away from the bustle and traffic of cities, far from the nervous excitements of an artistic "career," from the activities of business managers, concert societies, and public appearances. He has been favored far beyond most men, permitted to shape his life and his art entirely in concordance with his own ideals, without the need of earning a livelihood, winning celebrity, or competing with others, and, last but not least, without having to become a martyr to his ideals and succumbing in the fight, like Mozart, Schubert, and Moussorgsky. Can an artist be happier?

It is time to sum up. It would be extremely interesting to discuss at length what the younger generation in the various countries aspires to, what its aesthetic creed consists in. But it is forbidden by the limits set for this book and by the obvious impossibility of dealing authoritatively with trends that are constantly in flux, constantly changing, without having reached the status of a determined style. In the International Society for Contemporary Music — founded in 1924 and ably and wisely presided over by Professor Edward Dent of Cambridge University — all these various tendencies meet on common ground. The yearly music festivals of the society in various European countries show an interesting cross section through the radically modernistic achievements of the various nations. Experimentalism is welcomed, and masterpieces of mature art have been rare guests at these festivals. Germany, France, Austria, Italy, England, Hungary, Scandinavia, Spain, Poland, Czechoslovakia, and the United States have contributed to these festival programs, which represent a sort of experimental laboratory for trying out the effects of various new technical methods.

This new "International" in music is parallel in a way to the socialist or communist "International" in the labor movement. Only musical radicalism is patronized here. Certainly no union of this kind ever existed anywhere before the twentieth century. We even have, like the workers, three Internationals, each one characteristic of its epoch. The first International Society for Music, founded in 1899 and dissolved in 1914, was rather of the wealthy bourgeois type. It did excellent work through international collaboration in musicological research, through the publication of valuable scientific periodicals, and through incomparably brilliant and sumptuous congresses in Leipzig, Basle, Vienna, London, and Paris. Governments, city administrations, academies, universities, music publishers, eminent scholars, world-famous virtuosos, conductors, opera houses, orchestras, and cathedral choirs united their efforts — supported by money given by wealthy members and friends of music — to make those international congresses memorable festivals, equally fertile for science, art, culture, and social entertainment. After the war nothing so luxurious was possible for impoverished musical scholars and musicians. The "Second International," founded in 1921, is a very unpretentious gathering, a restricted club of professional musicologists, scholars, scientists. Its activities are a reflection of the spirit of *neue Sachlichkeit* or new objectivity, the cry of the years 1920–1930. A very sober, unsentimental attitude characterizes this Union Musicologique, whose quiet work has almost no public recognition. The "Third International," with its radically modernistic, revolutionary spirit, has been already described in some detail.

The present chapter has dealt with the chief problems of modern music, with its passionate striving, its agitated revolutionary spirit, its untiring search for new effects of sound, rhythm, and color, its great interest in formal problems. Technique of composition has been amazingly advanced, and one who really masters the manifold, intricate problems of modern composition ought not to have much difficulty in expressing anything that fills his mind and soul. But here the tragic shortcoming of recent music glares out: wonderful technique and few ideas, prodigious skill and emptiness of soul, great ingenuity wasted on paltry conceptions. Never in the entire history of music have young composers been accorded so much attention and honor as in the years 1920–1930. But this younger generation, at least in Europe, has distinguished itself rather by pretense and by an unscrupulous use of sensationalism than by honest artistic effort. The prevailing spirit of satire, the interest in the grotesque, the predilection for snobbisms of all kinds, the cheap pleasure of trying to *épater le bourgeois* — all these traits fit the art of music less than any other art. Caricature and satire, parody and burlesque, cannot without serious injury be made the main substance of music. A true ring is wanted in music, not a false one, and at present the false ring prevails. But how can it be otherwise in an age so distorted, so out of joint, so grotesque, and so deprived of sound reason? There is no lack of talent and skill in present-day music, but there is a decided lack of ethics, of seriousness, and of the spirit of responsibility.

I am perfectly convinced that this transitional age of ours is the low land between two chains of high mountains. Nature's creative power can be momentarily repressed but not destroyed. Out of the greatest destruction new life springs up again, and out of oppressive doubts a new clearness of mind must inevitably arise in due time. When this time will arrive cannot be predicted with any degree of certainty. But close observation makes it seem probable that the worst years of the artistic depression are past, that the spirit of negation is being superseded by a more positive belief. When that happens, the splendid technical material accumulated by our experimental activity will be properly utilized in the upbuilding of a truly great new art, and the nervous laboring of the postwar generation will not have been altogether futile after all.

POSTSCRIPT, 1947

MORE than ten years have elapsed since this book was written, and important changes in the musical situation have taken place, changes that demand attention in 1947. Most significant, American music, formerly almost negligible in the survey of international music, has advanced so considerably in artistic value and variety that it is beginning to assert itself as a power. The Hitler regime in Germany and the Second World War have caused not only a catastrophic decline of Germany's musical supremacy, but also more or less collapse in almost all other European countries. In the years from 1930 to 1947 America has greatly profited from this European debacle, since a great number of European celebrities have sought refuge and have been cordially welcomed here. Arnold Schönberg and Igor Stravinsky, the widely diverging leaders of the modern music movement, have both settled in America, and Bela Bartok, Paul Hindemith, Darius Milhaud, Ernest Bloch, Ernst Toch, Ernst Krenek, Kurt Weill, Castelnuovo Tedesco, and other European musicians of acknowledged rank, have in late years resided in the United States. All these by their teaching have influenced America's younger generation. The young German and Austrian composers referred to previously as champions of sensational and even subversive modernism have now, in America, come to maturity, and have stabilized their former reckless adoration of parody, grotesque, snobbism. A sounder, more serious spirit of artistic responsibility has in the last decade become manifest in American music. This change of mentality augurs well for the future.

American composers have advanced considerably on the road toward a national school. As far back as 1894 Antonin Dvořák pointed out the tunes of the Negroes and Indians as source material for a distinctive American music, but he found at that time more opposition than approval. Twenty-five years later, however, a younger generation of American composers began to be interested in building up a new national music. In the meantime the music of the Indians had been explored by competent folklorists; still more importance was attributed to the spirituals and the jazz music of the Negroes; and finally, the discovery of a vastly extended treasure of real, rural folk music all over the United States began to influence American compositions. About ten thousand of these genuine American folksongs have been assembled on records in the Library of Congress in Washington. American composers have at last become conscious of their national heritage and obligations.

This process has gone through several different phases. "Symphonic Jazz" became an ingredient of a number of American orchestral scores. Henry Gilbert, the first American composer intent on a characteristic American style derived from the folk music of the white people of English descent, with admixtures of Creole, Indian, and Negro tunes and rhythms, had a remarkable success at the International Festival in Frankfurt in 1927, with his orchestral work "The Dance in Place Congo." Three years earlier, in 1924, Paul Whiteman took Jazz to Germany for the first time, and George Gershwin, playing his famous "Rhapsody in Blue," was boisterously applauded on that occasion. Later in the twenties American composers vied with each other in depicting scenes from American life and landscape in compositions loudly acclaimed at that time, but forgotten a decade later. Programmatic scores like Frederick Converse's "Flivver

Ten Million," Carpenter's "Adventures in a Perambulator," Philip James's "Station WGBZX," Deems Taylor's "Through the Looking-Glass," Emerson Whithorne's "New York Nights and Days" and "Moon Trail" showed considerable progress in modern orchestral technique, but also a materialistic outlook on aesthetic problems that made these works appear somewhat out of style in the thirties, when a younger generation with new aesthetic ideas on a higher spiritual plane took over the leadership.

At present composers such as Roy Harris, Aaron Copland, Randall Thompson, Virgil Thomson, William Schuman, Walter Piston, Howard Hanson, and Samuel Barber represent American music at its highest level. Most of them have been more or less influenced by the neo-classicism of Stravinsky and Hindemith; their aim is not descriptive, programmatic music but "absolute" music of the Bach type, with its terse, logical structure, its rhythmic vigor and driving power, its contrapuntal virtuosity, its novel dissonant acrid harmony. They all stress Americanism, but differ in their approach to their goal. Roy Harris and Aaron Copland, for instance, show in their symphonic scores a thematic invention in close touch with the recently discovered American folklore, while Piston and Hanson believe that an American spirit and color will emanate from the music of a composer in whom the American spirit and idealism are really alive, even without actual quotation of American folksong or dance. Serge Koussevitzky, the famous conductor of the Boston Symphony Orchestra, has done more than any other conductor for the cause of American music. In his twenty-three years in Boston the new American music has been encouraged more liberally and systematically than anywhere else, while the Berkshire summer festivals and the music center at Tanglewood, which he directs, have become an incomparable source of musical education, for thousands of young professional students and for hundreds of thousands of music lovers.[1]

Music in Latin America, formerly completely unknown in

---

[1] For a more complete analysis of the various trends in recent American music see my *Serge Koussevitzky, the Boston Symphony Orchestra and the New American Music* (1946).

North America, has in the last fifteen years been explored and on rare occasions performed in a few of our music centers. Books by Nicolas Slonimsky, Gilbert Chase, Charles L. Seeger, and others [2] have surveyed the ground, and distinguished musicians from Central and South America have been invited to perform some of their works in New York, Boston, and elsewhere. Best known are Carlos Chavez from Mexico, and Heitor Villa-Lobos and Camargo Guarnieri, both representative Brazilian masters.

A hasty review of what has happened in the musical world outside of the Americas shows that its center is distinctly moving away from Berlin, Vienna, and Paris to America, as a result of the destructive activities of Hitlerism and the prolonged Second World War. Neither Germany nor Austria has been able in the last ten years to produce musical works of art fit to win access to other countries. Russia has been the only Continental country productive of music sufficiently elevated to claim international validity. Prokofieff's Fifth Symphony and Seventh Piano Sonata have been acclaimed in American concert halls, and his opera based on Tolstoy's monumental *War and Peace* has been accepted for performance by the New York Metropolitan Opera. Shostakovich, with his symphonies numbered 5 to 9, has caused quite an agitation in America. Besides these two leading Russian composers, Aram Katchaturian and Dmitry Kabalevsky have won attention, the former with a piano concerto based on the florid oriental folk music of the Caucasian people, the latter with a brilliant piano sonata. In England, the work of Benjamin Britten, a young composer hardly known at all in the thirties, has revealed a new personality of high rank in dramatic music. His "Peter Grimes," commissioned by the Koussevitzky Foundation, made a sensation when Leonard Bernstein conducted its first performance at the Tanglewood Music Center in August, 1946, while his second successful opera, "The Rape of Lucretia," has been acclaimed in several European opera houses. The new Fifth Symphony of Vaughan Williams, the most distinguished personality in English music, has been heard in New York and

---

[2] A more complete list of the books on Latin American music is found in Willi Apel's *Harvard Dictionary of Music* (1944), in the article "Latin-American Music," pp. 393, 394.

Boston. Not sensational or modernistic, contemplative rather than exciting, this music has intimate charms of its own, and a mellow, epic sound that makes it a late descendant of the great classic English music of the sixteenth and seventeenth centuries.

New French music has been conspicuous for its absence from American programs, although a few isolated works have been presented by guest conductors from Paris in New York and Boston. A new Symphony for Strings by Arthur Honegger reveals no new traits in the vigorous, unromantic, constructive style of this composer, who for twenty-five years has been a highly esteemed representative of modern French music. Darius Milhaud, a member of the famous "Groupe Les Six" of 1919, together with Honegger, has lately advanced to the front ranks of French music, but for about seven years he has been a resident of California, teaching at Mills College and creating numerous new works which reflect his Jewish descent, his French education, and his American affiliations. The most powerful of his recent works, his Second Symphony, was heard for the first time in a Boston Symphony concert, conducted by himself, December 20, 1946. A valuable addition to modern symphonic literature, this work, commissioned by the Koussevitzky Foundation, is dedicated to the memory of Mme. Natalie Koussevitzky. New names in French music, hardly known at all in America, are Jean Françaix and Olivier Messiaen. Françaix, a young musician endowed with the productivity of Hindemith, has been recommended to American attention by Nadia Boulanger in her lectures and concerts, where some of his pleasant minor works have been heard, but we are still waiting for his representative larger works. Messiaen's music has created quite a stir in Paris; bold modernism applied to music of an ecclesiastic character seems to be his characteristic formula. Pierre Monteux with his San Francisco Orchestra is just giving American audiences their first taste of Messiaen's controversial music.

Recent Czechoslovakian music at its best is represented by Bohuslav Martinu, who for a number of years has lived in America. His works are concerned more with a modern, cosmopolitan style of absolute music than with exploiting the rich Czech folksong material. His Second Symphony, commissioned by the Koussevitzky Foundation, is one of the most remarkable of modern symphonic works; while his Concerto Grosso, his Violin Concerto, his Concerto for Two Pianos, all written in America, may by their content and style claim a place in American as well as in Czech music.

Of recent music in the Scandinavian countries, Denmark, Norway, Sweden, and Finland, we are still ignorant, though the symphonies of the greatest Scandinavian master, Jean Sibelius, are frequently heard in America.

What has happened during the last ten years in Italy and Spain is almost totally unknown at present in America, and this statement applies alike to new works of accredited masters such as Malipiero, Casella, and Pizzeti, as well as to the activities of a number of newcomers. Manuel de Falla, the leading master of Spain, expatriated himself and spent the last years of his life in Argentina, where he died in 1946. His distinguished works have acquired universal validity and are constantly heard.

This brief sketch of the present status of the world's music presents indeed a sad picture of ruin and disorder. Its only bright spot emerges in the fact that North America has become the heir and trustee of the world's best music. This honors our country but also imposes new responsibilities. May they be recognized and fulfilled with wisdom and good will!

BIBLIOGRAPHY

THE following bibliography does not aim at completeness. The nature of this book and a regard for space have made it advisable to limit the list, with a few exceptions, to books dealing exclusively with music; consequently, only the most significant works in the immense literature of music have been chosen for inclusion. Good English translations of foreign works and modern reprints of old books have been listed whenever possible.

INTRODUCTION

Coussemaker, C. E. H., *Scriptorum de musica medii aevi novam seriem* . . . , 4 vols. (Milan, 1931).

Expert, Henry, *Les Maitres Musiciens de la Renaissance français*, 23 vols. (Paris, 1894–1908).

Gerbert, Martin, *Scriptores ecclesiastici de musica sacra potissimum*, 3 vols. (Milan, 1931).

CHAPTER I

Abert, Hermann, *Die Lehre vom Ethos in der griechischen Musik* (Leipzig, 1899).

—— "Die Antike," in Guido Adler, *Handbuch der Musikgeschichte* (Frankfurt, 1924).

Bellermann, Friedrich, *Die Tonleitern und Musiknoten der Griechen* (Berlin, 1847).

Fortlage, Karl, *Das musikalische System der Griechen in seiner Urgestalt* (Leipzig, 1847).

Gevaert, François Auguste, *Histoire et théorie de la musique de l'antiquité*, 2 vols. (Gand, 1875–81).

Jan, Karl von, *Musici scriptores graeci* (Leipzig, 1899).

Kralik, Richard von, *Altgriechische Musik* (Stuttgart, 1900).

Reinach, Théodore, *La Musique grecque* (Paris, 1926).

Riemann, Hugo, *Handbuch der Musikgeschichte*, vol. I (Leipzig, 1904).

Sachs, Curt, "Ein babylonischer Hymnus," *Archiv für Musikwissenschaft*, vol. VII (Leipzig, 1925).

—— "Die Musik der Antike," in Ernst Bücken, *Handbuch der Musikwissenschaft* (Potsdam, 1928).

Wolf, Johannes, *Handbuch der Notationskunde*, vol. I (Leipzig, 1913).

In addition, see Plutarch's *De musica*.

276 BIBLIOGRAPHY

CHAPTER II

Dreves, G. M., *Aurelius Ambrosius "der Vater des Kirchengesanges"* (Freiburg, 1893).

Fleischer, Oskar, *Neumen-studien*, 3 vols. (Leipzig, 1895–1904).

Flood, W. H. Grattan, *A History of Irish Music* (Dublin, 1913).

Gevaert, F. A., *Les Origines du chant liturgique de l'église latine* (Gand, 1890).

—— *La Melopée antique dans le chant de l'église latine* (Gand, 1905).

Huré, Jean, *St. Augustin musicien* (Paris, 1924).

Idelsohn, A. Z., *Hebräisch- orientalischer Melodienschatz*, 5 vols. (Leipzig, 1914–29).

—— *Jewish Music in Its Historical Development* (New York, 1929).

—— "Der Jüdische Tempelgesang," in Guido Adler, *Handbuch der Musikgeschichte* (Frankfurt, 1924).

Mocquereau, Dom André, *Paléographie musicale* (Solesmes, 1899).

Pothier, Dom Joseph, *Liber gradualis* (Tournai, 1883).

Riemann, Hugo, *Handbuch der Musikgeschichte*, vol. II, pt. 1 (Leipzig, 1913).

Schubiger, Anselm, *Die Sängerschule St. Gallens* (Einsiedeln, 1858).

Ursprung, Otto, "Die Katholische Kirchenmusik," in Ernst Bücken, *Handbuch der Musikwissenschaft* (Potsdam, 1928).

Wagner, Peter, *Einführung in die gregorianischen Melodien*, 3 vols. (Leipzig, 1911–21).

Wellesz, Egon, *Byzantinische Musik* (Breslau, 1927).

Werner, J., *Notkers Sequenzen* (1901).

See also St. Augustine's *Confessions* and *De musica;* Boethius' *De institutione musica;* Cassiodorus' *Institutiones musicae*, in Martin Gerbert, *Scriptores ecclesiastici de musica sacra potissimum* (Milan, 1931); the Solesmes edition of *La Messe et l'office* (Rome, Tournai, 1903); and Dom Cuthbert Butler's *Sancti Benedicti regula monachorum* (Freiburg, 1912).

CHAPTER III

Aubry, Pierre, *Trouvères et troubadours* (Paris, 1909).

Beck, Johann B., *La Musique des troubadours* (Paris, 1910).

Besseler, Heinrich, "Die Musik des Mittelalters und der Renaissance," in Ernst Bücken, *Handbuch der Musikwissenschaft* (Potsdam, 1928).

Guillaume de Machaut, complete edition of his works, ed. Friedrich Ludwig (Leipzig, 1926–34).

Hagen, Friedrich von der, *Minnesinger*, 5 vols (Leipzig, 1838–56).

Lavignac, Albert, *Encyclopédie de la musique*, 6 vols. (Paris, 1913–31).

Ludwig, Friedrich, "Mittelalterliche Musik," in Guido Adler, *Handbuch der Musikgeschichte* (Frankfurt, 1924).

Neumark, David, *Geschichte der jüdischen Philosophie des Mittelalters*, 2 vols. (Berlin, 1907–28).

The Oxford History of Music, vols. I, II (Oxford, 1901–05).

Riemann, Hugo, *Geschichte der Musiktheorie im IX–XIX Jahrhundert* (Berlin, 1920).

—— *Handbuch der Musikgeschichte*, vol. I, pt. 2, vol. II, pt. 1 (Leipzig, 1905–07).

Le Roman de Fauvel (facsimile, Paris, 1907).

Wolf, Johannes, *Sing- und Spielmusik aus älterer Zeit* (Leipzig, 1931).

See in addition the *Opus majus* of Roger Bacon and the *Physionomia seu de secretis naturae* of Michael Scotus.

CHAPTER IV

Ambros, A. W., and Leichtentritt, Hugo, *Geschichte der Musik*, chapter on Palestrina, vol. IV (Leipzig, 1911).

Isaak, Heinrich, *Choralis Constantinus*, in *Denkmäler der Tonkunst in Österreich* (Vienna, 1894–).

Kinkeldey, Otto, "Music and Music Printing in Incunabula," *Papers of the Bibliographical Society of America*, vol. XXVI (Chicago, 1932).

Leichtentritt, Hugo, *Geschichte der Motette* (Leipzig, 1908).

Orlando di Lasso, works (Leipzig, 1894–).

Palestrina, Giovanni Pierluigi da, works, complete edition (Leipzig, 1862–93).

Schmidt, Anton, *Petrucci* (1845).

Squire, William Barclay, *Notes on Early Music Printing* (London, 1896).

Ursprung, Otto, "Die Katholische Kirchenmusik," in Ernst Bücken, *Handbuch der Musikwissenschaft* (Potsdam, 1928).

Vogel, Emil, *Bibliothek der gedruckten weltlichen Vokalmusik Italians . . . 1500–1700*, 2 vols. (Berlin, 1892).

Winterfeld, Carl von, *Johannes Gabrieli und sein Zeitalter*, 3 vols. (Berlin, 1834).

See also Baldassare Castiglione, *Il Libro del Cortegiano* (1528), of which there are a number of English translations.

CHAPTER V

Blume, Friedrich, *Die evangelische Kirchenmusik* (Potsdam, 1933).

Forster'sches Liederbuch, modern score edition by Robert Eitner (Leipzig, 1902).

Hassler, Hans Leo, works, in *Denkmäler deutscher Tonkunst, Denkmäler der Tonkunst in Bayern,* and *Denkmäler der Tonkunst in Österreich.*

Leichtentritt, Hugo, *36 mehrstimmige Lieder alter deutscher Meister* (Leipzig, 1906).

Liliencron, Rochus von, *Deutsches Leben im Volkslied* (Stuttgart, 1884).

Locheimer Liederbuch, photographic reproduction (Berlin, 1925).

Moser, H. J., *Geschichte der deutschen Musik,* vol. I (Stuttgart and Berlin, 1930).

—— *Paul Hofhaimer* (Stuttgart and Berlin, 1929).

Otts'ches Liederbuch, modern score edition by Robert Eitner (Berlin, 1876).

Schünemann, Georg, *Geschichte der deutschen Schulmusik* (Leipzig, 1928).

Walther, Johann, *Ein Wittenbergisch-Gesangkbüchlein* (Wittenberg, 1524).

See in addition *Der Theuerdank* and *Der Weiszkunig* of the Emperor Maximilian; Albrecht Dürer, *Triumphzug Kaiser Maximilians; Epistolae virorum obscurorum;* and Martin Luther's translation of the Bible into German.

CHAPTER VI

Ambros, A. W., and Leichtentritt, Hugo, *Geschichte der Musik,* vol. IV (Leipzig, 1911).

Benevoli, Orazio, festival mass, in *Denkmäler der Tonkunst in Österreich.*

Burkhardt, Jacob, *Der Cicerone* (Leipzig, 1910).

—— *The Civilization of the Renaissance in Italy* (London, 1928), S. G. C. Middlemore, tr.

Denkmäler deutscher Tonkunst (Leipzig, 1892–1937).

Denkmäler der Tonkunst in Bayern (Leipzig, 1900–1937).

Denkmäler der Tonkunst in Österreich (Vienna, 1894–1937).

Gray, Cecil, and Heseltine, Philip, *Carlo Gesualdo, Prince of Venosa* (London, 1926).

Kretzschmar, Hermann, *Geschichte der Oper* (Leipzig, 1919).

Leichtentritt, Hugo, "Monteverdi als Madrigalkomponist," *Quarterly Magazine of the International Musical Society*, January–March 1910.

Lully, Giovanni Battista, works, complete edition of Henry Prunières (Paris, 1930–33).

Monteverdi, Claudio, works, complete edition of G. F. Malipiero (Asolo, 1926–32).

The Oxford History of Music, vol. III (Oxford, 1902).

Purcell, Henry, works, complete edition (London, 1878–1928).

Rolland, Romain, *Musiciens d'autrefois* (Paris, 1914).

—— *Les Origines du théâtre lyrique moderne: histoire de l'opera en Europe avant Lully et Scarlatti* (Paris, 1895).

Schering, Arnold, *Geschichte des Oratoriums* (Leipzig, 1911).

Schütz, Heinrich, works, complete edition of Philipp Spitta (Leipzig, 1885–94).

Vignola, Giacomo Barozzio, *Trattato degli ordini* (*c* 1550), of which there are English editions.

Wöfflin, Heinrich, *Kunstgeschichtliche Grundbegriffe* (Munich, 1915).

CHAPTER VII

In addition to the works of Bach and Handel, see the following:

Chrysander, Friedrich, *G. F. Händel*, 3 vols. (Leipzig, 1858–67).

Leichtentritt, Hugo, *Händel* (Stuttgart and Berlin, 1924).

Pirro, André, *J. S. Bach* (Paris, 1906).

Riemann, Hugo, "Das Generalbasszeitalter," *Handbuch der Musikgeschichte*, vol. III (Leipzig, 1912).

Schweitzer, Albert, *J. S. Bach* (New York, 1911).

Spitta, Philipp, *Johann Sebastian Bach*, 2 vols. (London, 1884–85).

CHAPTER VIII

Algarotti, Francesco, *Saggio sopra l'opera in musica* (1754).

Arend, Maximilian A., *Gluck, eine Biographie* (Berlin, 1921).

Bach, Carl P. E., *Versuch über die wahre Art das Klavier zu spielen* (1753; modern reprint, Leipzig, 1925).

Dent, Edward J., *Mozart's Operas, a Critical Study* (London, 1913).

Geiringer, Karl, *Joseph Haydn* (Potsdam, 1932).

Jahn, Otto, *W. A. Mozart*, 2 vols. (Leipzig, 1923–24), ed. by Hermann Abert.

Lessing, Gotthold, *Laokoon* (1766).

Pohl, Karl F., *Joseph Haydn*, 3 vols. (Leipzig, 1878–1927).

Tiersot, Julien, *Gluck* (Paris, 1910).

Winckelmann, Johann, *Geschichte der Kunst des Altertums* (1764; Vienna, 1934).

See in addition the essays of Jean Jacques Rousseau, and the symphonies of the Mannheim School in *Denkmäler der Tonkunst in Bayern*.

CHAPTER IX

Bekker, Paul, *Beethoven* (London, 1932).

Deutsch, O. E., *Franz Schubert* (Munich, 1913).

Flower, Walter N., *Franz Schubert: the Man and His Circle* (London, 1928).

Hohenemser, Richard, *Luigi Cherubini, sein Leben und seine Werke* (Leipzig, 1913).

Rolland, Romain, *Beethoven* (New York, 1927).

Schemann, Ludwig, *Cherubini* (Berlin, 1925).

Thayer, A. W., *The Life of Ludwig van Beethoven*, 3 vols. (New York, 1925).

CHAPTER X

In addition to the letters of Felix Mendelssohn-Bartholdy, the letters and critical writings of Franz Liszt and Robert Schumann, and the collected works of Richard Wagner, see the following:

Arnim, Ludwig, and Brentano, Clemens, *Des Knaben Wunderhorn*, 3 vols. (facsimile ed., Tübingen, 1926).

Berlioz, Hector, *Memoirs of Hector Berlioz* (New York, 1932), ed. Ernest Newman.

Haym, Rudolf, *Die romantische Schule* (Berlin, 1928).

Leichtentritt, Hugo, *Analyse der Chopin'schen Klavierwerke*, 2 vols. (Berlin, 1920–21).

—— *Frédéric Chopin* (Berlin, 1905).

Niecks, Frederick, *Frederick Chopin as a Man and Musician* (London, 1888).

Scharlitt, Bernard, *Chopin* (Leipzig, 1919).

Wagner, Richard, *My Life* (New York, 1924).

Weber, Max Maria von, *The Life of an Artist* (New York, 1865).

Weissmann, Adolf, *Chopin* (Berlin and Leipzig, 1912).

See also Kant's *Kritik der Urteilskraft*, Herder's writings and collections of folk songs, especially *Stimmen der Völker*, the poems of

Eichendorff and Novalis, the essays and poems of Heine, the novels of E. T. A. Hoffmann, Wilhelm Heinse's *Ardinghello* and *Hildegard von Hohenthal*, W. W. Wackenroder's *Herzensergiessungen eines kunstliebenden Klosterbruders* (Leipzig, 1904), and Mme. de Staël's *De l'Allemagne*.

CHAPTER XI

In addition to the letters and collected writings of Franz Liszt and Richard Wagner, see the following:

Adler, Guido, *Richard Wagner: Vorlesungen gehalten an der Universität zu Wien* (Munich, 1923).

Auer, Max, *Anton Bruckner, sein Leben und Werk* (Vienna, 1934).

Bekker, Paul, *Richard Wagner: His Life in His Work* (New York, 1931), M. M. Bozman, tr.

Berlioz, Hector, *Memoirs of Hector Berlioz* (New York, 1932), ed. Ernest Newman.

Cesari, Gaetano, and Luzio, Alessandro, *I Copialettere di Giuseppe Verdi* (Milan, 1913).

Glasenapp, Carl F., *Life of Richard Wagner*, 6 vols (London, 1900–08), W. A. Ellis, tr.

Göllerich, August, *Anton Bruckner, ein Lebens- und Schaffens-bild*, 3 vols. (Regensburg, 1922–32).

Fuller-Maitland, J. A., *Brahms* (New York, 1911).

Kalbeck, Max, *Johannes Brahms*, 4 vols. (Berlin, 1904–14).

Koch, Max, *Richard Wagner*, 3 vols. (Berlin, 1907–18).

Kurth, Ernst, *Bruckner*, 2 vols. (Berlin, 1925).

——*Romantische Harmonik und ihre Krise in Wagners "Tristan"* (Bern and Leipzig, 1923).

Lorenz, Alfred O., *Das Geheimnis der Form bei Richard Wagner*, 4 vols. (Berlin, 1924–33).

May, Florence, *The Life of Johannes Brahms*, 2 vols. (London, 1905).

Monaldi, Gino, *Verdi, 1839–1898* (Turin, 1899).

Newman, Ernest, *The Life of Richard Wagner*, 2 vols. (London, 1933–37).

Niemann, Walter, *Brahms* (New York, 1930).

Perinello, Carlo, *Giuseppe Verdi* (Berlin, 1900).

Pougin, Arthur, *Verdi: An Anecdotic History of His Life and Works* (London, 1887), J. E. Matthew, tr.

Weissmann, Adolf, *Verdi* (Stuttgart, 1922).

CHAPTER XII

Bekker, Paul, *Mahlers Sinfonien* (Stuttgart, 1921).

Bowen, Catherine D., and Meck, Barbara von, *"Beloved Friend": the Story of Tchaikowsky and Nadejda von Meck* (New York, 1937).

Busoni, Ferruccio, *Von der Einheit der Musik* (Berlin, 1922).

Calvocoressi, Michel, *Moussorgsky* (London, 1919), A. E. Hull, tr.

Cœuroy, André, *La Musique française moderne* (Paris, 1922).

Dent, Edward, *Ferruccio Busoni: a Biography* (London, 1933).

Fleischer, Herbert, *Strawinsky* (Berlin, 1931).

Hill, E. B., "Maurice Ravel," *Musical Quarterly*, January 1927.

Laloy, Louis, *Claude Debussy* (Paris, 1909).

Leichtentritt, Hugo, *Ferruccio Busoni* (Leipzig, 1916).

Manuel, Roland, *Maurice Ravel et son œuvre dramatique* (Paris, 1928).

Reich, Willi, *Alban Berg* (Vienna, 1937).

Riesemann, Oskar von, *Moussorgsky* (New York, 1929), Paul England, tr.

Rimsky-Korsakoff, Nikolai, *My Musical Life* (New York, 1923), J. A. Joffe, tr.

Schloezer, Boris F., *Igor Stravinsky* (Paris, 1929).

Slonimsky, Nicolas, *Music since 1900* (New York, 1937).

Specht, Richard, *Richard Strauss und sein Werk*, 2 vols. (Leipzig, 1921).

—— *Gustav Mahler* (Berlin, 1922).

Stefan, Paul, *Gustav Mahler, a Study of His Personality and Work* (New York, 1912), T. E. Clark, tr.

Stein, R. H., *Tschaikowskij* (Stuttgart, 1927).

Steinitzer, Max, *Richard Strauss* (Berlin and Leipzig, 1911).

Stravinsky, Igor, *Chronicle of My Life* (London, 1936).

Strobel, Heinrich, *Paul Hindemith* (Mainz, 1931).

Suarés, André, *Debussy* (Paris, 1922).

Vallas, Léon, *Les Idées de Claude Debussy, musicien français* (Paris, 1927).

Tchaikovsky, Modeste, *The Life and Letters of Peter Ilich Tchaikovsky* (New York, 1906).

Wellesz, Egon, *Arnold Schönberg* (New York, 1925), W. H. Kerridge, tr.

Wolfurt, Kurt, von, *Mussórgskij* (Stuttgart, 1927).

SUPPLEMENT

Here are listed some of the most important publications between 1938 and 1947.

Abraham, Gerald, *Eight Soviet Composers* (London, 1943).
Apel, Willi, *The Notation of Polyphonic Music* (Cambridge, Mass., 1942).
—— *Harvard Dictionary of Music* (Cambridge, Mass., 1944).
Calvocoressi, M. D., *Mussorgsky* (London, 1946).
Calvocoressi, M. D., and Abraham, G., *Masters of Russian Music* (New York, 1943).
Chase, Gilbert, *The Music of Spain* (New York, 1941).
—— *A Guide to Latin-American Music* (Washington, 1945).
—— *Music in Radio Broadcasting* (New York, 1946).
David, Hans, and Mendel, Arthur, *The Bach Reader* (New York, 1945).
Davison, Archibald T., and Apel, Willi, *Historical Anthology of Music* (Cambridge, 1946).
Einstein, Alfred, *Greatness in Music* (New York, 1941).
—— *Mozart: His Character, His Work* (New York, 1945).
—— *Music in the Romantic Era* (New York, 1947).
Ellinwood, Leonard, *The Works of Francesco Landini* (Cambridge, 1939).
Ewen, David, *The Book of Modern Composers* (New York, 1942).
—— *Music Comes to America* (New York, 1947).
Geiringer, Karl, *Haydn* (New York, 1946).
Graf, Max, *Composer and Critic* (New York, 1945).
Hewett, Helen, and Pope, Isabel, *Harmonice Musices Odhecaton A* (Cambridge, Mass., 1942).
Hindemith, Paul, *The Craft of Musical Composition* (New York, 1941–43).
—— *Elementary Training for Musicians* (New York, 1946).
Howard, John Tasker, *Our American Music* (New York, 1946).
Lang, Paul H., *Music in Western Civilization* (New York, 1941).
Leichtentritt, Hugo, *Serge Koussevitzky, the Boston Symphony Orchestra and the New American Music* (Cambridge, 1946).
Reese, Gustave, *Music in the Middle Ages* (New York, 1940).
Sachs, Curt, *The History of Musical Instruments* (New York, 1940).
—— *The Rise of Music in the Ancient World* (New York, 1943).
—— *The Commonwealth of Art* (New York, 1946).
Salazar, Adolfo, *Music in Our Time* (New York, 1946).
Schillinger, Joseph, *The Schillinger System of Musical Composition* (New York, 1946).
Slonimsky, Nicolas, *Music Since 1900* (New York, 1938).
—— *Music of Latin America* (New York, 1945).

—— *The Road to Music* (New York, 1947).
—— *Thesaurus of Scales and Melodic Patterns* (New York, 1947).
Smith, Moses, *Serge Koussevitzky* (New York, 1947).
Walter, Bruno, *Gustav Mahler* (New York, 1944).
—— *Theme and Variations, an Autobiography* (New York, 1946).

INDEX